Memoir of General Sir Hew Dalrymple

Memoir of General Sir Hew Dalrymple

Commander of the Portuguese Expedition During
the Peninsular War, 1808

Hew Dalrymple Ross

LEONAUR

Memoir of General Sir Hew Dalrymple
Commander of the Portuguese Expedition During the Peninsular War, 1808
by Hew Dalrymple Ross

First published under the title
Memoir of General Sir Hew Dalrymple

Leonaur is an imprint of Oakpast Ltd

ISBN: 978-1-78282-922-5 (hardcover)
ISBN: 978-1-78282-923-2 (softcover)

http://www.leonaur.com

Publisher's Notes

The views expressed in this book are not necessarily
those of the publisher.

Contents

The following narrative, as will be seen in the Introduction, was originally written by General Sir Hew Dalrymple, as a family record. Circumstances afterwards induced him to adopt the resolution of printing it, which his last illness alone prevented him from doing. I have therefore thought it a duty I owed to my Father's memory, to publish what he had prepared with much care, exactly as I found it, in his own handwriting.

I have added to the Appendix two letters, one from Brigadier-General Anstruther, the other from Lord William Bentinck, on the subject of the convention, conveying the opinions of two distinguished officers on the spot, as to the wisdom of allowing the French to evacuate Portugal with their arms and baggage.

Adolphus John Dalrymple.

Park-Street, Grosvenor-Square,
August, 1830.

Introduction

The first volume of Mr. Southey's *History of the Peninsular War* had long been before the public, and that of Lieutenant-Colonel Napier's incomparable work either published or on the eve of publication, when the Marquess of Londonderry's narrative appeared. I had early intimation that my name was everywhere unfavourably mentioned in that publication; but, as the share I had in the transactions of that period had now become, if I may be allowed to say so, matter of genuine history, I should, probably, have continued to disregard the small measure of justice afforded me in the marquess's narrative, had not an octavo edition, with an appendix of correspondence, been published. This correspondence contains expostulations from some highly-distinguished officers, against certain statements in the first edition of the narrative, of which each thought he had just reason to complain; and the justice those officers sought, was, by the noble author, most handsomely bestowed, by publishing their letters, with his replies, in an Appendix, prefaced by a frank acknowledgement of the deficiency of his work.

A publication which officers of rank and character thus thought it incumbent upon them to notice, it might not be becoming in me to overlook altogether; and, indeed, I am not wholly indifferent to the renewal of those misrepresentations of my conduct and character by which the people of England, twenty years ago, were misled. But the course pursued by those officers was not open to me, as I could scarcely have proposed to the author so very extensive a revisal of his work as would have been necessary to do justice, not to me only, but to the minister who, in communicating to me the king's commands, that I should forthwith proceed from Gibraltar, to take the command of the army, which I eventually found victorious in Portugal, attributed my appointment to His Majesty's high approbation of "the zeal and judgement which had marked the whole of my conduct under the late important events which had taken place in Spain."

Where, in the miscellaneous matter of Lord Londonderry's fourth chapter, in which the early transactions in Andalusia are alluded to, are the examples of that zeal and judgement to be found! It is true that I am once or twice alluded to as Governor of Gibraltar, and *my name* is once honoured by being joined to that of Lord Collingwood; but I cannot acknowledge much accuracy of statement in those passages where I am thus noticed. On the 14th May, when General Spencer's Corps sailed from Gibraltar, to join Admiral Purvis, off Cadiz, by *my authority*, and *under my sole responsibility*, (not "covered by the squadron of Lord Collingwood," but covered by a brig of war.) Lord Collingwood was off Toulon, as His Lordship's published correspondence will shew; as, also, that, whilst still off that place, it was in consequence of intelligence received from me of the events that were ripening into maturity in Spain, that His Lordship determined to resume his station off Cadiz, which he had quitted eleven months before.

This part of Lord Londonderry's narrative is, perhaps, not very clear; but, when His Lordship speaks of General Spencer's corps as having been the first British Force which "shewed itself upon the theatre of war," it is difficult to avoid the conclusion that it is intended to represent this corps as the one which, in the preceding sentence, the reader is told ministers were determined to send, contrary to the wish of certain deputies from the Asturias, as an efficient *nucleus* round which larger armies might gather.

During all this period the Marquess of Londonderry must have had access to my official correspondence, as well as that of Lord Collingwood. He was not only Under Secretary of State for his brother's department (with which it was my duty to correspond), but was actively engaged in the business of the office, as appears by a statement of Sir Henry Burrard's to the Board of Inquiry, "that, whilst at Portsmouth, he received a letter, of the 26th July," from the Under Secretary of State, "Brigadier-General Charles Stewart, expressing great impatience on the part of government that the armament should proceed," the 18th Dragoons, under the command of Brigadier-General Stewart himself, sailed soon after, as there is a letter in the appendix to the proceedings of the Court of Inquiry on the convention in Portugal, (No. 28,) dated the 4th August, in which Lord Castlereagh conveys to that officer His Majesty's commands to call off Oporto, to receive such instructions as Sir Harry Burrard might have left there for him. Though the circumstance is not mentioned in the marquess's narrative, there is no doubt that His Majesty's commands were obeyed.

It is most truly stated in the narrative, that, "on the 22nd of August,

I arrived from Gibraltar to take the command of the army," by that means superseding Sir Harry Burrard, who had assumed the command during the battle of the 21st; but I deny that, "before any definite course had been determined on, an event occurred, which gave a new turn to the general's deliberations." Immediately on my first interview with Sir Arthur Wellesley, I gave orders for the march of the army, the next morning, at daybreak, "undoubtedly as soon (as observed by the Board of General Officers composing the Court of Inquiry in its report) as it could be put in motion after his arrival;" and again:

> Considering the extraordinary circumstances under which two commanding generals arrived from the *Ocean*, and joined the army, (the one during, the other immediately after, a battle, and those successively superseding each other, and both the original commander, within the space of twenty-four hours), it is not surprising that the army was not carried forward until the second day after the action.

The account given in the narrative of the social discussions of all ranks of officers in their coteries, may afford a tolerable specimen of what those discussions usually are; but, I strongly object to its being made a vehicle for raising a doubt, what Sir Arthur Wellesley's opinion of the Armistice of Vimiera actually was; as, also, for inculating a belief, that the Oporto Intrigue, in all its circumstances, was well known in the army:

> During the period which intervened, between the conclusion of the armistice, and the return of the messenger, (namely, Lieutenant-Colonel, later Sir George Murray,) who carried a copy of the convention to Sir Charles Cotton.

The Marquess of Londonderry, then Brigadier General Stewart, joined, at headquarters, on the 24th of August; and, as appears by the correspondence itself, was the bearer of the first of a series of letters, from Brigadier-General the Baron Von Decken, who had recently arrived England, on a special mission to Oporto. This first letter, received on the 24th of August, contained the first intimation I received, that, in consequence of Baron Von Decken's own suggestion, the Bishop of Oporto had consented to take the Government of Portugal upon himself. The transfer of "the executive" (as it is called in the narrative) to Oporto, was the subject of a subsequent communication; and I cannot admit, that what I was wholly unacquainted with in the morning, and knew but imperfectly at noon, could have been well known in the army before night; for it was in the night of the 24th, not on the 26th, as is erroneously stated in the narrative, that Lieutenant-Colonel Murray arrived with Sir Charles Cotton's decision, upon the subject of the armistice.

The question whether Sir Arthur Wellesley did, or did not, approve the armistice at the time it was concluded, was, I should have hoped, set at rest by his letter, to Lord Castlereagh, of the 6th of October, 1808, of which the following is an extract: the letter itself has long been before the public, in the Appendix to the Proceedings of the Inquiry (No. 152), and is not a bad supplement to the extract from the Report of the Board already given, as shewing the fruits, as the latter does the immediate consequences, of the measures adopted by His Majesty's Ministers, in the outset of the Peninsular War.

Extract—

At the same time, adverting to the situation which I held in Portugal, previously to His Excellency's arrival, I think it but just to inform your lordship, that I concurred with the commander of the forces in thinking it expedient, on the 22nd of August, that the French Army, in Portugal, should be allowed to evacuate that kingdom with their arms and baggage, and that every facility for this purpose should be afforded to them. I deemed this to be expedient in the relative state of the two armies on the evening of the 22nd, considering that the French Army had resumed a formidable position between us and Lisbon; that they had the means of retiring from that position to others in front of that city; and, finally, of crossing the Tagus into Alemtejo, with a view to the occupation, in strength, of the forts of Elvas, La Lippe, and, eventually, Almeida. As Lieutenant-General Sir John Moore's corps had been diverted from the occupation of the position at Santarem, which had been proposed for them, there were no means to prevent, and no increase of numbers could have prevented, the French Army from effecting these objects.

I give this long extract the rather, as Lord Londonderry has thought it right ("before dismissing the subject of Cintra altogether") to give the extract of a letter, from a correspondent of his own, upon the same subject; it would appear, from the narrative, that the extract refers to what the noble author would call the *Convention of Cintra*; but that this is not the case, is evident from the first sentence:

> The tumult of our joy, on Wellesley's glorious conduct and success, has been cruelly disturbed by the communication of a *supposed convention*.

Obviously alluding to a copy of the armistice communicated, by the Portuguese Minister, to Mr. Secretary Canning, the day after the news of the victory of Vimiera was received, and published; of which document ministers affected to disbelieve the authenticity. Moreover, this correspondent's seven objections to the treaty, principally relate to the supposed recognition of Bonaparte as Emperor of the French, and the acknowledgement of the neutrality of the Tagus to the Russian Fleet; matters which are not so much as alluded to in the definitive convention, as a reference to that instrument will prove.

With reference to a discussion which arose between Don Josef Galluzzo (Captain-General of Estremadura) and myself, it is observed, by Lord Londonderry, that:

> *I consented* that Colonel Graham should repair to *Elvas*, with full powers to conciliate the Spanish general; the colonel was moreover furnished with ten thousand dollars, as a means of enforcing his arguments, should they be violently opposed.

The noble author was misinformed in this matter; to Lord Lyndock I appeal, that no such dollars were either furnished or bestowed; and I disclaim the feelings with which I am said to have been actuated on this occasion, and the absurd declaration I am represented to have made—namely:

> That, if my wish were not promptly attended to, I should withhold all succours from the Spaniards, and cease all correspondence with them.

Don Josef Galluzzo was, like some other great men, a dupe to the Bishop and *Junta* of Oporto, and took the field accordingly, for the express purpose of obstructing the execution of the convention; but Galluzzo was not more opposed to my measures than to those of the Spanish authorities at Madrid; and I can scarcely be supposed so entirely devoid of consistency, as to speak or think of abandoning the cause of the Spanish Nation, to which I had from the first been so zealously devoted, because one of their own officers was regardless of his duty to this country. Had the Marquess of Londonderry known me better, he would not have believed so improbable a tale.

I shall abstain from farther remarks upon detached passages of the Marquess of Londonderry's narrative; if that had never been published, the following statement of all my proceedings, as connected with the insurrections in Spain and the Peninsular war, would have continued to be,—that for which it was originally intended,—a family record. I deem it now expedient to place it in the hands of such persons as may take an interest in me and my conduct, in order to supply the omissions and correct the mistakes in those parts of the Marquess of Londonderry's narrative, which treat of the transactions in which I bore a part. To posterity and those who are capable of judging, Colonel Napier's *History* leaves me nothing to wish for or explain.

CHAPTER 1

Gibralta, Affairs of Spain Before the Juntas were Established

In June, 1806, I received orders to proceed to Gibraltar, to take the command of that fortress, in the absence of the lieutenant-governor, (General Fox,) who was about to be employed on another service. Upon my arrival in the garrison, on the 2nd of November, I found that the intercourse with Spain was considerable; and, having fully ascertained that no possible danger could accrue to the place from its continuance, (as the garrison was sufficiently numerous, the troops in a high state of health and discipline, and the duty done with scrupulous exactness,) I cultivated the friendly disposition which seemed to prevail, and soon had direct and confidential communication with General Castaños, (who commanded the Spanish troops in that part of Andalusia,) upon the occurrences to which this intercourse occasionally gave rise.

That this state of things was well known to the Spanish Government could not be doubted; it was productive of mutual convenience, and, to the garrison, it produced an ample supply of many useful articles of provision, and, at the same time, afforded to the British merchants the means of carrying on their commercial speculations with facility and advantage. Towards the end of the year 1807, columns of French troops began to enter Spain, for the avowed purpose of taking possession of Portugal, which materially changed the face of affairs; and, on the 7th day of October, it was officially notified to me, by the brigadier-general commanding in the Spanish lines, that:

> Lieutenant General Don F. Xavier de Castaños had received the orders of government, to stop all manner of communication with Gibraltar.

And, from this date, the fortress was held in as rigorous a state of blockade as the enemy had the power to enforce.

Soon after this, I received advices from several quarters, confirmed, and more fully detailed, in an official despatch from Lord Strangford, the British Minister at Lisbon, that it was certainly a part of Bonaparte's plan of operations to possess himself of Gibraltar; and, it must be confessed, that the mode of attack, he was said to have in contemplation, displayed much local knowledge and great information of those circumstances which were most likely to contribute to the success of his design. Although the danger was comparatively distant, no time was lost in making the necessary preparations to meet it when it should arrive.

On the 24th of October, Captain Rosenhagen, of the *Volage* frigate, brought me despatches from England. He was proceeding, without delay, for Sicily, with orders to Sir John Moore, which he was anxious to deliver before the embarkation of a body of troops with which Sir John had been previously ordered to leave that island. These orders, however, did not arrive in Sicily till after Sir John Moore's corps had embarked and sailed.

On the 1st of December, those troops from Sicily arrived in the bay. On the 4th, Sir John Moore sailed for the Tagus, in the *Chiffonne* frigate, for the purpose of communicating with Sir Sydney Smith, whom he expected to find cruising off that river. On the 10th, he returned, bringing to us the first intelligence of the departure of the royal family of Portugal for the Brazils; and, on the 15th, Sir John Moore, with the troops under his command, sailed for England.

About the time that Sir John Moore arrived in England, an expedition sailed from thence under the command of Major-General Spencer, destined for a particular service, and which was to rendezvous at Gibraltar. Those ships encountered a violent gale of wind, by which they were dispersed. The general, with the convoy, and the greater part of the transports were driven back to England; the remainder of the fleet, with detachments of various regiments on board, arrived in Gibraltar-bay on the 23rd January, 1808.

Whilst those ships lay in the bay, exposed to heavy gales of wind which at that time prevailed, we had intelligence from a ship, detained by the *Hydra* frigate, that a French squadron had escaped from Rochfort, and had, in the night, passed Gibraltar into the Mediterranean; and, on the 10th of February, Sir Richard Strachan, with seven sail of the line and one frigate, (having communicated with the garrison and ascertained the course the enemy had steered,) passed through the Straits in pursuit.

As it appeared to me, from a variety of circumstances, that Sicily would be exposed to considerable danger, should that island be the destination of the enemy's squadron, particularly now, when so large a body of troops as that under the command of Sir John Moore had been withdrawn from its garrison, I took it upon myself to send the detachments of General Spencer's corps, then in the bay, under the command of Colonel Walker of the 50th regiment, to reinforce the British troops in Sicily. The transports sailed, on the 11th February, under convoy of the *Phoebe* frigate.

On the 10th of March, General Spencer, with the remainder of his corps, arrived at Gibraltar, and when the original object of his expedition was relinquished, (for reasons wholly unconnected with the temporary diminution of his force by the absence of the detachments sent to Sicily,) the transports were secured in the Mole, and the troops placed in such accommodations as could be provided for them, until His Majesty's pleasure, as to their future destination, should be made known. This additional force at Gibraltar soon became peculiarly seasonable; for, although General Spencer's corps formed no part of the regular garrison, and was, in fact, a separate command, its presence gave weight to my subsequent communications with the Spanish authorities, and General Spencer himself expressed the greatest readiness to act under my authority, for the public service, whenever occasion should require it.

When the French troops first entered Spain and marched through Irun, on their route to Portugal, the strength of each column and a description of the troops composing it, regularly appeared in the Madrid *Gazette*; but, early in March of this year, it was ascertained that large columns had passed the frontier by other routes, and for other purposes: the French had taken possession of Pamplona and Barcelona by force or fraud; and at the moment when the insurrections at Madrid, and at the royal residence of Aranjuez had terminated in the abdication of Charles IV.; the imprisonment of the favourite Godoy; and the elevation of Ferdinand VII. to the throne of his father; Murat was advancing. upon Madrid (under pretext of proceeding on his route to Cadiz) at the head of the divisions of Moncey and Dupont.

I never failed to communicate to His Majesty's government the earliest and best intelligence I could obtain of the transactions in Spain at this interesting period; but, on the 8th of April, the arrival of a confidential agent from General Castaños, to inform me of the actual state of things, with an accurate detail of the late events; and to commence that confidential communication which henceforward subsisted between us, gave, to my subsequent reports to government, a new and more interesting character.

By this Spaniard I was informed of all the circumstances which preceded and accompanied the revolution which had placed Ferdinand VII. on the throne; and, from his account, it appeared that the turn affairs had taken was not anticipated by Bonaparte; and that, when Murat arrived at Madrid, he found a state of things for which he was wholly unprepared; and a government in full activity, which he had no authority, and probably no will, to acknowledge.

This gentleman further stated:

> That all the political talents in Spain, long sanctioned by public opinion, now surrounded the throne of the new sovereign; that the nation itself had caught the impulse, and was preparing, in the most energetic manner, to support its monarch; that Catalonia, Arragon, and Valencia, had already offered to raise and maintain an army of 150,000 men; and that it was not doubted that the example would be universally followed: in short, he believed (or affected to believe) that should the perfidy of the French, already suspected, be proved, by subsequent acts of the generals or troops, the latter would, notwithstanding their discipline and numbers, be overwhelmed by the energy of an enraged and formidable population, thus roused into action by wrongs and insults.

That those opinions, so truly Spanish, were those of the multitude, and perhaps of the individual who now uttered them, I thought most probable; neither did I doubt that the population of Spain was actuated by the feelings described; but it was from the sequel of the discourse of this accredited agent, that I drew more reasonable conclusions as to the objects of his mission; for he was authorised to inform me that, had matters taken an unfavourable turn, and the Prince of the Austurias been constrained to fly, he was to have taken refuge at

Algeciras, and from thence to have passed over to Gibraltar, preferring that port of embarkation to any other, from the confidence he was inclined to repose in the generosity of the English, added to the personal consideration which was known to subsist between General Castaños and the officers commanding that fortress.

In consequence of this communication, of which I had an opportunity that very day of sending the details to His Majesty's government, I concluded my letter to Lord Castlereagh in the following terms:

> I must now observe to your lordship, that, though the sanguine hopes, at present entertained from the firm, (or rather as they themselves describe it.) from the ferocious character of the Spanish Nation, when roused into action by wrongs or insult, prevents any immediate contemplation of reverse or disaster, I think I can perceive that, in such an extremity, *this* would be the point to which the new King of Spain would direct his retreat. In affording an asylum to an illustrious fugitive from French oppression, I feel confident I should be fulfilling the wish of the king; but, beyond this point, I should proceed with diffidence and caution, if not first honoured with His Majesty's commands.

From the circumstances thus described, I felt the fullest confidence that no time would be lost by His Majesty's ministers in furnishing me with at least provisional instructions; but, though this important despatch of the 8th of April was received by Lord Castlereagh in the course of that month, His Lordship's answer to it was not *dated* until the 25th of May; and, in the margin of this answer, was acknowledged ten despatches from me, on the affairs of Spain, from the 24th of March up to the 8th of May, inclusive. (A letter to Colonel Gordon, conveyed by the same vessel that took my letter of the 8th of April, was answered the 27th of that month.)

Whatever measures General Castaños and the friends of the Spanish monarchy might have had in contemplation at this crisis, to assert the independence of their country, were frustrated by the unexpected and most unfortunate journey of FerdinandVII. to Bayonne, of which, I am quite sure, those faithful Spaniards had no previous intimation. The first accounts General Castaños received from one of the ministers, who accompanied the king to Bayonne, appeared to him to be, in a certain degree, favourable. They announced that, upon the 20th of April, an interview had taken place in a country house upon the frontiers, between Bonaparte and Ferdinand, in which it had been agreed upon—that Ferdinand should be acknowledged King of Spain and the Indies, and that he should have the administration of Portugal until a general peace; but that Spain should accede to the confederation of the Rhine, furnishing a contingent of 50,000 men, and should give the French a free port in South America.

It is difficult to imagine what motive could have induced any individual about the person, and in the confidence, of the King of Spain to concur in the propagation of these falsehoods: it is, however, certain that, under such authority, the treaty I have mentioned was received at Algeciras. Those delusions were not, however, of long continuance; the bloody transactions at Madrid, of the 2nd of May; and, finally, the deposition of Ferdinand VII. and the other atrocious measures which attended that proceeding, roused into action that determined resistance to Bonaparte's power, which ultimately contributed so materially to its annihilation.

After the important communication from General Castaños, which I have mentioned, our intercourse was carried on through the medium of a native merchant of Gibraltar, named Viali.

★★★★★★

Mr. Viali acquitted himself of the service for which he had been selected by General Castaños with zeal and fidelity; but when the *Juntas* were established, and my intercourse with the Spanish authorities was direct and official, I had no further communication with Mr. Viali on political subjects; indeed he never was further in my confidence than was necessary for the communication with General Castaños.

★★★★★★

This person was intimately acquainted with General Castaños, and much in his confidence, and was employed by him to introduce the accredited agent already alluded to. The communications from Algeciras to this gentleman were frequently by letter, under feigned names and figurative expressions; but on more important occasions, by meetings, in the Spanish lines, between Mr. Viali and the Secretary of General Castaños, or some other confidential person employed by that general.

My general instructions to Viali were, in the first place, upon every proper occasion, strongly to dwell upon the (indeed, self-evident) proposition, that, under the present circumstances, which were not, and could not have been, foreseen by His Majesty's government, I had no authority to treat, and could therefore stipulate little or nothing, except with reference to the pleasure of the king, my master, consequently that any agreement I might enter into (beyond what it was in my power immediately to fulfil) must be of such a nature as, in my judgement, to merit His Majesty's approbation.

When the events at Bayonne were known, I desired Viali to urge, that this last stride on the part of France towards universal monarchy, rendered it peculiarly necessary for England to obtain military means and commercial advantages, to enable her to sustain the contest in which she was engaged, for the common cause of all independent nations. That it was not easy, nor, perhaps, *immediately* necessary, to suggest particular arrangements, as those must depend on circumstances as they arose. Loose suggestions might, however, be thrown out of those measures, which might possibly soon be advisable, as being likely to have a material influence on the future conduct of the war.

Of those measures, the first and the most important was, by some conjoint operation, to get possession of the French fleet in Cadiz. The next was to secure Ceuta, by our assistance, from falling into the hands of France; and that no difficulty could arise, on the part of the British government, to a fair and honourable compromise, respecting future possession, in the event of a peace. In the meantime, the Spanish troops then in garrison in Ceuta would be of essential service in the field.

Minorca was, also, at this moment, an object of consequence, on account of the Spanish fleet in that harbour; and it was essential to know how that island and the fleet were commanded, and what was their disposition.

On the 8th of May, Mr. Viali had an interview with the general's secretary, (see Appendix 1), in the Spanish lines, in which many of the above suggestions were discussed. The general's secretary first informed him, that should the Duke of Berg (Murat) endeavour to possess himself of the regency by force, that the province would arm, and join the regular troops; and that the general would, at their head, move to the Sierra Morena, to occupy the passes, and to check the advance of the enemy; and that, if the other provinces concurred, and followed his example, he would apply to me for such assistance as I could afford.

That General Don Manuel de la Peña commanded at Cadiz, of whose co-operation General Castaños had full assurance; and that the general had written to Don Ventura Escalante, the Captain-General of Grenada, of whose assistance he had no doubt: that if the perfidy of Bonaparte should extend to the removal of the reigning dynasty, timely measures would be concerted to secure the possession of South America.

When Mr. Viali spoke of securing the Spanish fleet, the Secretary alleged the probability that, as soon as the nation should consider itself at war with France, the Spanish fleet would sail, (either with or without an escort of British ships,) to convey the Infant Don Francisco to South America; when the British fleet, assisted by the Spanish batteries, might take possession of the French ships. Upon many points which entered into the present discussion, the general's secretary was fully prepared, and occasionally referred to notes in writing; but upon other topics introduced by Mr. Viali, he spoke his own opinion, and as if the subjects were new to him; when, however, the temporary possession of Ceuta by us was touched upon, he was ready in his reply, and as if the measure had been considered.

To this proposition he answered, that they had nothing to apprehend for Ceuta from the French, as the measures already mentioned would prevent their passing the Sierra Morena; but that, when the Spaniards came to a full understanding with us, they would, probably, remove the garrison of Ceuta, to reinforce their army in the field; and might also transfer some of the convicts now there, to some of the other *Presidios*. When at this point, Mr. Viali interrupted him, to propose sending a small British garrison, to enable the Spaniards to remove *all* their troops from Ceuta.

The Spaniard observed, that they would require from us at least 8,000 or 10,000 men, (besides money); and asked, whether, independent of that number, we had more to spare for Ceuta? This observation, probably made at the moment by the general's secretary, to parry the proposition about Ceuta, was the ground on which His Majesty's government, when the receipt of this despatch was acknowledged, authorised me to offer General Castaños 10,000 men.

At the time, when this conference took place, the massacre at Madrid was known; but nothing upon which reliance could be placed as to the transactions at Bayonne. The treaty of the Five Articles, as it was called, though transmitted to Algeciras, from what seemed official authority, began to be doubted; and, although the Infant Don Antonio and the Spanish authorities at Madrid had (as it was understood) refused to allow the Infant Don Francisco to depart for Bayonne, such strong suspicions of Bonaparte's designs began, at length, to prevail, that, when the general's secretary was asked, what might be the consequence if the French should actually destroy or remove the whole royal family, when Spain would be left without an acknowledged head or leader, he answered, that even that event was provided for; and he was authorised to say, that the Archduke Charles, of Austria, was the person on whom, in that case, their choice would fall; and that I should be requested to have a British frigate in readiness to proceed to Trieste, for the purpose of bringing the archduke to Spain, and to inform the Emperor of Austria of the actual state of things in that country.

In reply to these observations, I desired that it might again be intimated to General Castaños that, in discussing those important matters, a marked line of distinction must be drawn between such assistance to the Spanish cause as the British government might eventually be dis posed to afford and such aid as it could be in my power immediately to give, circumstanced as I was, in the command of a fortress which it was my duty to hold in a constant state of preparation effectually to resist the enemy, should he be enabled to appear before it. That I thought the general's plan of operations good; but that its success seemed to depend on the early possession of the Sierra Morena, in order to anticipate the enemy in occupying those important passes, of which the French generals well knew the value.

That accidental circumstances, at the present moment, placed at my disposal (by the consent of General Spencer, who commanded them) a few thousand men. That, probably, this corps, (to which an addition was shortly expected from Sicily, by the return of a part which had been detached to that island,) augmented by such troops as I could spare from the garrison of Gibraltar, might be usefully employed, in con junction with the British fleet now off Cadiz, in making a diversion in favour of the Spanish Army; but to this sort of measure the British admiral's consent and co-operation must be obtained; and, whilst a combined French and Spanish fleet lay at anchor in Cadiz, the British admiral could not be expected to consent to any conjoint operation that had not for its first object the capture of the French ships, and the secure possession of the Port of Cadiz by the Spanish Royalists.

That, with respect to money, public money was not at my disposal; I could, therefore, make no engagement on that point without His Majesty's authority. That a frigate might, probably, be kept in the bay in readiness to proceed to Trieste, but that it would be necessary to know the exact state of the negotiation which would render the service of that frigate necessary, before I could propose the measure to the British admiral. Early on the 9th of May, before the above observations upon the general's proposals had reached him, I received notice from General Castaños:

That the time was now come to carry into execution what had been so long in contemplation.

But that it was important to avoid any unnecessary demonstration that might attract the attention of the enemy, until the return of Don Joachim Novarra, an officer he was sending off to Cadiz to communicate with Don Manuel de la Peña, and to urge him to commence reprisals, and revenge the outrages committed by the French in various places, which the general enumerated, dwelling particularly on the barbarity displayed by "Murat and his satellites," on the day of the tumult, "even upon the bodies of the dead."

I had at all times made an unreserved communication to General Spencer of every information I received, which could eventually affect the operations of his corps; and lost no time in making him acquainted with this important notice from General Castaños. In consequence, General Spencer became most anxious to embark his corps, and hold it prepared to move; but as this operation seemed to be in opposition to General Castaños's anxious wish to avoid any demonstration that might create suspicion in the enemy (who had ample means of knowing all our movements) before the return of the adjutant-general, Novarra, from Cadiz, I assented to the measure with some reluctance; but the reasons urged by General Spencer were so many, and so forcible, that I could not but acquiesce in his proposal; and the troops were, as soon as possible, embarked, and the transports prepared for sea.

In the meantime I had it again intimated to General Castaños, in reply to this notice of the morning of the 9th, that the measure of forcing the French fleet out of Cadiz was one of immediate necessity, for the reasons already urged; and that, by producing an effect greatly beneficial to the common cause, it would, I had no doubt, produce some decisive steps on the part of England. I also furnished the general with a letter, to be transmitted by him to Admiral Purvis, (with whom I had been in correspondence upon the passing events in Spain,) to inform that admiral of the real state of things, should a Spanish force, at or near Cadiz, have the means of friendly communication with him, before a despatch I also addressed to him by sea could reach him.

Early on the 12th of May I wrote an official letter to General Spencer, (see Appendix 2), putting him in possession of my views in detaching his corps to join the fleet off Cadiz, and repeated the most important parts of my agreement with General Castaños, of which I had before verbally apprised him.

It unfortunately happened that the same day, and soon after this letter was sent to General Spencer, a communication was received from General Castaños, which evidently showed that something untoward had occurred, sufficient, at least, to postpone, if not to frustrate the plans we had concerted. In, this letter the general speaks of:

> His indifference as to any misfortune which might befall himself in an attempt to save his country, but that everything would be lost if the enemy should come to the knowledge of what we had been concerting.

This letter, however, stated that the adjutant-general, Don Joachim Novarra, had not yet returned from Cadiz.

★★★★★★

In a vindication of himself, which General Castaños put forth, after his defeat at Tudela, dated the 27th of January, 1809, he dwells much upon the communication he entered into with me in the month of April, 1808, and the beneficial consequences to the common cause which it was calculated to produce.

★★★★★★

I immediately communicated this letter to General Spencer, from which it was evident that every hope was extinguished of the accomplishment of the objects set forth to him in my letter of that morning, which was written with reference to an effectual co-operation with the Spanish authorities, of which there could no longer be any reasonable grounds of immediate expectation. It, however, happened, at this critical juncture, that a despatch arrived from Admiral Purvis, containing a report from the captain of a line-of-battle ship, stationed close off Cadiz, by which it appeared that insurrections against the French actually existed in many parts; and that the town of Cadiz itself was in such a ferment that the French Consul, and the merchants of that nation were compelled to seek refuge on board the French admiral's ship, in order to escape a general massacre, with which they were threatened. This letter concluded with a suggestion to the admiral, that the presence of His Majesty's ships close into Cadiz, at such a moment, might influence the minds of the people, and induce them to ask assistance.

These details naturally excited in General Spencer an anxious wish to join Admiral Purvis forthwith; which I very reluctantly gave him authority to do, in a second official letter, in which I did not fail to observe that, although I was induced, by the despatch just received from Admiral Purvis, to concur with him in the decision that he should forthwith join that officer off Cadiz, he must by no means now expect any of that sort of Spanish co-operation, upon which, the resolution of detaching his corps to join the fleet was originally grounded.

I was not informed, till after General Spencer had sailed, that it was the removal of Don Manuel de la Peña and the return of General Solaño to his government of Cadiz, and the adherence of the latter to the French interest, that had effectually frustrated General Castaños's plans of operations. Had I been apprised of that circumstance in time, I certainly should not have given my sanction to General Spencer's joining Admiral Purvis, (see Appendix 3), a measure which, in that case, could not (in my opinion) be productive of any beneficial result.

From this period until the end of May I received no intelligence from Spain of much interest, except that at times there were obscure allusions to the exertions about to be used to rescue the Spanish Nation from the thraldom preparing for them; but, certainly, those expressions had no reference to the extraordinary events then on the eve of accomplishment, and of which I received the first notice on the 31st of May, confirmed the next day by the arrival, in the garrison, of Don Joachim Novarra, with a letter from General Castaños, announcing the establishment of a *Junta* of Government at Seville. (See Appendix No. 4.) This officer was accompanied by Don Bantista Esteller, First Secretary to this new government, by which he was sent to Gibraltar to negotiate with me.

I found that, of this new government, General Castaños immediately acknowledged the authority, and was, in consequence, appointed to the command of its army; but that General Solaño, (the Marquess del Socorro,) having pursued a different course, was barbarously murdered by the populace of Cadiz, as being an avowed partisan of the French. It seems, so far from having been known, at this period, that *Juntas* of Government, similar to that of Seville, had, within the last few days of May, been established in every place not actually under the power of the French, that, when General Castaños wrote to announce to me the formation of the new government, he used the following expressions:—

In the city of Seville has been established a Supreme *Junta* of

Government for the four kingdoms of Andalusia.

At no very distant period, however, the general found that each of the four kingdoms of Andalusia—*viz.* Seville, Grenada, Jaen, and Cordova—had a *Junta* of its own; and that the *Junta* of Grenada was so far from acknowledging the supremacy of that of Seville, that it only allowed its troops to join those of Seville, and to act under the command of General Castaños, in opposition to the French under Dupont, in consequence of a regular treaty negotiated (see Appendix No. 5), and ratified by the authority of the respective *Juntas*, in which the independence of Grenada was affirmed and acknowledged

Don Bantista Esteller was a young officer of artillery, probably selected not more for his talents than for his ardent zeal in the cause he had embraced. He spoke confidently of the resources of the government he served; he represented those resources, in point of money, as considerable; in point of men, as immense. He estimated the four kingdoms of Andalusia at 300,000, and that, in truth, it would be more difficult to select the men to be embodied than to excite the population to arm; the enthusiasm, he said, was general, excited and directed by men of energy and influence, and kept up by the whole *body of the clergy.*

This gentleman was sent by the *Junta* of Seville to communicate with me confidentially on the present state of things, and to court the most cordial amity with England. But, although he was charged to negotiate with me certain minor articles, which were not of difficult arrangement, and, amongst others, that I should, without delay, send a confidential person to Seville, to keep up the necessary communication between myself and the *Junta*, he never claimed for that body the character of a National Government, authorised to treat, as such, with foreign powers in the name of the Spanish monarchy.

General Castaños having forwarded to me open despatches addressed to General Espeleta, at Barcelona; and the governors of Valencia, Majorca, &c. announcing to them the state of things in Andalusia, and the steps he had himself pursued in reference to the Supreme *Junta* of Seville; I applied to Lord Henry Pawlet, commanding His Majesty's ships in the Bay of Gibraltar at the time, who immediately forwarded those important despatches, by a brig of-war, to their destinations. On the 2nd of June, His Lordship sailed for Cadiz, taking with him, on board His Majesty's ship *Terrible*, Don Bantista Esteller, and my military secretary, Captain Dalrymple, whom I had selected to proceed with the former to Seville, in compliance with the requisition of the *Junta* to that effect. (See Instructions, Appendix No. 6.) Captain Dalrymple, also, carried with him a letter to Admiral Purvis, communicating the nature of his mission, and expressive of my confidence, that the admiral would concur with me in opinion as to the urgent necessity of transmit ting, express to England, the important despatches to government, of which Captain Dalrymple was the bearer.

On the 1st of June (the day that this officer, from the *Junta* of Seville arrived at Gibraltar) General Oakes and General Lumley came from England, on their way to Sicily; and with them Captain Whittingham, who was appointed to serve with that army in the quartermaster general's department. This officer, who had passed much of his early life in Spain, took a lively interest in the events now opening to view; and gladly accepted the proposal which, by General Oakes's permission, I made him, of being attached, by me, to General Castaños's headquarters. I never saw Captain Whittingham before, and only knew him by character; but by what I had heard of that, I was fully persuaded that, in him, good fortune had placed at my disposal the very man I wanted; and the result amply justified my choice. General Castaños, on his part, received my proposal of having Captain Whittingham at his headquarters with the most flattering expressions of satisfaction—although he was then but little aware of the value of the officer, whose attachment and assistance I thus procured him.

On the 4th of June, General Castaños received orders to take the command of the army, and on the 6th he set out, accompanied by Captain Whittingham, for Seville, to communicate with the government on the measures to be pursued. On the 4th of June, also, the garrison of Ceuta landed in the Bay, on its route to join the army, and, at the same time, a supply of money being necessary to put the troops in motion, the Gibraltar merchants (to their honour be it recorded) subscribed, in a few minutes, above forty thousand *hard* dollars, without premium, and on the security of the *Junta* of Seville.

From contrary winds and other causes, it so happened, that I had little or no intelligence from General Spencer, from the time he sailed until the 4th of June, when Colonel Bathurst, his quartermaster-general, came with despatches over land from Cadiz. The principal object of this officer's mission was to communicate to me the proceedings of a sort of negotiation, which General Spencer and Admiral Purvis had been induced to enter into with Morla, who had succeeded to General Solaño, as Governor of Cadiz. As I felt confident that Morla had no authority, even from the *Junta* of Seville, to treat for the objects he originally proposed; and having, from the first, a bad opinion of this Spaniard, which every day's experience tended to confirm, I declined entering upon the subject officially with Colonel Bathurst, or taking any part in the proceeding. Finding that the admiral and General Spencer had thought it advisable not to allow Captain Dalrymple to proceed to Seville, even though he was sent there in compliance with the desire of the *Junta*, I sent him orders to return to Gibraltar forthwith. (The despatch, which Captain Dalrymple carried to Admiral Purvis to be forwarded, was acknowledged by Lord Castlereagh, the 6th of July.)

On the 6th of June, General Spencer's detachments, which had arrived from Sicily on the 2nd, sailed to join their corps, and, on the 9th, the 6th regiment, part of the garrison of Gibraltar which I could spare, and which I had promised General Spencer to furnish, together with a proportion of field-artillery, sailed to reinforce his corps.

On the 8th of June, Captain Dalrymple returned to Gibraltar; and, on the same day, I received Lord Castlereagh's long looked-for reply to my interesting report, (see Appendix 7), dated the 8th of April. It was (as I have already noticed) dated the 25th of May, and it acknowledged nine of my despatches, on the affairs of Spain, up to that of the 8th of May, inclusive, which last contained the details of Mr. Viali's conference with General Castaños's secretary on that day. I was now gratified with the assurance of His Majesty's entire approbation of all my proceedings; and I received instructions for my conduct in future, that seemed entirely founded on the intelligence I had sent.

With reference to Mr. Viali's report of his conversation with the Spanish secretary, Lord Castlereagh informed me, that the utmost exertions would be made to send out a reinforcement from England, so as to enable His Majesty to afford the loyal party in Spain the assistance of the 10,000 men, which General Castaños seemed to require, including what could be spared from the garrison of Gibraltar; and a confidence was expressed, that, should any requisition for troops have been already made to me, I had afforded them under such precautions as to ensure the communication with our fleet. I was finally flattered with the assurance, that:

> His Majesty entertained a full reliance upon my vigour and discretion in the present juncture; that as, on the one hand, I should not commit either the faith of his government, or the force under my command unnecessarily, or for an inadequate

object, I would, on the other, act with determination and spirit, according to circumstances on the spot, relying on the disposition of His Majesty's Government to give my exertions the fullest support.

Although on this occasion it was not signified in direct terms either to myself or General Spencer, that his corps was to be considered as part of the "force under my command," relative to the employment of which I was so particularly cautioned, the whole tenor of the instructions could not, I think, convey any other meaning; be that as it may, however, before these instructions reached me, General Spencer's corps, with such augmentation from the garrison as I could afford it, had joined the fleet off Cadiz, and was no longer, to any useful purpose, under my direction or control.

CHAPTER 2

Gibralter, Affairs of Spain After the Juntas were Established

Having been in the constant habit of confidential correspondence with Lord Collingwood, ever since my arrival at Gibraltar, I did not fail to inform His Lordship, who was, during this period, high up in the Mediterranean, of the various occurrences in Spain, as they arose, and as opportunities offered; but when, from the result of Mr. Viali's conference with Castaños's secretary, on the 8th of May, it seemed that an important crisis was at hand, in which the able co-operation of His Lordship would be most desirable, I communicated the important intelligence by a sloop of war, which found him off Toulon. In consequence of this notice Lord Collingwood sailed for Gibraltar, where he arrived in the *Ocean*, accompanied by Captain Legge, in the *Repulse*, on the 9th of June. (See Lord Collingwood's Letters of the 29th of May to Mr. Drummond, at Palermo, and the Archduke Charles of Austria, in the volume of his *Correspondence*.)

Having been fully informed, by me, of all the events which had recently happened in Spain, as also of the feelings of the Spanish people, and consequently of their government, as to the measures they were inclined to adopt, whether of war or alliance, Lord Collingwood sailed on the 10th, to take the command, off Cadiz, carrying with him Major Cox, of the 61st regiment, whom I had selected to reside as confidential agent at Seville. (See Appendix 8, Cox's Correspondence.) Through that officer my communications with the Supreme *Junta*, and generally those of Lord Collingwood, were conveyed, and he certainly acquitted himself of the duties confided to him with singular discretion and ability.

The *Junta* of Seville, like the others which were about the same period formed in every province of Spain, arose out of the simultaneous insurrection of the Spanish Nation against French violence and usurpation; but the individuals of which it was composed, being named by popular acclamation, were not very judiciously chosen; and certainly few of them, in the sequel, displayed extraordinary talents as statesmen; or were found to possess much disinterestedness or enlarged patriotism; but their early proclamations and addresses to the Spanish people were admirably composed, and produced a great effect, in animating the zeal, and directing the energies of the nation; at the same time raising the reputation, and increasing the influence of the body from which they proceeded. General Castaños, from the integrity of his character, and the important situation in which he was placed, possessed the confidence of the President, and considerable influence with the *Junta*; particularly when the approach of the enemy threatened Seville itself; but when, Dupont having surrendered, that danger was past, the influence of Morla, the Governor of Cadiz, became more conspicuous.

General Castaños placed a just confidence in British honour, and was desirous of concerting measures with British officers, for the furtherance of the common cause. Morla, on the contrary, was hostile to England, used his influence with the *Junta* to excite suspicions of our views and intentions, and in his intercourse with the British officers commanding off Cadiz, before Lord Collingwood's arrival, displayed much of that duplicity of character, for which he was at the last so disgracefully distinguished.

When Major Cox arrived at Seville, he requested, at the outset, that some members of the *Junta*, or some individual, authorised by that body, should be appointed to communicate with him officially, through whom every proposition of the Supreme Government should be conveyed to him. (Cox's Correspondence, June 15.) The suggestion was immediately adopted, and Padre Gill, the most able, and one of the most influential members of the *Junta*, was appointed to communicate with Major Cox, in the name of the government, on all necessary occasions.

General Castaños, accompanied by Captain Whittingham, arrived at Xeres, on the 8th of June, where he received orders from the *Junta*

30

to repair immediately to Seville. It was at this time and place that the general first received intelligence that a body of Spaniards, principally peasants, had been defeated at the Bridge of Alcolea; and that General Dupont was in possession of Cordova.

On the 9th, General Castaños arrived at Seville, and after having had an interview with Don Francisco Saavedra, the President of the *Junta*, set out for Carmona, where he established his headquarters.

Before the general left Seville, he sent Captain Whittingham to Cadiz, to propose to General Spencer to land his corps, and to advance with it to Xeres, where General Castaños offered to meet him, in order to concert their plan of operations. (See Appendix 9, Whittingham's Correspondence.)

General Spencer did not accede to this proposition, but determined upon sailing immediately to Ayamonte, in the hope of intercepting a French column, of between three and four thousand men, which (as he had been made to believe) was marching along the coast, and making preparations to pass the Guadiana at Ayamonte. (See Appendix 10, Lord Collingwood's Correspondence.)

With this report of his mission Captain Whittingham joined General Castaños, on the evening of the 11th of June, when the general sent him forthwith to Gibraltar to inform me that he had his headquarters at Utrera, where his force amounted to 5,000 men, and that he occupied Carmona with three thousand; Captain Whittingham was further instructed to inform me of the measures General Castaños intended to pursue, under the various circumstances which the enemy's movements might probably produce.

When Captain Whittingham returned from Gibraltar to the Spanish headquarters, he found that General Castaños had got together, at Utrera, 8,000 regulars, with whom he had incorporated 12,000 men, selected from the mass of the peasantry. He had thus assembled and formed, in a wonderfully short space of time, an army (exclusive of the advanced guard at Carmona) of 20,000 men; he had also organised the staff of the army, and, upon the whole, placed his army in such a state of equipment, as to be fit for offensive operations against the enemy; Dupont remaining all this time inactive at Cordova.

From Captain Whittingham I received constant accounts of the operations of this short campaign, which terminated in a victory obtained over the French, at Baylen, and the consequent capitulation, not only of Dupont's corps, but also of a strong reinforcement, under the command of General Wedell, which, during the time, and while the convention was negotiating, attacked General Reding's corps, (by which Dupont's retreat had been cut off, in the course of the action,) and had surprised and taken prisoners the battalion of Cordova. As General Wedell's retreat was open, and his force by no means inconsiderable, his having consented to be included in General Dupont's capitulation seems rather a singular occurrence. It is understood that a body of his cavalry, commanded by an officer, who refused submission to the proposed capitulation, effected its retreat to Madrid, without molestation.

In consequence of this conversation, on two succeeding days, the divisions of Dupont and Wedell filed off before the Spanish Army, and piled their arms; the former consisting of 5,500 men (of which number 1,200 cavalry) and 20 pieces of cannon: the latter of 9,100 men, of which 1,500 cavalry.

It was calculated, that, in the course of this short campaign, the French lost 2,600 men killed and wounded, and 1,100 deserted after the battle, and before the surrender. (Whittingham's Correspondence, July 26.) It is probable that a considerable proportion of this number were Swiss soldiers in the French Army, who eventually enlisted into the Swiss regiment of Reding. The entire loss of the Spaniards was estimated at 1,200, killed and wounded. The Spanish Army, before the battle, was estimated at 25,000 men, of which number nearly one-half were peasants; and of those a battalion of 3,000 men, in General Reding's division, fled at the commencement of the battle, and returned no more.

When the news of this victory reached Seville, the *Junta* and people became so much elated by this proof of their power, that the subsequent accounts of the convention were received with strong marks of disapprobation. Nevertheless, on the 1st of August, General Castaños and Don Tomas Morla (Governor of Cadiz) were received at Seville with great ceremony, a deputation of the *Junta* meeting them outside the gates of the city. (Cox's Correspondence, August 3.) This reception of Castaños was in consequence of the victory he had obtained.

It was alleged (Whittingham's Letter), that Morla was associated with him in the triumph to *prevent jealousy.*

Those two generals were, for some hours, shut up with the *Junta*, where it was said that the debates were warm.

From the first, Morla was a strong advocate for breaking the convention with Dupont, and was known to be the author of rather an able paper, industriously circulated, recommending that measure, to which Castaños, as a man of honour, and pledged to the fulfilment of the engagements which he himself had made, was most warmly op-posed. At last the *Junta*, being strongly inclined, if not fully resolved from the first to break the treaty, sanctioned by the popular clamour which Morla had contributed to excite, and utterly regardless of the public faith and the national character, adopted Morla's opinion and broke the capitulation.

On the 3rd of August, a despatch arrived at Seville addressed to General Castaños from General Grouchy, the French *commandant*, in Madrid, (Cox's Correspondence, August 5,) in which it was stated that the troops under his command being destined for another service, he could wish that General Castaños would detach part of his army to occupy the capital; to ensure its tranquillity, to protect the French sick left in the hospitals, and, also, the French families established in the place: but, at all events, whatever the general's determination in that respect might be, he (General Grouchy) requested that an of-ficer might be sent to treat of matters which would probably be of advantage to both nations. In consequence of this notice, Major-Gen-eral Moreno (the Quartermaster General of the Spanish Army) was sent off to Madrid, which was soon evacuated by the French. General Castaños himself did not enter the capital until the 23rd of August.

The glorious result of the campaign, and the popular enthusiasm which the ostentatious reception of the victor, and the pompous cel-ebration of the victory could not fail to inspire, contributed to exag-gerate the pretensions, and excite the ambition of the *Junta* itself, and to foster a disposition which had before been manifested in that body, to assume the supreme and sole government of Spain; and, at this pe-riod, in a debate which arose upon the refusal of the *Junta* of Granada to acknowledge the supremacy of Seville, Count Tilly (the leader of the party which espoused those ambitious projects) had the hardi-hood to propose, in the *Junta*, that a division of the Army of Andalusia should be marched into Granada, to reduce that kingdom to submis-sion. It was in answer to this proposal that General Castaños made the following remarkable reply:—

He should like to see who dared to order a division of the army, under his command, to move without his authority; that he knew no distinction of provinces; he had the command of part of the *Army of Spain*, and he should never suffer it to be the vile instrument of civil war. (Cox's Correspondence, Sept. 7.)

Count Tilly and his party had not, upon this occasion, sufficient influence to carry the violent measures they proposed; and the prevalence of wiser councils was manifested in the very able address to the Spanish Nation which the *Junta* of Seville put forth on the 3rd of August, recommending the establishment of a supreme national government, to be composed of two delegates from each of the provincial *Juntas*. This able paper deprecates the discussion of subjects, or the adoption of measures, likely to create disunion, particularly the subject of the right of succession to the crown, upon which great difference of sentiment prevailed in Spain; one party supporting the Salique law and advocating the pretensions of the house of Naples; the other maintaining the old Spanish laws contained in the great code called *Las Partidas*, by which was enacted the right of female succession to the crown.

It was singular that a body, from which had emanated a document so wise should have followed up the measure they recommended, by selecting (by ballot) the Conde de Tilly and Don Vicente Hore to represent them in the Supreme Government. (Cox's Correspondence, August 18.) Of the former I have already spoken, he was, in fact, a man of infamous character; of the latter it is only necessary to observe that he was a person of no respectability, and only politically distinguished as having been a warm friend and partisan of the Prince of the Peace. Thinking, perhaps, that his known attachment to a detested favourite might not recommend him to favourable notice at Madrid, he declined the appointment, (Cox's Correspondence, August 27,) and the Archbishop of Laodicea was chosen deputy to the Central *Junta* in his stead.

Don Andres Miñano was appointed to replace Count Tilly, as member of the *Junta*, with Castaños's army, with a salary (as at first decided) of 12,000 hard dollars a year; but this scandalous misapplication of the pecuniary resources, which the British Government had at this time so liberally supplied, excited so much popular indignation, that the grant was, for the present, rescinded. It was afterwards settled to allow this field-deputy 500 dollars a month; and the same was granted to Count Tilly, as deputy to the Central *Junta*.

★★★★★★

On the 3rd of September, the British Consul arrived at Seville, to place, at the sole disposal of the *Junta*, a million and a half of dollars and forty thousand stand of arms, with the hope, expressed by Mr. Canning, to the Andalusian deputies, "That the aid now granted may be considered as applicable to the general service of the country." Upon what was this hope founded? Certainly not upon a just estimate of the character of the body to which the sole disposal of the aid was consigned. (Cox's Correspondence, Sept. 5.)

★★★★★★

As soon as the capital was evacuated by the French Army, the Council of Castile resumed its functions, and began to issue orders and decrees as the supreme tribunal of the nation. This was a measure not unlikely to create dissensions and discord amongst the provinces, as they might each be inclined to acknowledge or deny the power of this tribunal. Major Cox discovered that a letter written to me by the Council of Castile had been stopped by the *commandant* at St. Roque, and sent to Seville by order of the *Junta*; and in answer to his warm remonstrance against this breach of confidence, Padre Gill alleged, in excuse, that the *Junta* wished to save me the embarrassment of being drawn into a correspondence with an assumed authority which could not be acknowledged; the *padre* promised that the letter should be forwarded; which, however, he did not enable Major Cox to do before the 30th of August, when, doubtless, it was no longer deemed important to withhold it. (Cox's Correspondence, August 30.)

Whilst the progress of the campaign against Dupont, and the other occurrences which arose during this interesting period, furnished occasion for frequent reports to the Secretary of State; the letters I received from him were few, and had little or no reference to the substance of my communications.

I have said that on the 8th of June I received the satisfactory despatch of the 25th of May, approving of my past, and giving me instruction for my future proceedings.

Somewhere between the 20th and 25th of June I received a despatch from Downing-Street, (without a date,) containing, for my information and guidance, copies of further instructions, ad dressed to Admiral Purvis, then supposed to be in the command off Cadiz. In those documents, dated the 4th of June, were fully explained the conduct to be observed towards the Spanish patriots, particularly in regard to the advance of money for their use. Those papers were received by Lord Collingwood, who had taken the command off Cadiz.

On the 16th of July, Mr. Adair came to Gibraltar, on his way to Constantinople, and brought me two letters from Lord Castlereagh, dated the 28th of June. The one contained copies (for my information and guidance) of letters directed to Vice-Admiral Purvis and Major-

35

General Spencer, announcing the appointment of Lieutenant-General Sir Arthur Wellesley to the command of a force destined to act, as circumstances should point out, in support of the efforts of the Spanish Nation. In consequence of directions those letters contained, I forwarded to Sir Arthur Wellesley, through Lord Collingwood, (see Appendix 11), a long despatch, containing all the information respecting the affairs of Spain which it was in my power to impart.

The other letter brought by Mr. Adair was to direct me to reinforce General Spencer from the garrison of Gibraltar to whatever amount I might deem advisable. Those directions I had anticipated long before this letter of Lord Castlereagh's was written.

On the 27th of July I received two despatches from the Secretary of State, both dated the 6th of that month. The one transmitted several copies of the king's speech to Parliament, and an order of His Majesty in Council for a cessation of hostilities with Spain: an order which I had, under my own responsibility, practically anticipated above two months before.

The other letter, of the 6th of July, from Lord Castlereagh, acknowledged the receipt of two letters from me, the one dated the 2nd, the other the 4th of June. The former was the letter I sent by Captain Dalrymple to be forwarded by Admiral Purvis, announcing the arrival at Gibraltar of the deputies from the *Junta* of Seville; and of my having, in consequence of an intimation from the *Junta*, sent my military secretary to reside at Seville. The latter was to inform His Lordship of the reasons which induced me to order Captain Dalrymple back to Gibraltar.

A copy of this letter of the 6th of July was laid before the Court of Inquiry, and is inserted in the Appendix to its proceedings: I annex a copy of a part which it seems to have been thought prudent to omit, and which greatly contributed, with other circumstances, to convince me, that, subsequent to the 25th of May, my opinions were little regarded, and that the confidence of ministers was transferred from me to Admiral Purvis and General Spencer; and, also, that, so late as the 6th of July, they (the ministers) were ill informed of the probable course of events in Andalusia and of the character of the people and the authorities in that part of Spain.

★★★★★★

The correspondence relative to General Spencer's movements, after his return from off the Tagus, is to be found in Cox's Correspondence, 28th June, and Appendix, No. 12.

★★★★★★

The instance I allude to is as follows:—

I thus write to you under the impression of the intelligence received from General Spencer, dated, off Cadiz, the 6th of June, at which time preparations were making for taking possession of the French squadron, and our commanders were waiting for a ratification by the *Junta* of Seville of the conditions proposed by them for their co-operation. The despatches of the admiral and general leaves us little room to doubt that their propositions have been in the main acceded to; and that His Majesty's forces are acting in alliance with the *Junta* of Seville.

To this extent, as it appears, were the admiral and general the dupes of Don Tomas Morla and his confederates.

At length, on the 8th of August, His Majesty's ship, *Orestes*, arrived at Gibraltar, with despatches from England, of which the following is a copy, of the most important, at least to me, as proving, that, between the 6th and 15th of July, a considerable change had taken place in the opinions of His Majesty's ministers, respecting my proceedings in the affairs of Spain, and the reliance to be placed on my communications.

Downing-Street,
July 15, 1808.

Sir,

I am to acquaint you, that His Majesty, highly approving the zeal and judgement which has marked the whole of your conduct under the late important events which have taken place in Spain, has been graciously pleased to entrust to you, *for the present*, the chief command of his forces, to be employed in Portugal and Spain, with Sir Harry Burrard, second in command. Lord Collingwood will be directed to place a frigate at your disposal, in order that you may have the means of transferring yourself to whatever point of your command your personal presence may, according to circumstances, be most required; the charge of the garrison of Gibraltar being entrusted, *during your absence*, to Major General Drummond, or the officer next in command.

I enclose copies of the instructions which have been given to Sir Arthur Wellesley, Nos. 1, 2, 3, and enclosures; in the execution of which he is directed to proceed, transferring his orders to any senior officer in command.

I am, &c.

(Signed)   Castlereagh.

To Lieut.-Gen. Sir Hew Dalrymple.

The instructions, Nos. 1 and 2, alluded to in this letter, had reference to the corps which, on the 30th of June, when they were written, was supposed to be under the immediate command of Sir Arthur Wellesley; No. 3, on the contrary, which announced the approaching reinforcement of 10,000 men, related to the objects which the army, when assembled, would have to provide for, and was dated the 15th of July, the same day as my appointment to the command. Of this paper the following is an extract:—

The motives which have induced the sending so large a force to that quarter, are—

1st. To provide effectually for an attack upon the Tagus. And

2nd. To have such an additional force, disposable, beyond what may be indispensably requisite for that operation, as may admit of a detachment being made to the southward, either with a view to secure Cadiz, if it should be threatened by the French force, under General Dupont, or co-operate with the Spanish troops in reducing that corps, if circumstances should favour such an operation, or any other that may be concerted.

His Majesty is pleased to direct that the attack upon the Tagus should be considered as the first object to be attended to. As the whole force, (of which a statement is enclosed,) when assembled, will amount to 30,000 men, it is conceived that both services may be amply provided for.

The precise distribution, as between Portugal and Andalusia, both as to time and proportion of force, must depend on circumstances, to be judged of on the spot; and should it be deemed advisable to fulfil the assurance, which Lieutenant-General Sir Hew Dalrymple appears to have given to the Supreme *Junta* of Seville, under the authority of my despatch of the 6th of July, that it was His Majesty's intention to employ a corps of his troops, to the amount of 10,000 men, to co-operate with the Spaniards in that quarter; a corps of this magnitude may, I hope, be detached, without prejudice to the main operation upon the Tagus; and may be reinforced according to circumstances, after the Tagus has been secured.

When I received these instructions the campaign in Andalusia was over; and it was no longer of consequence what assurances of support had been given to the Supreme *Junta* of Seville in His Majesty's name, or by whom they were conveyed. I certainly gave such assurances to General Castaños, under the authority of Lord Castlereagh's letter of the 25th of May, written before the *Junta* of Seville existed; but in the despatch of the 6th of July, here referred to, there was no such authority, and, indeed, not one word upon the subject.

Besides the official despatches, I received, by this opportunity, a private letter from Lord Castlereagh, offering me, in the first place, his personal thanks for the zeal and ability with which I had (as His Lordship was pleased to observe) discharged my public duties during the late important period. His Lordship then proceeds to recommend to my particular confidence, Sir Arthur Wellesley, whose high reputation in the service, as an officer, would in itself dispose me (His Lordship was very justly persuaded) to select him for any service that required great prudence and temper, combined with much military experience. The letter concluded as follows:—

> The degree, however, to which he has been for a length of time, in the closest habits of communication with His Majesty's ministers, with respect to the affairs of Spain, will, I am sure, point him out to you as an officer of whom it is desirable, on all accounts, to make the most prominent use the rules of the service will permit.

Under all the circumstances of the case, I think it can scarcely be wondered at, that I received these communications with, at least, as much surprise as satisfaction. This ebb and flow of approbation and confidence was not satisfactory; and something seemed to lurk under this most complicated arrangement, which bore, I thought, a most unpromising aspect. But I was at a distance from government; had no means of stating difficulties, or of receiving explanations or advice; and could, therefore, only hasten, as far as circumstances would allow, to obey His Majesty's commands, by repairing to Portugal, there to assume, "for the present," the command of an army already in the field, and actually engaged in active operations against the enemy.

When busied in preparing for my departure, a question arose, upon which I was obliged to come to an immediate decision; in direct opposition, as it appeared at the time, to the foreign policy of His Majesty's Government, although not officially pronounced.

At a late hour, on the 9th of August, His Majesty's ship, *Thunderer*, arrived from Sicily, having on board Prince Leopold, second son of the King of Naples; and the Duke of Orleans, with a large suite of attendants upon the former.

Near ten at night the Duke of Orleans, attended by Captain Talbot, of the *Thunderer*, came to my quarters, when His Highness put into my hands a letter from Mr. Drummond, (see Appendix No. 13.) His Majesty's minister at the court of Palermo. At the same time, Captain Talbot delivered a despatch, with several enclosures, (see Appendix 14), from Admiral Sir Alexander Ball, by whose orders Captain Talbot was authorised to give the Duke of Orleans a passage on board the *Thunderer* to Gibraltar, but to the Duke of Orleans only, as the admiral had received no intimation of Prince Leopold's intended voyage.

From the Duke of Orleans, as also from Mr. Drummond's letter, I understood that Prince Leopold was come to establish himself at Gibraltar, for the avowed purpose of negotiating for the Regency of Spain; of which measure Mr. Drummond not only expressed his entire approbation, but frankly acknowledged that he had urged it upon the King of Naples, as one which His Majesty was called upon to pursue. The Duke of Orleans anticipated so little difficulty on my part, that he proposed to make with me the necessary arrangements for the formal reception of Prince Leopold and his suite into the garrison in the morning.

Though neither the Duke of Orleans nor Mr. Drummond alleged any official authority from His Majesty's ministers for this strong and decisive proceeding, I could have no doubt that they felt confident of approbation and powerful support at home.

I at once, however, told the Duke of Orleans, that I would consent to no measure which should appear to throw the weight of Britain (with an army collecting on the coast) into the scale of any competitor for the Regency of Spain, without distinct orders from His Majesty's Government for that purpose; I, therefore, declined, in the first instance, to allow Prince Leopold to land at Gibraltar, and sent off an express to Cadiz, to Lord Collingwood, to inform him of the embarrassing situation in which I was placed; in the meantime I took every step I could to convince the authorities in Spain, civil and military, that this act of the Court of Palermo was wholly unauthorised by the British Government and unexpected by me.

Before the return of the express from Cadiz, Captain Talbot announced his intention of sailing, and his disinclination to keep his illustrious passenger on board, I therefore, on the 11th, addressed a letter to Prince Leopold, expressive of the concern I felt at having been compelled, by a sense of duty, to expose His Royal Highness to the inconvenience of remaining so long in a state of uncertainty on board ship, and also to say, that I should give orders for the reception of His Royal Highness into the garrison, with all the honours due to his illustrious rank, upon certain conditions, which I mentioned, for the regulation of his intercourse with Spain and communication with the Spaniards. It was at the same time understood, that the Duke of Orleans was to proceed immediately to England.

Prince Leopold having most readily acceded to the conditions proposed, landed in the garrison, on the 12th of August, when I transferred the command to Major-General Drummond, preparatory to my embarkation next morning for Portugal.

That His Majesty's minister at the Court of Palermo should have recommended such a measure as this, and that a British line-of-battle-ship should have been employed in its execution, were occurrences for which I was by no means prepared; but that such an intrigue, carried on by inferior agents, was in active operation, I had for some time been aware.

Towards the end of June, I had good reason to believe that the Court of Palermo had acquired an able, and not very scrupulous, embassy in Gibraltar; and, in the middle of July, a sort of accredited minister to the Spanish Nation, named the Chevalier Robertoni, arrived for the double purpose of protesting, in the name of his sovereign, against the late renunciations at Bayonne, and of asserting His Majesty's claim to the succession. As I was not disposed to allow a British fortress to be the seat of this sort of diplomacy, and had also reason to believe that Robertoni was charged with papers for circulation, of which he did not choose to communicate to me the contents; and, moreover, being assured by Mr. Adair, who was then at Gibraltar, that the object of this mission would not be approved by government at home, I had it intimated to the Chev. Robertoni that I wished him to return to Palermo.

Just before the arrival of Prince Leopold, the celebrated address from the *Junta* of Seville to the Spanish Nation was received at Gibraltar. This instrument, as I have already mentioned, deprecated the discussion of any subject that might create disunion, particularly *that of the succession*. This publication placed an effectual bar to the object of Prince Leopold's voyage, at least for the present.

CHAPTER 3
Portugal, Landing, Armistice, and Convention

Lord Collingwood having been directed to place a frigate at my disposal, in order that I might have the means of transferring myself to whatever point of my command my personal presence might be required, His Lordship appointed the *Phoebe* frigate, commanded by Captain Oswald, for that duty. On the 13th of August I embarked, and having passed the Straits by the first fair wind, after I received my orders, I communicated the same day with Lord Collingwood, off Cadiz, as I did, on the 19th, with Sir Charles Cotton, off the Tagus.

From Sir Charles Cotton I received information that Sir Arthur Wellesley had landed in Mondego Bay, and being joined there by General Spencer's corps, was advancing, along the coast, towards Lisbon, deriving his supplies from victuallers, &c. which attended the movement of his army. The admiral also told me of the arrival upon the coast of Brigadier-General Ackland with a corps of troops, seeking an opportunity to land, to join Sir Arthur Wellesley. The admiral had not then heard of the action of Roliça, and did not seem to anticipate much opposition from the enemy to Sir Arthur Wellesley's advance to Lisbon.

Having ordered the 42nd regiment to be embarked at Gibraltar for Portugal, I arranged with Sir Charles Cotton that, upon its arrival, it should remain with the fleet for the present, and, on returning on board the *Phoebe*, I desired Captain Oswald to direct his course towards the Mondego, for the purpose of joining the reinforcements expected from England, with Lieutenant General's Sir Harry Barrard and Sir John Moore.

On the 21st, when sailing along the coast, a fleet of ships was descried under the land, and the first lieutenant of the ship and one of my *aide-de-camps*, being sent on shore for intelligence, they returned, about one o'clock in the morning, with information, that a victory had just been obtained, and that Sir Harry Burrard was on shore and had taken the command of the army. Upon receiving this intelligence, I made for Maceira Bay, at the place where the ships were at anchor, and, landing on the beach, proceeded to the village of Maceira, where I found Sir Harry Burrard, and established my headquarters.

Sir Harry Burrard sailed from Portsmouth on the 31st of July, on board His Majesty's ship *Audacious*, together with a fleet of transports, containing Sir John Moore's corps of 10,000 men. (See Proceedings

Court of Inquiry.)

On the 16th of August, when off Cape Finisterre, Sir Harry shifted on board the *Brazen* sloop, and made sail for Oporto, where he arrived next day, and, learning that Sir Arthur Wellesley had landed at Mondego, he proceeded southward, and, on the 18th, arrived off the Mondego, where he found despatches from Sir Arthur Wellesley, in which it was recommended that Sir John Moore's corps should land at Mondego, and proceed to Santarem, to confine the movements of the enemy on that side.

This suggestion Sir Harry Burrard determined at first not to accede to; but afterwards found cause to send back orders to Sir John Moore to land in the Mondego Bay, and (under a knowledge of Sir A. Wellesley's despatches, which were sent for his information) to act as he might think best for Sir Arthur's support. (See Proceedings Court of Inquiry.)

On the evening of the 20th, Sir Harry Burrard arrived off the landing-place at Maceira, when Sir Arthur Wellesley came on board to report his proceedings and the actual state of things, and ended by saying he had intended to march next morning, at five o'clock, by the Mafra-road, to turn the enemy's position at Torres Vedras.

Of this plan Sir Harry Burrard did not approve; and gave orders to Sir Arthur Wellesley that the army should not move next morning. He at the same time sent orders by land, and by the *Brazen* sloop, to Sir John Moore, to proceed forthwith to Maceira, and, if any of his troops were on shore, to order them to embark and follow.

Sir Arthur Wellesley being of opinion that, if the army remained on its ground, it would be attacked by the enemy, he made such dispositions as he thought necessary in consequence. Sir Arthur was not disappointed in his expectations, for, soon after eight o'clock, a. m. on the 21st, the enemy appeared in force on the left of the position.

On the 21st, about nine o'clock in the morning, Sir Harry Burrard landed from His Majesty's ship *Alfred*, where he had passed the night; and, upon receiving notice from an officer, sent by Sir A. Wellesley, that large bodies of the enemy were seen moving towards the left of the position, Sir Harry hastened to Vimiera, where he arrived about ten o'clock; at which time he found Brigadier-Generals Anstruther and Fane's brigades vigorously attacked by the enemy.

Here Sir Harry Burrard was informed of, saw, and approved all the steps taken by Sir Arthur Wellesley to repulse the enemy, and directed him to proceed in the execution of an operation he had so happily begun; but he afterwards, before the Court of Inquiry, indignantly repelled the supposition that he had, at any time, (but particularly at that time,) an intention of giving up the command of the army to another. (See Proceedings Court of Inquiry.)

The enemy being repulsed in all parts, and in full retreat, Sir Arthur Wellesley proposed to Sir H. Burrard to take advantage of the victory, by pursuing them; which, however, the latter, from the view he had taken of the state of things, deemed it best to decline; and the army remained on the ground where the battle had been fought, and where I found it when I landed on the 22nd.

Upon my arrival at Maceira, Sir Harry Burrard gave me the necessary information respecting the recent transactions; and (to use his own words to the Court of Inquiry) "*how* and *why* he had acted." Soon after, Sir Arthur Wellesley (whom I had never before seen) came into the room, and expressed much anxiety that the army should advance. As soon as I could ascertain whether any orders had been issued by Sir H. Burrard for the morrow, I acceded to the proposition, and desired Sir A. Wellesley to hold the army in readiness to march next day at daybreak, (as stated in the Report of the Court of Inquiry):

> Undoubtedly as soon as it could be put in motion after his arrival;—and, considering the extraordinary circumstances under which two new commanding-generals arrived from the ocean and joined the army, (the one during and the other immediately after a battle, and those successively superseding each other, and both the original commander within the space of twenty-four hours,) it is not surprising that the army was not carried forward until the second day after the action.

Between one and two o'clock, p. m. a report came in that the enemy seemed to be advancing, I, therefore, desired Sir A. Wellesley (who was soon upon the spot) to take up the position as the day before. This, however, soon proved to be a body of French cavalry, with a flag of truce; and, soon after one o'clock, General Kellermann arrived at Sir Arthur Wellesley's quarters, at Vimeira, where he found Sir Harry Burrard, Sir Arthur Wellesley, and myself.

The object of General Kellermann's mission was to propose, on the part of the general-in chief of the French Army, a suspension of hostilities, in order to settle a definitive convention for the evacuation of Portugal by the French troops, with their arms and baggage. Lieutenant-Generals Sir Harry Burrard and Sir Arthur Wellesley assisted in the discussions which took place upon this occasion; and I need urge no other reason for my assenting to the measure proposed than that it was recommended by Sir Arthur Wellesley, whose opinion, as being the most competent judge of the relative situations of the two armies at this point of time, I should have thought it my duty to follow, even if his judgement had not been so particularly recommended to my attention by the Secretary of State.

Sir Arthur recommended the measure of allowing the French to evacuate Portugal with their arms and baggage, (Proceedings and Appendix to Inquiries), and that every facility for this purpose should be afforded to them, from the relative state of the armies on the evening of the 22nd, considering that the French had then resumed a formidable position between us and Lisbon; that they had the means of retiring from that position to others in front of that city; and, finally, of crossing the Tagus into Alemtejo, with a view to the occupation, in strength, of Elvas la Lippe, and, eventually, Almeida, (see Sir A. Wellesley's Letter, of 6th Oct. 1808, to Lord Castlereagh, in the Appendix to the Proceedings of the Court of Inquiry):

> As Sir John Moore's corps had been diverted from the occupation of the position at Santarem, which had been proposed for them, there were no means to prevent, *and no increase of numbers could have prevented*, the French Army from effecting these objects.

The suspension of arms was therefore agreed upon, to terminate at forty-eight hours' notice. The basis of the proposed treaty was also settled, but not to be considered as in force without the concurrence of Admiral Sir Charles Cotton; for I was quite determined to conclude no definitive convention with the French commander-in-chief, to which the British admiral should not be a party as well as myself.

The armistice being copied fairly, and signed by Sir Arthur Wellesley and General Kellermann, the latter retired; when immediately an *aide-de camp*, from General Bernardin Friere de Andrada, was introduced to me, being sent, as he said, by his general (who had heard of my arrival) to ask my commands.

That there was a Portuguese force somewhere, I had probably heard; and, in the forenoon, I had seen a Portuguese detachment marching to occupy the post assigned it in the position; but, as neither General Friere nor his army had been mentioned to me during the recent discussions, or spoken of as having had any share in the battle of the 21st, I was not prepared to find them so near at hand; I could only, therefore, desire the *aide-de-camp* to give my respects to his general, and to say that I should be glad of the honour of seeing him next day at Ramalhall, where I intended to have my headquarters.

On the 23rd, the army advanced to a new position, within the line of demarcation; and, soon after my arrival at Ramalhall, I was visited by the Portuguese General Friere de Andrada. The general soon entered upon the subject of the treaty, and the whole proceedings of the day before, with which he seemed to be much offended; particularly, as he thought that he himself, and the *Government of Portugal*, (for such he considered the *Junta* of Oporto to be,) had been treated with disrespectful neglect.

I was not prepared, at the moment, fully to discuss this matter, but gave him to understand that no disrespect was meant; and that, however meritorious the exertions of the *Junta* of Oporto might have been, I could not consider that body to be the government of Portugal, and the legitimate representative of its prince. In the meantime, that I should furnish him with a copy of the armistice, provisional though it was, and subject to the admiral's approval, in order that I might receive such observations as he should think it necessary to make, that they might be considered during the negotiation of the treaty.

In paying this respect to the Portuguese general, which I thought due to him under the present circumstances, I committed a grievous error, as the sequel proved, and as I shall have occasion to shew. Early on the 23rd, in the morning, Lieutenant Colonel Murray, Quarter-master-General, set off for the fleet, to communicate to Admiral Sir Charles Cotton the terms of the agreement, provisionally concluded with the French general, but subject to his approbation and concurrence.

On the 24th, at night, Colonel Murray returned from the fleet, with information, that the admiral objected to an article in the armistice which regarded the Russian fleet; as he was ready himself to enter into an agreement with Admiral Siniavin upon that point. But that he had no objection to join me in negotiating with General Junot upon the remaining articles.

Sir Charles Cotton having thus declined to sanction the Russian article in the basis, I conceived the armistice to be at an end, and determined on sending to announce the recommencement of hostilities at the end of forty-eight hours. In consequence, I sent Lieutenant-Colonel Murray to Lisbon, on the 25th, with a letter, informing General Junot of the admiral's decision; but, at the same time, I gave authority to Lieutenant-Colonel Murray, should Junot manifest a wish to negotiate on the remaining articles of the former agreement, (that respecting the Russian fleet being expunged,) to enter upon such negotiation, and to conclude a convention upon the terms specified in a paper of memoranda, which Sir Arthur Wellesley had previously drawn up. Lieutenant-Colonel Murray was further empowered to prolong the suspension of hostilities for a *definite period*, should the negotiation be entered into.

During the night between the 26th and 27th, a French officer arrived with letters from Lieutenant-Colonel Murray and General Junot, in forming me that the negotiation was in progress; but as General Junot, by his letter, affected to understand that the cessation of hostilities was now to be for an unlimited period, and to depend upon Sir Charles Cotton's negotiation with Admiral Siniavin; whilst Lieutenant-Colonel Murray distinctly reported that, according to his instructions, he had only offered a continuance of the truce for a limited period; it seemed necessary to Sir Arthur Wellesley and myself to send Lieutenant-Colonel Murray instructions, (which were drawn up by Sir Arthur Wellesley,) immediately to clear up this misunderstanding; and, if that could not be satisfactorily done, to break off the negotiation, and come away. In the other case he was to continue it; and, for that purpose, was authorised to prolong the armistice for a further period of twenty-four hours. These instructions were sent by Sir Arthur Wellesley's *aide-de-camp*, Lord Fitzroy Somerset, to Lisbon.

On the 29th, in the morning, Captain Dalrymple, who had accompanied Lieutenant-Colonel Murray to Lisbon, brought a treaty, which that officer had concluded with General Kellermann, who had been appointed to negotiate with him; some of the provisions of which seeming objectionable, I assembled all the lieutenant-generals I could immediately collect, namely, Lieutenant Generals Sir Harry Burrard, Sir John Moore, the Hon. J. Hope, Mackenzie Frazer, and Sir Arthur Wellesley; when the treaty was read, article by article, and the objections and proposed alterations minuted down by Sir Arthur Wellesley, which, being copied, was sent by my *aide-de camp*, Captain Fanshawe, to Lieutenant-Colonel Murray, for his guidance.

On the 31st, at an early hour in the morning, Lieutenant-Colonel Murray, accompanied by Lord Fitzroy Somerset and Captain. Fanshawe, together with an *aide-de-camp* of General Kellermann's, arrived at Torres Vedras, (Report of the Board of Inquiry), where my headquarters were then established, with the definitive convention, in which some of the articles of the treaty of the 28th, which had been objected to, were altered, and some other "good alterations inserted, not before suggested." At all events the season for negotiation was past; I, therefore, immediately convened the lieutenant generals I could assemble—Sir Harry Burrard, Sir John Moore, Hon. J. Hope, and Mackenzie Fraser; and, in their presence, and with their approbation, I ratified the *definitive convention.*

During these negotiations Sir John Moore arrived at Maceira, and disembarked his troops as fast as the state of the weather would allow. Two regiments of infantry, two brigades of artillery, and the German cavalry, landed on the 26th, but the last division did not land until the 29th of August; and the disembarkation was not effected without great difficulty, and, latterly, some loss.

On the 29th, at noon, the term for the suspension of hostilities having expired, I moved my headquarters to Torres Vedras, in front of which was, at the same time, placed Major-General Paget's advanced guard; on the 28th, the corps, originally under the command of Sir Arthur Wellesley, had marched towards, and near to Torres Vedras; leaving Brigadier-Generals Anstruther's and Ackland's brigades, with part of Sir John Moore's corps, in camp at Ramalhall.

On the 31st, early in the morning, Sir Arthur Wellesley's corps moved to the left, and the divisions of Lieutenant-Generals Hope and Mackenzie Fraser took up the ground in the rear of Torres Vedras, which Sir Arthur's corps had occupied. Sir Arthur Wellesley proceeded by Sobral de Monte Agraça to occupy the position assigned to his corps.

The definitive convention having been concluded, on the 1st of September, the troops under my immediate command began their march towards the positions they were to occupy during the embarkation of the French; and, on the 2nd, I established my headquarters at Cintra, where I learned that the treaty having been ratified by the admiral, our troops had that day occupied the forts upon the Tagus; from Cintra, therefore, my despatches, giving an account of the recent transactions, were dated, and sent off.

On this march, I was met by two Russian officers, charged with a letter to me from Admiral Siniavin, desiring to know what flag would be displayed when we took possession of the forts on the Tagus, and whether, if the Portuguese flag were hoisted, the port of Lisbon would be considered as neutral? and his squadron entitled to the benefit of the neutrality?

In reply to this letter, I intimated to the Russian admiral, that his query should have been addressed to Sir Charles Cotton; for that I did not think myself at liberty to interfere in a matter which that admiral had reserved to himself.

Had I thought it proper to enter into any discussion with Admiral Siniavin, I should have assured him that the Portuguese flag would certainly be hoisted on the forts when occupied by British troops; for, although Sir Charles Cotton's negotiation with the Russian admiral might be facilitated by a contrary proceeding, I thought it was of the utmost importance, that so great and so just a cause of jealousy and offence should not be afforded to the Portuguese Nation, as to appear to usurp the sovereignty which we had just compelled the French to relinquish.

On the 3rd of September, at a very early hour in the morning, the long looked-for despatches from England reached me, of which the most important were—Instructions for the establishment of a provisional government at Lisbon, when the French should be expelled from Portugal; and a confidential communication from Lord Castlereagh upon the subject of the future conduct of the war, when that great object should be accomplished: the former of these documents was dated the 19th, the latter the 20th of August.

On the 4th of September, Captain Dalrymple and Captain Halsted, first Captain of the *Hibernia*, embarked for England with my despatches and those of Sir Charles Cotton, *each* containing a copy of the convention with General Junot which we respectively had ratified. (See *London Gazette*, Sept. 16, 1808.) Captain Halsted was also charged with another despatch from the admiral, containing the convention Sir Charles Cotton had himself concluded with the Russian admiral, Siniavin, in which I had no share, and of which I had at the time no cognisance.

I must not forget to mention that Sir Charles Cotton, as soon as he had ratified the treaty with the French general, and the forts on the Tagus were, in consequence, evacuated by the French, landed the 3rd and 42nd regiments from the fleet, took possession of the forts, and caused British colours to be hoisted. As soon as the fact was made known to me, I ordered the Portuguese flag to be substituted for the British; but this error, though soon rectified, was used at Oporto as a means of inflaming the popular discontent.

On the 5th of September, the army advanced and took up ground in front of St. Julian, the left extending to the Heights of Bellas; the same day my headquarters were transferred from Cintra to Oeyras.

Whilst the embarkation of the French was in progress, the situation of our troops was changed, and headquarters removed, first to Prayas and afterwards to Bemfico, both sufficiently near Lisbon for every purpose of business. I never fixed my residence in that capital.

To avoid long and minute details of the measures pursued to carry the provisions of the convention into effect, I shall insert that part of the report of the Board of General Officers which relates to that particular subject. It was formed, after minute inquiry into all the circumstances of the case, and, being an official document upon record, requires no reference to vouchers placed in the Appendix.

> It appears that the forts on the Tagus were taken possession of, on the 2nd of September, by the British troops, and the port was then opened to our shipping; that, on the 5th, the army had its right at St. Julian's, and its left on the Heights of Bellas; that, on the 8th or 9th, a British corps marched into Lisbon to ensure the tranquillity of that city during the embarkation of the enemy, who were all sent off (except the last division, purposely detained, by orders from home,) before the end of the month, and part of the British Army was then actually on its route to the Spanish frontier.
>
> It appears that, during the discussion, and afterwards during the execution of the convention, much firmness was shewn in resisting the pretensions and interpretations of the enemy; every stipulation being restricted to its fair, honourable, and grammatical meaning; and the French not allowed to carry off, but obliged to disgorge plunder which they affected to consider as private property.
>
> It appears that pains were taken to misrepresent and raise a clamour, in Portugal, against the convention; but, when it was generally known, and its effects felt, the people of Lisbon and of the country seem to have expressed their gratitude and thanks for the benefits attending it.
>
> On the whole, it appears that the Convention of Cintra, in its progress and conclusion, or at least the principal articles of it, were not objected to by the five distinguished lieutenant-generals of that army; and other general officers who were on that service, whom we have had an opportunity to examine, have

also concurred in the great advantages that were immediately gained to the country of Portugal, to the army and navy, and to the general service, by the conclusion of the convention at that time.

★★★★★★

The name Cintra was improperly and unluckily applied to this treaty; as it produced an opinion, that it was actually negotiated and concluded in that village, in a certain hall, in the Marialva Palace, whereas Cintra was in rear of the "formidable position," the possession of which was obtained by the convention.

★★★★★★

Pains were, indeed, taken by the Bishop of Oporto, his partisans and adherents, to misrepresent and raise a clamour against the convention, not only in Portugal but in England also. In the former their misrepresentations were soon contradicted by the evidence of facts; not so in England; they were there so powerfully seconded by the language held by ministers, and the measures they pursued, that the erroneous impression thus made upon the public mind was confirmed and perpetuated.

The main agents in propagating disaffection in Portugal were General Friere and an officer, called Sousa, whom the general asked leave to attach to my headquarters, whilst the definitive convention was negotiating. This officer was, certainly, not sparing in his observations upon the stipulations which formed the basis of the treaty, principally founded upon the assumption, that the *Junta* of Oporto was the lawful government of Portugal, which I never failed to deny. But both this officer and his general were deaf to my requests, that they should state their observations in writing, and in an official shape, when every possible attention would be paid to their representation. When, however, the treaty was ratified, and the question was decided, both those officers began to write, and their correspondence abounded in some animadversions upon the provisions of an instrument which it was now my duty to abide by.

Although the letters of both those officers, a memorial from the general, a remonstrance and a protest, were directed to me, they were, in fact, addressed to the passions and the prejudices of the people. I was, therefore, aware of the necessity of replying to those vexatious addresses with civility and temper, as it was evident the correspondence would be immediately submitted to the public: but when, in his memorial and protest, General Friere indulged in false and injurious animadversions upon the general character of the British Nation and government, I thought it time to put an end to this sort of correspondence, and closed my reply to those insinuations by saying:

> I hasten to assure Your Excellency, and shall use the necessary means to give publicity to the pledge, that I serve in Portugal as commander of a force acting in alliance with the sovereign of that country; and that I, therefore, consider myself to be bound, by duty and honour, (as far as my judgement and abilities stand,) to pay as strict a regard to the interests of the prince regent; the dignity and security of his government; and the welfare of the nation of which he is the lawful ruler, as even Your Excellency yourself.

Amongst the papers which I received on this occasion, one that was addressed to me by Pinto de Sousa, in the form of queries, requires notice, as it shews the connexion between General Friere and Don Josef Galluzzo, Captain General of Spanish Estremadura, to whose proceedings I shall have, by and by, occasion to refer. The question I allude to was as follows:—

> If the *Provisional Government of Portugal*, approving the conduct of General Friere, for not having taken any part in the arrangements made with the French, should order him to move forwards in combination with the Spanish Army in Alemtejo, would the English Army, in that case, offer any opposition?

To this query I thought no reply necessary. About this time, another Portuguese general, from the south, was introduced to my notice quite as unexpectedly as had a few days before been General Friere, from the north. This general enclosed, in a letter to Sir Charles Cotton, a protest against the convention, and demanded that all the vessels, in which the French troops were embarked, should be embargoed in the Tagus, until the pleasures of the King of England, or the Prince Regent of Portugal, should be made known. The writer of this letter was no less a personage than "Francisco Mello del Cuhna de Mendonça Menezes, Count of Castro Marino, Montiero Mor, &c. &c. &c. &c. General of the Army of the South, and President of the Supreme *Junta* of the Kingdom of Algarve." His letter contained a pompous account of his exploits, he states:

> Having driven the enemy from Algarve, and pursuing him into Alemtejo, causing him to abandon all his posts, and march away

until the Portuguese Army of the south took up its position on the south bank of the Tagus, &c.

Although this nobleman must have been a very respectable person, as being the individual whom the prince regent, on his departure, named to supply any vacancy which might occur in the regency; of his military exploits, as described by himself, I had considerable doubts; as, however, the letter and protest were addressed to Sir Charles Cotton and not to me, I left it to the admiral to reply to his expostulation.

I found it more difficult to deal with Don Josef Galluzzo, Captain-General of Spanish Estremadura, with whom General Friere thought he might be ordered by the *Junta* to combine his operations.

As soon as the convention was ratified, I took steps to communicate the fact to Galluzzo; but soon found, by a letter from him, that he had not received, or did not choose to acknowledge, the receipt of that intimation. In reply, I gave him full information of what had been agreed on, and that, therefore, there was no longer war in Portugal; that the Spanish troops, detained by the French in the Tagus, would speedily be armed and equipped, and would, ere long, join one of the Spanish Armies now marching to expel the enemy from Spain; and, in conclusion, observed:

> That, as we were all engaged in the same cause, it would be very satisfactory to me to be informed to what point it was his intention to direct the march of the army under his command; for I knew that the Spanish Armies were assembling to act against the enemy at this favourable juncture; and that His Excellency, with the Army of Estremadura, was anxiously looked for to take his place in the line.

I thought this observation, which Galluzzo knew to be the truth, would have had some effect upon him; but I was mistaken; Galluzzo had other views, and his present object was, to oppose every obstacle he could to the fulfilment of the convention with the French.

In consequence of this determination, I learnt, from Colonel Ross, of the 20th regiment, whom I had sent in the command of a corps to take possession of Elvas and Fort la Lippe, and to escort the French troops occupying those places to Lisbon, that, having sent forward an officer to communicate to the French commandant the approach of the British troops, and the object of their march, he found that a Spanish force from Estremadura, of from four to five thousand men, had appeared before the place, and that the French had retired into the forts, which they were preparing to defend. The officer, however, obtained admission into Fort la Lippe, and delivered to the French commandant a letter from General Kellermann, of which the latter did not pretend to doubt the authenticity; but desired leave to send an officer to the French headquarters to receive further instructions, before he gave up the important place committed to his charge.

To this proposition, when communicated to me, I saw no cause to object, neither did the officer commanding the Spanish corps before the place make any opposition; but, though he allowed of this communication between the French commandant and his general in-chief, he would not permit him to conform to the instructions he had received, but pretended to force him to submit to certain conditions, which General Galluzzo had determined to impose, but which he certainly had not the power to enforce.

Soon after receiving Colonel Ross's report, which was dated the 15th of September, from his camp, one league beyond Estremos, I received a letter from General Paula Liete, who commanded the Portuguese troops in Alemtejo, dated on the 16th, from Estremos, informing me that he had received an order, by an officer from the *Junta* of Oporto, dated the 1st of September, directing him to take possession of Elvas as soon as it should be evacuated by the French. The general expressed his opinion that this order was given in consequence of the conduct of the Spanish troops in Alemtejo, which was marked by a system of plunder and devastation, and that it was against them that this precaution was taken.

In this General Liete was mistaken; the order was given that he should act in co-operation with those very Spanish troops; but it fell out otherwise; for Liete having, the day before, seen a body of English troops pass Estremos, on its route to Elvas, and "knowing (as the general observed) that, in a combined army, no officer should undertake an operation intended for another," he had sent his quartermaster-general, the Marquess de Tornay, to deliver that letter, and to communicate with me upon the subject of its contents. I found the Marquess de Tornay a reasonable and intelligent man; and he went back to his general with explanations that proved entirely satisfactory to him, and upon which he regulated his future proceedings.

My correspondence with General Galluzzo, though conducted in terms of civility and respect, not promising any successful result, as he abated nothing of the violence of his proceedings; and all the French troops at Lisbon being embarked, it becoming necessary to extend the cantonments of the army and to push part of it forwards towards the Spanish frontier; I directed Lieutenant-General Hope, with his own division, and the advanced guard commanded by Major General Paget, to occupy advanced cantonments upon the Tagus, in Alemtejo; and I, at the same time, sent Colonel Graham to expostulate with Galluzzo and the *Junta* of Estremadura upon the hostile operations carrying on against the fortress of La Lippe and its dependencies, which could only tend to create delay, at a moment when expedition was most desirable. Colonel Graham was directed, if he found Galluzzo obstinate, to proceed to Madrid, to lay the case before the Central Government of Spain.

These measures had soon a favourable result, and, by the judicious language held by Colonel Graham, and probably from Galluzzo himself being convinced of the unreasonableness of his pretensions, and the insignificance of his means of supporting them, he withdrew his troops (composed of undisciplined peasantry) from the neighbourhood of Elvas, which, with La Lippe, were delivered up, by the French commandant, to the British troops, and the French garrison marched to Lisbon for embarkation.

CHAPTER 4
Portugal, Establishing the Regency

Amongst the papers which were put into my hands, when I first landed in Portugal, was an Address from the bishop and *Junta* of Oporto, to Sir Charles Cotton, dated the 4th of August, upon the subject of the *form of Government with which they meant* to govern Portugal, immediately the City of Lisbon was free from the French." (Appendix to Inquiry, No. 124, 125.) This document began by announcing the glorious resolution the *Junta* had taken "of restoring the Portuguese monarchy in all its extent, and of restoring the crown of Portugal to its lawful sovereign, Don John the Sixth." For that purpose, they proposed that they should themselves install the individuals composing the regency originally established by their prince on his departure, with the exception of those who had accepted office under Junot.

But, in order to identify the bishop and *Junta* with this new regency, it was proposed that one of their own body should formally install the new government, of which he was himself to be a member, and when it should be *acknowledged by the Junta of Oporto*, "and not before," it should assume "the reins of government of all the kingdom, in the manner ordered by the prince regent." The whole, however, concluded with a *proviso*, that, in case "this newly named regency should be interrupted by a new invasion of the French, (which God forbid,) *or by any other thing,*" that the *Junta* of Oporto should *resume the Government of the kingdom.* By this arrangement it was intended to establish the Government at *Lisbon*; and in enumerating the individuals of the original regency, who were to be restored, the name of the principal Castro (half-brother to the Bishop of Oporto) was omitted, as having accepted, from Junot, the office of *Ministre des Cultes*; a strange one for a Romish ecclesiastic of high dignity to accept.

When I perused this paper I did not conceive it possible that the British Government could sanction such a project, or contribute to the establishment of such a phantom of a government, claiming to represent the sovereign, but in fact the mere creature of a revolutionary and local government, like that of Oporto. Strongly impressed with this conviction, I did not hesitate, in my conference with the Portuguese general, Friere, to deny the attribute of sovereignty which he claimed for the *Junta* he served; but, in less than twenty-four hours afterwards I began to doubt the soundness of my judgement upon that point, and to suspect that the views of the bishop and *Junta* of Oporto had powerful supporters in England.

It was the policy of His Majesty's Ministers, at this period, to send officers to the Peninsula, upon a sort of separate, but confidential duty, with instructions to report to the commander of the forces in Portugal, but to correspond with government at home. In pursuance of this system, Brigadier Generals the Baron von Decken and Sontag embarked, on the 11th of August, at Plymouth, for the Asturias; but on the same day received notice from Lord Castlereagh, that their destination was changed, and that they were to proceed to Oporto, where they arrived on the seventeenth.

At a late hour that same night, the bishop desired to see Baron von Decken in private, when the conference began by the former explaining the motives which had induced him to assume the *Government of Portugal*, (see Appendix No. 16)—but hypocritically added, that, as the prince regent, on leaving Portugal, had established a regency, he considered it his duty to resign the government into the hands of that regency as soon as possible.

Against this plan the baron (although he professed that he had no instructions upon the subject) took it upon himself decidedly to object, as he alleged that the persons who formed that regency had deservedly lost the confidence of the nation, by their attachment to the French; but suggested to the bishop, the propriety of his *retaining the Government of Portugal in his own hands* until the pleasure of his sovereign could be known.

The bishop allowed that the former regency did not possess the confidence of the people; that several of the members had shown themselves partisans of the French, and that certainly all the members of that regency could not, with propriety, be restored. Upon the whole, Baron Decken became persuaded that, although the bishop declared the contrary, he was not averse to retaining the government, if it could be done by the interference of the British Government; in the meantime it was agreed that the baron should communicate to our ministers the sub stance of this conference, and (to save time) was also to inform *the general officer commanding His Majesty's forces in Portugal* of the bishop's wish, that he should be pleased to write him an official letter, expressive of his desire, that the bishop should retain the government until the pleasure of his sovereign should be known; neither the bishop nor the baron seemed to have any doubt, that the commander of the forces, whoever that might chance to be, would write the sort of letter he was thus called upon to transmit.

This first letter from Baron von Decken was brought to me by Brigadier-General Stewart, (later Marquess of Londonderry,) who having called at Oporto, on his way out, for any orders that Sir Harry Burrard might have left for him, joined at headquarters, on the 24th of August; the letter I did write to the baron, the very day I received this communication, was of a very different import, as I could not but express my extreme surprise at the whole proceeding, conducted, as it professed to be, without any formal authority from His Majesty's Government: before this letter could reach its destination, two more letters were despatched from Baron von Decken to me, in which the whole arrangement made with the Bishop of Oporto, for the future provisional Government of Portugal, was fully detailed.

It was decided upon that the bishop should preside over the new government, of which the members of the *Junta* of Oporto were to form a part; to them were to be added such individuals of the original regency as had not, according to the bishop's account, joined the French; but in this number his Excellency did not fail to include his half-brother, the Principal Castro, Junot's *Ministre des Cultes*. But as the Bishop of Oporto could not be spared from that City, Baron von Decken was induced to consent that Oporto should be the seat of the new government. The bishop admitted that this would be highly displeasing to the inhabitants of Lisbon and its environs, but Baron von Decken was made to believe that those people were much attached to the French, it was, therefore, agreed on that the ancient capital should be made a military post, occupied by a strong British garrison, which would thus be employed in supporting the Bishop of Oporto's usurpation of the sovereign power, by overawing a justly incensed population.

During the whole of these transactions I remained in total ignorance of the intentions of His Majesty's Government as to the sort of regency that was to be established in Portugal, after the French should be expelled; in fact, no later instructions, of any sort, had been received by me, than those of the 15th of July, which reached me at Gibraltar; but I could not suppose, from the rank and general character of the Baron von Decken, that he would so suddenly, and so soon after his arrival from England, have entered into the sort of negotiations I have described, without being aware that the views of the bishop and *Junta* of Oporto had powerful supporters at home.

As I have already mentioned, I received at Cintra, on the 3rd of September, instructions for the formation of a Council of Regency, *at Lisbon*, after the French should be expelled; and that they were dated at the very time when Baron von Decken was occupied in making arrangements for its establishment *at Oporto*. In this one material point the brigadier-general does not seem to have been fully aware of the intentions of His Majesty's Ministers; in other respects, allowing for the exercise of that discretionary power, which they certainly contained, he might have referred to the instructions I at length received, to sanction his proceedings.

In the first place, the instructions (as the baron had done in his first audience of the bishop) assumed as a fact, that the regency appointed by the prince, on his departure for the Brazils, or at least a considerable number of them, were strongly suspected of a close connexion with the French interest; and stated that it had been suggested to His Majesty's Ministers that, when the French were removed, those individuals would lay claim to resume their functions; that to such a pretension it would be impossible for His Majesty to assent; and that I was, in that case, to consider the authority of that regency of no effect.

In the next place, for the purpose of establishing a regency at Lisbon, with similar powers to those exercised by the regency thus set aside, I was to take measures, in conjunction with such leading individuals in Portugal, as had given proofs of their own fidelity to their sovereign to form a council of regency, composed of such persons of rank, character, and talents, as might be found ready and qualified to discharge so important a trust.

★★★★★★

Baron von Decken found (was, perhaps, directed to find) those individuals at Oporto. The interests and pretensions of the bishop and his associates were powerfully supported by the Chevalier de Sonha, the accredited Minister of Portugal.

★★★★★★

If, however, from circumstances which might have taken place in Lisbon, I should find the establishment of such a regency either impracticable, or, in my judgement, inexpedient, I was, in that case, authorised *myself to assume*, in the name and behalf of the Prince Regent of Portugal, the chief civil as well as military authority. After the measures here proposed should be completed, either by the appointment of a regency, or by myself having assumed the chief civil as well as military authority, it was intimated that:

As several of the provinces of Portugal, which have risen against the French, have appointed temporary authorities for their internal government and organisation, it may be advisable that those authorities should be allowed to remain for a time in the administration of the respective provinces after the appointment of the regency, unless they voluntarily submit to a central government; and, in case you should yourself be obliged to assume the chief civil authority, it will be expedient for you to act in concert with those authorities until His Majesty's pleasure can be known.

With reference to those instructions, it is necessary to observe, that His Majesty's Government did not seem to have been informed, that, of the regency left by the prince on his departure for the Brazils, composed of five individuals, one, the Marquess of Abrantes, was absent in France, (whether voluntarily, or by constraint, did not appear, and was of no consequence); two, the Principal Castro and another, had accepted office under Junot; consequently, none of these three persons had any claim, or right to expect a place in a new Provisional Government; but in the Act of Regency itself, promulgated by the prince regent, upon his departure, one individual, namely, the Monteiro Mor, was named to supply the first vacancy which might occur; and, if more vacancies should eventually arise, it was especially provided that those should be supplied by the suffrage of the remaining members.

Thus there remained three members of the regency named by the sovereign, whose conduct for loyalty remained unimpeached; and it had not fallen in my way to know, or to hear of individuals in Portugal, who had given such undoubted proofs of their fidelity and loyalty to their prince, as to entitle them to more confidence than the three personages above mentioned, either to be chosen themselves, or to select others, to complete the number of which a regency, similar to that originally established, ought to be composed.

By adhering to the rule prescribed by the original constitution of the regency, in supplying the place of those who had, by their misconduct, forfeited the confidence of the nation, I felt confident that the new government would appear most respectable, and would be most acceptable to the nation; and that I should, by that means, be under no necessity to resort to the very strong, and certainly to the people of Portugal, offensive measure, of assuming the chief civil authority to myself. In truth, no council of government, which could have been selected by me, according to that part of my instructions, could have possessed that legal and constitutional character, necessary to silence the clamour, and frustrate the ambitious and selfish designs of the factious.

It may be presumptuous in me to question the policy, under any circumstances whatever, of permitting the co-existence of the revolutionary local *Juntas* which had at that time arisen in the Peninsula, with a National, or what was called a Central Council of Government; but I saw plainly that no such plan would be expedient in Portugal, when a regency should be installed. In fact, there were but two of those *Juntas*, that of Oporto, which had extended its power over the north of Portugal and Alemtejo; and that of the kingdom of Algarve, of which the Monteiro Mor, himself a member of the prince's regency, was President. Under these circumstances, for me to have placed a feeble pageant of a regency in Lisbon to represent the sovereign, but whose power would not have extended far beyond the environs of the city, would have been impossible; and then I must of necessity have, myself, assumed the civil as well as the military power; and the capital would have become, according to the suggestion of the Bishop of Oporto, a British military post, whilst that prelate and his *Junta* would have governed Portugal in effect.

Upon these considerations, I determined that the regency should be restored as nearly as possible according to the original constitution of that body, and that they should continue in the exercise of their authority, until the pleasure of their own sovereign (not that of the

Junta of Oporto) should be made known.

As I had sent Lieutenant-General Hope into Lisbon, in the command of a body of troops, to protect the embarkation of the French Army, I availed myself of the assistance of that most excellent officer, to communicate with those individuals with whom it was necessary to concert arrangements for carrying this important measure into effect; and, on the 19th of September, a proclamation was issued, by which the two admissible members of the original regency, and the Conde Monteiro Mor were invited to assume the functions of government; and all the tribunals were called upon to obey the orders of the regency thus restored. The regency then met, and proceeded to complete their number by the election of the Bishop of Oporto, and the Marquess de las Minas.

It appeared both to General Hope and myself a matter of considerable importance, that the Bishop of Oporto should be elected into the regency, and even placed at its head; it would then remain for him to accept or decline the proposed distinction. In order to prepare the bishop to accede to this proposition, when it should be made to him, I directed Brigadier General Anstruther—(who went, on the 7th of September, to Almeida, to superintend the evacuation of that fortress by the French, and to make the necessary arrangements for the early advance of the army into the adjoining provinces of Spain)—to take Oporto in his route, and to endeavour to persuade the bishop to adopt my views.

The general succeeded completely in his mission, with the understanding, however, (to which he was not aware of the objection,) that the Principal Castro should be a member of the new government; but, although disappointed in this object, the bishop returned a favourable answer to the letter I wrote him, announcing his election to a place in the regency, of which I urged his acceptance in the most flattering and respectful terms I could use. He had not, however, arrived in Lisbon when I left Portugal.

Having thus installed the regency in Lisbon, and the troops, under the command of Lieutenant-General Hope, having moved across the Tagus into Alemtejo, I established Major-General Beresford in Lisbon, as a channel of communication between the commander of the British forces and the Portuguese Government.

It is somewhat remarkable that, in the course of little more than a month, it became my duty to defeat measures *recommended* by two more or less accredited diplomatic agents of His Majesty's Government; the first to give a regent to Spain; the second to establish a regency in Portugal. And, although both those individuals disclaimed any official authority for the measures they proposed, neither of them anticipated the slightest opposition to their execution from me.

When I arrived in London, I requested, from Lord Castlereagh, some intimation of His Majesty's sentiments upon those two transactions; and had the satisfaction of receiving, in reply, the assurance of His Majesty's entire approbation of my conduct in both those cases.

CHAPTER 5

Portugal, For the Advance of the Army, and Ulterior Operations

By a private letter which I received from Lord Castlereagh, at Cintra, (dated the 20th August,) upon the subject of ulterior operations, when the French should be expelled from Portugal, I was informed that the objects of His Majesty's Government would be, to aid the Spaniards in expelling the enemy from their country, and, in the mode of doing so, to aim, if possible, at the destruction or capture of the whole or a part of the French Army.

The amount and dislocation of the British force, which was to co-operate in the accomplishment of those designs, (exclusively of what might be eventually spared from Sicily,) consisted of 30,000 men in Portugal, and 10,000 infantry held ready for embarkation in England; the proportion of cavalry depended on the means of conveyance.

In discussing the modes in which this force might be most advantageously employed, His Lordship dismissed from present consideration the whole line of coast, from the Tagus to the French frontier of Roussillon; and the plans of offensive operations were limited to the following:

1st, That such part of the force, under my command, as could be spared from Portugal, should pass the Spanish frontier, and act, in co-operation with the armies of that nation, against the enemy in front; or,

2ndly, Under the supposition that the native force of Spain could *bear up* against the enemy in front, and that the British troops might act from the northern provinces with more effect than *entering on the side of Portugal*, it was supposed that a British corps, say of 20,000 men, with a proportion of cavalry, and supported by the Spanish levies, would not be too much exposed in the Asturias, or the Principality of St. Andero, taking into consideration the defensive nature of the country; and when reinforced with 10,000 men more from Portugal, (leaving the remaining 10,000 for the service of that country,) it did not seem to be doubted that this army of 30,000 British troops, in co-operation with the force of the country, might act against the French line of communication and the flank and rear of their army: it seems also to have been confidently believed that those operations, combined with the pressure by the main army of Spain in front, would render the future advance of the enemy impracticable; and that there was not then in Spain, nor likely soon to be assembled in that quarter, such an amount of force as would enable the French to defend themselves against such an attack. These reasonings seemed to have been founded on the supposition that the enemy should not have advanced further than Segovia and Burgos.

This letter was evidently written under a most exaggerated and erroneous opinion of the efficiency of the Spanish Armies; as well as of the time that it would require for the French to assemble an amount of force capable of resisting measures of tedious and difficult accomplishment, which were only in discussion so late as the 20th of August; and, although the plan of advancing from Portugal, to join the Spanish Armies assembling to cover the capital, and to act against the enemy's position, was not over looked, the difficulties and disadvantages of that system of warfare were so much dwelt upon, that it was evident the other was the favourite plan of operations. Before my reply to this letter could have reached England, (nearly, indeed, as soon as it was written,) the operations which Sir John Moore was fated to conduct were *almost* determined upon.

Lord Castlereagh's letter concluded with the following sentence, *viz.*:—

In the meantime, and whilst the necessary measures are pursuing to collect information, I trust you will not hesitate to use the full discretion with which you have been invested in such manner as your own excellent judgement may point out to you to be for the advantage of His Majesty's service, without deeming it necessary to wait for authority or instructions from home; and I can safely assure you that you will find, not only in me, but in my colleagues, the most sincere and cordial disposition to support you in the exercise of a responsibility which I am persuaded you will not shrink from, in any instance, where the good of the service may be promoted by your acting without reference home.

The day I received this letter, and, indeed, for ten days afterwards, when I undertook to answer it, it was quite impossible that I could have obtained such information as to enable me to reply satisfactorily to the propositions it contained, particularly as to the amount of force the enemy actually had, and still less as to what he was likely soon to have, assembled in the north of Spain, upon which the whole question turned; I, therefore, thought it best, in order to show the impression upon my mind, under such information as I possessed, of the plan of ulterior operations it was most advisable to adopt, to apprise His Majesty's Ministers of the course I intended to pursue when acting under the discretional power I was thus authorised, or rather urged, to exercise. I could not help, however, prefacing my reply by observing, that although I should dismiss from consideration, according to His Lordship's desire, the whole line of coast from the Tagus to the French frontier of Roussillon, I could not help thinking, as I had before expressed to His Lordship, in a letter from Gibraltar, that the force which might be sent to or might eventually arise in Catalonia, would have a material influence on the result of the war.

I then informed His Lordship that I should, as soon as circumstances would permit, place the army in such cantonments as might enable the whole to assemble and march from Portugal into Spain, in co-operation with the Spanish Armies, against the enemy *in front*, but that the actual advance of the army must depend, 1st, on the real disposition of the Spanish Nation and its generals, as to having a formidable British force enter their country; and, 2ndly, what means the Spaniards would undertake to furnish for the supply of such an army in the field. By the efficacy of those arrangements the more or less inconvenience would be felt, from the length of the line of operations from Portugal; lastly, that, whether the aid of a British force would or would not be required to oppose the enemy in front, (a query proposed by Lord Castlereagh,) would depend, besides the force of the enemy, not on the numbers only, but on the degree of *union* of the Spanish Armies and the state of discipline of each.

Upon the plan of operations to the northward I professed myself unable to give any decided opinion, as far as it might depend on local knowledge of the country; but that I thought the question could not be argued as if thirty thousand British troops could be brought to act at once in that quarter: certainly the 10,000 infantry from England might soon be conveyed to the Asturias or the principality of St. Andero; and that 20,000 more, from Portugal, might, at no distant period, arrive there also; but then the question arises, where may the French Army be when those troops land and what plan of operations may their landing suggest? It is impossible to suppose that the enemy should remain at Burgos all this time inactive, or that he should not take the most prompt and decisive measures to dispose of an enemy thus taking, by detachments, a position to act on his communications.

In conformity to this opinion, I immediately set about the necessary preparations for the movement of the army into Spain as soon as the French should be embarked, by forming the divisions and brigades of the army, and issuing all the necessary orders preparatory to its early advance; and, what was most important, I sent Lord William Bentinck to Madrid, to consult with the Spanish generals then assembled in that Capital, and to concert with them the necessary arrangements for the supply of our army, if it should enter Spain. I also sent Brigadier-General Anstruther to Almeida to obtain every necessary information, should the army eventually enter Spain by that route. He was also to superintend the evacuation of Almeida by the French garrison. I have already mentioned that as soon as the French were out of Lisbon, and the regency installed, Lieutenant-General Hope's presence being no longer necessary there, he was ordered to occupy advanced cantonments with a considerable body of troops.

No time was lost, after it could conveniently be done, to arm, accoutre, and equip a Spanish corps of between three and four thousand men, which had been disarmed and imprisoned on board of ships in the Tagus, by the French, when the insurrections broke out in Spain and Portugal: and by ordering the commissary-general to advance 10,000 dollars to the Marquess of Villadares, who was in command of a Spanish corps which had been serving with the Portuguese northern army, that corps was enabled to march immediately to join General Blake in the north of Spain. As soon as the troops which had been imprisoned by the French were likely to be rendered effective, that corps was claimed by the *Junta* of Seville, and an officer sent to receive it; but he brought no money for its supply, relying upon *the funds* (as they were called) of the British Army, to defray all the necessary expense. Just before this time His Majesty's Ministers had thought it wise to place at the disposal of the *Junta* of Seville a million and a half of dollars and 40,000 stand of arms, with the hope, as Mr. Secretary Canning told the Andalusian Deputies, that the aid then granted, might be considered as applicable to the general service of the country; but the *Junta* thought differently, and the Secretary of State was mistaken in reposing this confidence in the *Junta* of Seville. The corps in question was soon given over by the *Junta* of Seville to that of Estremadura, and Don Josef Galluzzo sent a general officer to command it.

Ultimately, in consequence of an application from the Marquess del Palarios, supported by one from General Castaños, both brought me by a deputy from Catalonia, after I had received His Majesty's commands to transfer the command of the army to Sir Harry Burrard, and return to England, (by the desire, also, of Galluzzo,) I embarked those troops in British transports, with the consent of Sir Harry Burrard, but under my own responsibility, and sent them to Rosas, with 90,000 dollars, for the remount of the cavalry, and 10,000 stand of arms for the use of the province of Catalonia.

At this time, when the sum of a million and a half of dollars was entrusted to the management of the *Junta* of Seville, so much difficulty was found in procuring money for the payment of our army, without raising the exchange to a degree highly disadvantageous to the public, that the commissary-general was directed to procure money for his bills at Gibraltar and Cadiz.: such were the *funds of the British Army*.

In completing the history of this Spanish detachment, I have somewhat anticipated the course of events to which I now return.

About the middle of September, I received two letters from Lord Castlereagh, by the same conveyance, the one dated the 2nd, the other the 4th of September, to which last, I shall, by and by, have occasion to revert. The letter dated the 2nd of September, which was the day the news of the victory at Vimiera was communicated to the public, was evidently written before those advices were received by Government. Here follows the copy:—

Downing-Street,
Sept 2, 1808.

I am to acquaint you that it is the opinion of His Majesty's Ministers, (subject, of course, to alteration from any subsequent information they shall receive,) that it may be expedient, as early as possible after the enemy's force shall have been either reduced or expelled from Portugal, to direct as large a British corps as can be conveniently assembled to the north of Spain, there to co-operate with the armies of Spain in expelling the enemy from the Peninsula.

Ten thousand infantry, and a proportion of cavalry, are held in readiness here, to be united with such part of the army in Portugal as may be rendered disposable after due provision shall have been made for the garrison of Lisbon, and of the forts on the Tagus. It is presumed that 20,000 men may, in that case, be appropriated from the force under your command, for the ser vice in question; and that 10,000 British troops, with the Por-tuguese levies, will amply provide for all the immediate wants of the country as long as the enemy shall be kept at a distance from the frontier of Portugal.

I am, therefore, to convey to you the king's pleasure, that you do hold such proportion of your force, as you may be of opinion could be spared for such a service, consistently with the princi-ples above stated, in such a state of preparation as may admit of its being detached upon receipt of His Majesty's commands to that effect; and as circumstances may come to your know ledge, which might render the immediate employment of your dis-posable force, in the north of Spain, of the utmost importance to the common cause, without waiting for orders from home, I am to acquaint you, that it is not His Majesty's pleasure that you should consider the present instruction as depriving you of the latitude of discretion, which you now possess, of acting in such cases as the good of His Majesty's service may appear to you to demand, without waiting for express orders from hence. In this case, however, you will lose no time in notifying your determination to me, in order that the movements of the corps, now held in readiness for service here, may be combined with those of the troops from Portugal.

(Signed)   Castlereagh.

From this letter it appeared, that what had been thrown out as a subject for consideration in Lord Castlereagh's letter, of the 20th of August, had now become the plan of operations decided upon by His Majesty's ministers, subject to such alterations as further information might produce, and with this improvement, that the 20,000 men from Portugal were at once to be united to the 10,000 from England, in the north of Spain, instead of by detachments of 10,000 men each; but how that union was to be effected does not seem, at any time, to have formed a part of the ministerial arrangements. It was, however, in my opinion, most probable, that, should this plan be persevered in, orders would be received for the embarkation of the troops in the transports which were quite ready for their reception in the Tagus; for it did not seem probable that a part of a corps, collecting in the Asturias, and deriving its security from the defensive nature of the country, would be ordered to enter Spain from the side of Portugal.

But besides my own opinion, that our early junction with the Spanish armies was the only means (if there were any means) of rendering those armies effective, there was so much of uncertainty in this official communication, depending, as it did, on further information; and so much discretional power was still left to me, that I determined to proceed in the preparatory measures which I had commenced for an advance by land; I did not, however, think that I should be justified in incurring a considerable expense in the purchase of baggage animals, which the next despatches from England might render useless. To establish magazines, on the routes through Portugal never occurred to me; but measures were taking for the supply of the troops, with provisions, on the march, moving in small divisions, and by several routes; and it was thus, I believe, the army moved to the Spanish frontier at last, when the decision of the question, in what manner the army should move, was left to Sir John Moore.

Whatever difficulty or delay Sir John Moore might have experienced from the want of the equipments which I *did not* provide, it was not from that cause that the worst consequences ensued, but from the total want of the necessary preliminary arrangements, for the proper reception, at Corunna, of the troops from England; from whence arose much inconvenience, and the delay of the junction of that corps with Sir John Moore. The necessity of marching a column of the army from Portugal to the north of Spain, by the Escurial, was not suggested when I left Portugal.

By Lord Castlereagh's letter of the 2nd of September, discretional power was limited to operations in the north of Spain, but no favourable report from Lord William Bentinck was received, whilst I remained in the command; and in point of fact, there did not exist, in the Spanish Government or armies, at that period, that unity of purpose, or subordination to authority, which could render any combined operation safe or expedient, as will, I think, appear by the following statement of what the Spanish Armies actually were, and how they were commanded and distributed.

General Castaños did not enter Madrid until the 23rd of August at the head of General La Peñas's division of 7,000 men, belonging to the victorious Army of Andalusia; he was received in a sort of triumph, amidst the acclamations of the people.

The Army of Andalusia, commanded by General Castaños, amounting to about 28,000 regular troops, had one division in Madrid, one in La Mancha, and two at Puerto del Rey Carolina, and St. Helena.

The Army of Estremadura, commanded by General Gulluzzo, was at Badajoz, the infantry principally composed of the peasantry, the exact force not mentioned.

The Army of Gallicia, commanded by General Blake, of from 20,000 to 23,000 regular troops, stationed at Astorga and Leon.

The Army of Castile, commanded by General Cuesta, from 18,000 to 20,000 peasantry, but including 2,000 cavalry stationed at Salamanca and the places adjacent.

The Army of Arragon, commanded by General Palafox, of from 20,000 to 30,000 peasantry and in habitants of the town of Saragossa, stationed at Saragossa and Tudela.

The Army of Valencia, commanded by General Llamas, had one division of 12,000 men at Madrid, and one division of 16,000 men at Tudela. In the Madrid division there were 6,000 regular troops.

Of the force in Catalonia I had no official accounts at this time. The troops I have enumerated were destined to cover the Capital; to capture or expel the French force, then in the neighbourhood of Burgos, to the amount, as was supposed, of about 40,000 men; and to recover the fortresses, and occupy the passes of the Western Pyrenees.

On the 4th of September, a meeting of the generals, commanding the Provincial armies, was held at Madrid, to consider of the measures to be pursued, and the plan of operations to be adopted, in order to effect the above important designs. Here follows the result of their deliberations: *viz.*—

General Llamas, when he should have occupied Tarazona and Agreda, was to take post at Cascante, Corella, and Calahorra. This movement was to take place as soon as General Peña, with the Army of Andalusia, was in readiness to support his left, by moving to Logrono and Najera; and then (but not before) General Palafox was to take up the position of Sanguessa. It was intended that General Cuesta should fill up the space between La Peña and Blake, who was supposed to have advanced to Palencia: at this time, it was calculated that the head of the Andalusian Army would arrive at Soria, about (but not before) the 17th of September.

Whatever might be the merits or the objects of this disposition, there was not much chance that either that or any other arrangement of the sort could be carried into execution.

In the first place, the *Junta* of Seville had given strict orders to their general not to advance beyond Madrid; at least, until the Central *Junta* should be installed; and, to ensure his compliance with those injunctions, the *Junta* withheld the necessary funds for the supply of his army.

Don Josef Galluzzo, as we have already seen, had formed an engagement (announced in a letter of the 27th of August, to General Bernardin Freire) to march a force into Alemtejo, an engagement which he faithfully fulfilled. General Cuesta, instead of advancing with his army to Burgo del Orma, as had been agreed upon at the meeting of generals, (at which he had himself been present,) fell back upon Segovia, for the purpose of arresting the Captain-General Valdes, (a Counsellor of State and Deputy from Leon to the Supreme *Junta*,) and lodging him a prisoner in the Tower of Segovia.

General Palafox, who, though son of a *grandee* of Spain, was, before this war, a person of no rank or consideration as an officer, now found himself a captain-general, and in the command of an army which was in the position assigned it by the meeting of generals; but he had become so elated by the renown he had acquired by the glorious defence of Saragossa, that he was not much disposed to submit to any control, and had even written in terms of authority to the Council of Castile, telling that body that he should make it responsible for not immediately sending forwards to him all the troops at Madrid, in which Castaños's army was included.

It is not to be wondered at, therefore, that, in spite of what had been decided upon at Madrid, this presumptuous young man determined *immediately* to send a corps of 7,000 men, to take post at Sanguessa, by this means turning (as he alleged) the flank of the enemy, and threatening his rear and his retreat; and this was done before the army under General Llamas could be sufficiently advanced to support the corps, thus taking a position within seven leagues of Pampeloña, and at least seventy miles from Saragossa. In short, every general commanding a Provincial Army thought himself completely independent, except, perhaps, of the instructions from the *Junta* of the province to which his army belonged.

On the 9th of September, Major Cox remonstrated, in emphatic terms, with the *Junta* of Seville, upon their having withheld from General Castaños the pecuniary supplies which were necessary to enable him to move the Andalusian Army to Soria, the place assigned for it by the Council of Generals at Madrid. Next day the *Junta* replied to this representation in lofty terms, contrasting the efforts made by Andalusia in support of the common cause, with those of the other Provinces of Spain. To this reply Major Cox made a spirited rejoinder, which seems to have produced the desired effect.

On the 17th, the *Junta* published a manifesto, in which was inserted an extract of a letter from that body to General Castaños, giving him full powers to exercise his own discretion, and assuring him of pecuniary supplies. To persuade the people that this was their own spontaneous act, the *Junta* inserted the 8th of September as the date of their letter to General Castaños, being the day preceding that on which Major Cox's representation was made. General Castaños having published the same letter at Madrid, with its true date, (the 11th,) this mean device of the *Junta* was exposed, and it became evident that the measures they had at length adopted were, in consequence of Major Cox's judicious interference, and, probably, in no small degree from the apprehension of the popular indignation, and the consequences to themselves, individually, which that might produce.

About the same time Lieutenant-Colonel Doyle, who was one of the officers at this time employed by our government on a sort of military mission in Spain, and who was at this juncture at Madrid, took it upon himself to raise money for the immediate use of the Andalusian Army, drawing bills for the amount upon the British Consul at Seville, by whom his bills were honoured. The consul (as has been said) had not long before arrived from England with a remittance of a million and a half of dollars, to be placed at the disposal of the *Junta* of Seville, which durst not object to this mode of its application.

General Cuesta's conduct was in part explained to me in a letter from Major Cox, in which was enclosed the copy of a paper from the united *Juntas* of Leon, Castile, and Gallicia, dated the 5th of September, and signed by Valdes. This document, which was addressed to the *Junta* of Seville, besides accusing Cuesta of having betrayed Blake at the battle of Rio Secco, and by that means having procured his defeat, enclosed two letters from Cuesta, the one to the *Ayuntamiento* of Leon, dated the 30th of May, and another of the 2nd of June, to the Supreme *Junta* of the same kingdom, strongly maintaining the legality of the renunciations at Bayonne, and dissuading the people from any *revolutionary* movements.

It was generally thought, at this time, at Seville, that Cuesta was opposed to the popular cause. It was, nevertheless, considered as a suspicious circumstance, the long silence of the accusers, supposing that their allegations were founded in fact. His conduct at last, with respect to Valdes, proved, at least, that he was more actuated by private resentment than by zeal for the public service or the cause in which he was engaged. The remedy for all this disorder was looked for in the appointment of General Castaños to the command of the army, by that means placing all those discordant elements under one supreme head. Castaños, soon after his arrival at Madrid, proclaimed himself captain-general and commander-in-chief of the army at *Madrid*; but this, though giving him local authority in the capital, could have no beneficial effect upon the armies assembling to occupy the positions assigned them.

As early as the 26th of September, Count Florida Planca, the First President of the Central *Junta*, assured Lord William Bentinck that the appointment of General Castaños to the chief command would immediately take place. This salutary measure was, however, never adopted; on the contrary, in a letter from Lord W. Bentinck to me, of the 2nd of October, it is stated that the *Junta* had come to the strange resolution of making the several commands separate and in dependent. This determination His Lordship thought the more extraordinary, as General Castaños was without a competitor, and enjoyed in a marked degree the esteem and confidence both of the Supreme Central *Junta* and the public.

Such was the state of the Spanish Armies when I left Portugal, and such was the force which, in co-operation with a widely-separated British Army of 30,000 men, was expected to drive the French beyond the Pyrenees.

Conclusion

I have already mentioned that, when General Freire visited me the day after the provisional agreement with General Kellermann was concluded, I, incautiously, furnished him with a copy of that instrument for his own information and guidance. (See Appendix 17.) He well knew that its validity depended on the British admiral's concurrence. Freire, however, sent it off, together with a letter from me, which enclosed it, express to Oporto, and, doubtless, gave due notice to the bishop, by the same conveyance, that he would not find in me a partisan of his ambitious pretensions.

The bishop seized the opportunity, and immediately sent off those documents, (together with a characteristic report, from Freire, of his own proceedings, from the time of his departure from Lyria, until the 25th of August, the date of his despatch,) to the Chevalier de Souza, the Portuguese minister, in London; the whole accompanied by a letter from himself, (see Appendix 18,) written in the most acrimonious spirit, and containing observations upon the several stipulations of the armistice, equally remarkable for virulence of style, and total disregard of truth and justice.

This communication from the bishop had so quick a passage from Oporto, that the Chevalier de Souza was enabled to present the whole to Mr. Canning, with a diplomatic note from himself, couched in terms sufficiently hostile, on the 3rd of September, a very few hours after the publication, in the *London Gazette*, of Sir Harry Burrard's report of the victory at Vimiera.

In consequence of this, by the same conveyance which brought me Lord Castlereagh's letter, of the 2nd of September, already alluded to, I received another letter from His Lordship, professing to enclose copies of the whole of the documents lodged by Souza in the Foreign Office, together with Mr. Canning's note in reply. In this letter, I am informed that:

> The king could not permit himself to attach any credit to such a convention (meaning the armistice) having been agreed to, under the relative circumstances in which his fleet and armies were placed, towards those of his enemies, at the time when it professes to bear date.

And His Lordship concludes by observing:

> His Majesty thinks it unnecessary that I should do more, under the present circumstances, than submit to you the communication which has been received from the Chevalier de Souza, together with His Majesty's sentiments thereupon, as contained in Mr. Canning's note.

Lord Castlereagh certainly intended that all the documents to which he referred should be transmitted with his letter; but, in fact, the Bishop of Oporto's letter to Souza, to which it behoved me most particularly to reply, was withheld, and another irrelevant document substituted in its place. I could only, therefore, say, in answer to Lord

73

Castlereagh's letter, that an armistice, or, subsequently, a definitive convention, had been concluded, as His Lordship must, by that time, have learnt by my despatch of the 3rd, from Cintra.

Although, upon the receipt of this letter, I began to abate much of my confidence, in the assurances of support which I had been flattered with in a former communication, I, nevertheless, could not but consider that, taking together the despatches of the 2nd and 4th of September, which arrived at the same time, and came by the same conveyance, I remained vested with the discretional power which the former of those letters had, to a certain extent, confirmed; and, as the period, when the enemy's force could have been otherwise expelled from Portugal, was considerably anticipated by the convention, I was willing to believe that, when my despatches of the 3rd, should have been received by government, the unfavourable impression which the Chevalier de Souza had succeeded in exciting would be removed. But, at all events, whatever might be the issue, I was determined to pursue, with unabated firmness, the course I had thought it my duty to adopt.

On the 28th of September, Captain Dalrymple returned with despatches, and, by the same opportunity, newspapers and letters were received, by which the army and the people of Portugal were informed of the reception which the news of the conventions in Portugal had met with in England. The popular violence which prevailed on that occasion is now matter of history; and, I believe, no measure was ever so little under stood, or even inquired into, or so universally reprobated, as was the convention, miscalled, of Cintra. To that treaty, which was attributed exclusively to me, was ascribed every obnoxious provision, not only in the convention negotiated at Lisbon, by Lieutenant-Colonel Murray, under Sir Charles Cotton's instructions and mine, but, also, in that concluded with the Russian Admiral Siniavin, which Sir Charles Cotton reserved for himself. (See Southey's *History of the Peninsular War*.)

The partisans of the Oporto intrigue, informed, on the 3rd of September, of the terms of the Armistice of Vimiera, on the basis of which it was probable some definitive convention would soon be concluded; and being also, no doubt, apprised of my decided opposition to their views, contrived to prepare a strong reaction in the public mind, when the truth should be disclosed, by circulating rumours of further successes in Portugal, the inevitable consequences, as the public were taught to believe, of the splendid victories already obtained there.

What greatly contributed, also, to the popular delusion, was a hasty

and not very accurate account of the victory of Vimiera, early addressed, by Lord Castlereagh, to the Lord Mayor of London, (see Appendix No. 19), in which my abrupt assumption of the command, the
moment I landed, was placed in invidious contrast with the supposed
generosity of Sir Harry Burrard, who was untruly stated to have declined taking the command from Sir Arthur Wellesley, when he landed, during the battle. As my arrival was in the same letter very truly
stated to be nearly simultaneous with that of Kellermann to treat for
terms, the public were prepared to credit some impudent falsehoods
put forth in a ministerial journal, when my despatches arrived, and
to receive my account of the convention with increased indignation.

I found that, after Captain Dalrymple had received from Lord Castlereagh himself the despatches intended for me, he set out for Ply
mouth, where he was to embark, nothing doubting, from his conversation with Lord Castlereagh, that the letters with which he was
charged only required from me some further explanations of the circumstances which led to, and the inducements which had recommended, the treaty with the French general for the evacuation of Portugal by his army. When he arrived at Plymouth, he received orders,
by telegraph, to wait for further instructions, which soon arrived by a
special messenger, to whom he was ordered to deliver the despatches
Lord Castlereagh had given, and to convey to me others, with which
the messenger was charged.

I have ever been inclined to believe that Lord Castlereagh was
sincere in the promises of support he had given me; and, in a private
letter, of which Captain Dalrymple was the bearer, His Lordship expressed his concern at being obliged to convey to me Commands
from His Majesty, which would give me uneasiness. But he seems to
have undertaken too much, when he answered for his colleagues; and
the change of the despatches at Plymouth proved that then a hostile
influence preponderated in the Cabinet; and the system respecting me
then determined upon was ever afterwards pursued.

One of the official despatches which I received on this occasion, in
speaking of the definitive convention, adopted, and in a great measure
applied to that treaty, all the invective and much of the misinterpreta-
tion which the Bishop of Oporto had bestowed on the Armistice of
Vimiera. The other letter was, properly speaking, my letter of recall:
it dwelt upon the surprise felt by His Majesty that so important an
agreement as the armistice should have been signed so far back as the
22nd of August, and no step taken to communicate it to His Majesty's

Ministers until the 4th of September, together with the considerations which had induced me, under the relative circumstances of the two armies, to sanction such an agreement.

I am, then, once more told of the embarrassment occasioned to His Majesty's Ministers, by their receiving this communication, in the first place, through the Chevalier de Souza, His Lordship affirms:

> To whose representations they have been obliged to reply, not only under a total ignorance, but under an absolute disbelief of the facts thus brought under their notice.

The letter concluded with His Majesty's commands:

> That you do forthwith return to England, to give explanations with respect to your conduct, transferring the command of the army, together with your instructions, to the general officer next you in command.

It cannot be doubted that, from the despatches of the two general officers who preceded me in the command, and from Sir Arthur Wellesley's *aide-de-camp*, who brought them, and was recommended, by both those generals, as an officer well qualified to give every necessary information, ministers were fully informed what the relative circumstances of the two armies actually were when the command devolved on me; and considering (as the public were informed by the letter from Lord Castlereagh, above referred to) that, before this confidential *aide-de-camp* left the army, General Kellermann had arrived to treat for terms, some judgement might have been formed what the sort of terms were which the French general had been sent to treat for.

It is, therefore, upon a view of the whole case, somewhat difficult to account for the total ignorance and absolute disbelief with which ministers received Souza's communications. It is most true that I did not send home the agreement provisionally concluded by me, and signed by Sir Arthur Wellesley upon the 22nd; and which, from the admiral's refusal of his concurrence, became a dead letter upon the 24th; and whilst I acknowledge, I do not altogether mean to justify the omission.

As soon as the most pressing business was concluded, and the Spanish corps embarked for Catalonia, I was prepared to obey His Majesty's Commands; and on the 2nd of October I transferred the command of the army, with my instructions, to Lieutenant-General Sir Harry Burrard; and, on the 5th, embarked on board the *Phoebe* frigate, and sailed for England.

Thus recalled, to account for my conduct, in sanctioning a treaty recommended by Sir Arthur Wellesley in all its most important provisions, and negotiated under the joint instructions of Sir Charles Cotton and my own, it became my first duty, on arriving in London, to wait upon the Secretary of State.

Lord Castlereagh received me with much courtesy, but soon asked me, whether I wished my conduct to be investigated by a general court martial, or by a court of inquiry: The question somewhat surprised me, but the suggestion was, perhaps, a friendly one; for, if I had embraced the former alternative, ministers could not have adopted the course they afterwards pursued.

My reply was, (in substance) what I afterwards observed to the Board of General Officers, when alluding to those who, from friendship to me, or any other motive, suggested the alternative of a general court martial, namely, that I was not aware that any charges, capable of being supported by evidence, could be exhibited against me, that could come under the cognisance of a courtmartial; that if such charges were brought, I must summon as witnesses some of the principal officers serving with the army in Portugal; and, for my own share, I was impatient for an early opportunity of repelling the false and injurious imputations with which my character had been assailed. A Court of Inquiry was consequently ordered; and to its published proceedings (soon afterwards put into the hands of each member of both Houses of Parliament) I appeal for the accuracy of what follows.

When the court (consisting of four generals and three lieutenant-generals) assembled, I found, when His Majesty's warrant was read, that my conduct was not more submitted to investigation than that of Sir Harry Burrard or Sir Arthur Wellesley: it seemed a question to whom blame attached; and, in fact, whether blame was imputable to anyone. I was, also, surprised to find, that no official letters were produced to the board, by the Secretary of State, except the despatch which contained my appointment to the command; and another, relative to *booty and prize of war.* some important documents which had reference to the views and proceedings of the bishop and *Junta* of Oporto being of the number of those withheld.

As I had reason to believe that it was to the influence of the bishop and his adherents, with some, at least, of those in power at home, that I had to attribute all the vexatious injustice I experienced, I wrote to Lord Castlereagh to express my disappointment, that the above documents had not been produced; and, also, to inform His Lordship, that I had thought it advisable to insert in the narrative (which each of the three generals were directed by the board to prepare) the full powers I was, in such flattering terms, urged to exercise, in his letter of the 20th of August, as also the strong assurances of support which that letter contained.

His Lordship informed me, in answer, that he did not consider his private letter, of the 20th of August, as in any degree material to my case, being only a repetition, in an unofficial shape, of the full powers and assurances of support conveyed, by His Majesty's commands, to Sir Arthur Wellesley. As to letters referring *to the immediate matter of my recall, they did not appear to His Lordship to contain information material to be laid before the board.*

In consequence of this (as I thought) unequivocal declaration, combined with the very general terms in which the king's warrant was couched, I was induced to write to the judge advocate-general for permission to withdraw that part of my narrative which adverted to Lord Castlereagh's letter of the 4th of September, with its enclosures, received from Souza, the Portuguese minister, containing comments upon the Armistice of Vimeira, highly reflecting upon that treaty, and the officers by whom it had been sanctioned, and totally unfounded in justice.

The request was acceded to, and the papers withdrawn. I took care, however, that this my application, and Lord Castlereagh's letter which suggested it, should be placed on the face of the proceedings. It was evidently the wish of ministers to withhold the Oporto intrigue from public exposure; and, having been led into the belief that I was to be no longer held forth to a prejudiced public in the light of a culprit, I waved the privilege I undoubtedly possessed of bringing forwards the subject myself. (Lord Liverpool *was reported* to have said, in his place in the House of Lords, that those documents were withheld by desire of the Chevalier de Souza.)

The unanimous decision of the board was in favour of all the generals into whose conduct they were instructed to inquire; and when, after the proceedings were closed, the separate opinion of each member was required, as to the merits or demerits of the armistice and definitive convention, a majority of the members decided in favour of *both*. Upon this last question (the proceedings having been closed) no opportunity was afforded me of urging that, whatever opinion the majority of the members might pronounce upon the definitive convention, I was not more responsible than Admiral Sir Charles Cotton for that treaty, or any of its provisions; a circumstance which ministers seemed to forget, or wish to have forgotten by the public.

The investigation being over, it was officially announced *to me* that the proceedings of the Board of General Officers "*having been fully considered*" by His *Majesty's Ministers,* "and their opinion thereupon humbly submitted to His Majesty's consideration," a severe censure was addressed to me in the king's name, *and to me only*, upon those very transactions which Lord Castlereagh called *the matter of my recall.*

A short time afterwards, when it became the duty of the Board of Admiralty, under an order of the House of Commons, to furnish such documents as it might possess, on the subject of the convention concluded with General Junot for the evacuation of Portugal, instead of merely producing the admiral's letter, of the 3rd of September, in which that treaty, as ratified by himself, was enclosed, application was made to Sir Charles Cotton (who was then in England) for any paper he could furnish which might bear upon the subject.

A letter from Sir Charles Cotton to me, of the 27th of August, with my reply of the 28th, together with a paper also directed to me, and purporting to be the enclosure in Sir Charles's letter, were laid before Parliament by the Board of Admiralty, and speedily published in the newspapers, with a high panegyric upon the admiral for having been, as it seemed by this paper, opposed to the convention, but particularly to those stipulations to which the pretended enclosure seemed to refer.

As soon as this publication came to my know ledge, I informed the First Lord of the Admiralty that a spurious paper had been laid before Parliament instead of the genuine enclosures which I received in Sir Charles Cotton's letter, of the 27th of August, of which I enclosed the originals, with the admiral's signature to each. A correspondence ensued, of which the result was that Lord Mulgrave promised to substitute the true for the pretended enclosure, presenting the former to the House of Lords, with the following explanation, *viz.*:—

That the papers to be presented, at your request, were those to which the letters of the 27th and 28th of August refer; and that paper, previously printed, were articles, the adoption of which Captain Halsted was instructed to exact, and *which were, in fact, inserted in the treaty.*

Thus, Sir Charles Cotton, from his own mistake, is *recorded* for having objected to those very stipulations in the treaty of which he was, in fact, the author.

His Majesty's pleasure being pronounced, and the Board of General Officers dissolved, Sir Harry Burrard resumed the command of the London district, which he held before he was ordered to Portugal; but, as it seems to have been the policy of ministers to hold me out to the people of England as the cause of the disappointment of what they were taught to consider their just expectations, and an object, also, of His Majesty's displeasure, there was no question of my being permitted to resume the command at Gibraltar, which I had been instructed *to entrust, during my absence,* to another general officer; nor were the representations I made to Lord Liverpool, on the subject of my wrongs, when His Lordship succeeded to the war department, in the smallest degree attended to.

At last, in the year 1814, when peace was supposed to be established, and Lord Castlereagh stood deservedly high in public estimation, I addressed to His Lordship a letter, of which the following is a copy:—

London,
July 20, 1814.

My Lord,

The war on the Peninsula being at an end, government and the country seem to vie with each other, in testifying their gratitude to those who have contributed, by their talents, or their exertions, to the glorious result of the contest; your lordship, therefore, cannot wonder if I feel myself peculiarly hurt by remaining, as I do, under the censure, with which it pleased His Majesty's Ministers to dismiss me from employment, in January, 1809, although I had the good fortune, by the line of conduct I observed, so successfully to cherish and promote the rising enthusiasm of the Spanish people, that expressions of gratitude to my country and its government were mingled with the popular acclamations over a large portion of the South of Spain, before I was honoured with that communication, from your lordship, of the 25th of May, 1808, which first acknowledged the receipt of my important despatches, on the affairs of that country; and at the same time communicated to me the pleasing assurances of His Majesty's entire approbation of all the measures I had pursued.

Your lordship must too sensibly feel the value of well-earned reputation and esteem, not to form an idea of what I must suffer, should I be doomed by government to unmerited and perpetual reproach; to avert such an indignity is a duty I owe to myself and my family, and I anxiously wish, that by some public testimony of the royal approbation of those services, of which, separately, I have received from your lordship the assurance that the king approved, I may be set right in the estimation of my country, which cannot fail to have formed a very erroneous opinion of my conduct, from the manifold delusions which have been practiced to mislead.

I have even supposed, that if circumstances had allowed, the promises of support which your lordship gave me, in your private letter of the 20th of August, 1808, (accompanied, as they were, by too flattering compliments to the excellence of my judgement) would not have proved a mere repetition, in an unofficial form, of those conveyed by His Majesty's command to Sir Arthur Wellesley, transferred to me when I took the command, and of course, devolved to Sir Harry Burrard, at the moment I most wanted, and, perhaps, thought, I had a right to expect, the support that had been promised.

If there is any justice in this supposition, I should be happy to be allowed an interview, whenever your lordship may appoint, when I shall explain the nature of the applications I have officially, at different times, made to Lord Liverpool upon this subject.

I have the honour to be, &c. &c.

H. W. Dalrymple.

In consequence of this letter (in the style and tenor of which I hope there is nothing that can be deemed servile, or unworthy of myself) I had, on the 25th of July, an interview with Lord Castlereagh, in which I fully explained to His Lordship my feelings and my wishes, to which he listened with kindness and attention, and did me the honour to observe—that during the course of our official intercourse there was only *one point* upon which he had ever differed from me in opinion' I was not there to enter into a discussion of that, so took my leave, very well satisfied with my reception, though nothing was promised.

A short time afterwards, Lord Castlereagh took me aside, at the *levée* of the prince regent, where we chanced to meet, and told me my business was settled; and, in fact, very soon afterwards my name was placed at the head of a list of baronets; and as a mark that the honour was conferred, as a reward for public services, it was especially provided, in the patent, that it was given free from all the usual charges, which became an item in the public accounts laid before Parliament. This circumstance gave a value to the honour conferred, in comparison of which the cost, whatever it may have been, sunk into utter insignificance.

Appendix

(No. 1.)

To Lord Castlereagh.

Gibraltar,
8th May, 1808.

My Lord, A wish having been expressed that General Castaños's confidential Secretary should meet Mr. Viali at the Spanish lines this morning, an interview, by my desire, took place accordingly. I have the honour to enclose to your lordship Mr. Viali's report of the result.

A particular degree of anxiety seems to have been expressed, as to the certainty of having the frigate always in readiness, to despatch to Trieste; but this does not altogether accord with the nature of the service that vessel is proposed to perform, which depends upon many, and some of them improbable, events. This matter will, I trust, be more fully explained at the next interview, which, I think will be soon, and perhaps between the general and myself.

The commanding officer in the bay has despatched a vessel, with a copy of the enclosed paper, to Lord Collingwood, and I will furnish Admiral Purvis with another, by the earliest opportunity, as it discloses some important circumstances, which it is necessary both those officers should be apprised of.

If events succeed each other with the rapidity there is reason to expect, and if the Spaniards are constrained to act before His Majesty's pleasure can be known, any diversion in their favour must, of course, depend on naval co-operation; for I can scarcely foresee a case that could justify the committing any British troops, that could be brought into action from hence, beyond the safe and easy communication with the fleet; with that precaution, situations certainly might be imagined where a combined operation of army and fleet, added to a favourable disposition on the part of the Spaniards, might produce the happiest effects; and though from the substance of the enclosed communication, (in which the extensive scale of the Spanish general's views is displayed,) Minorca and Ceuta are for the present, I think, not to be bargained for, the seizure of the French Ships in Cadiz is a measure of a different description, and one which, under my present conception of the subject, I think it might be right to require.

Although I cannot foresee the result of the very extraordinary and critical situation in which I find myself placed, I think it incumbent upon me, by every opportunity, to apprise your lordship of the effect the strange course of events has upon my mind, and the general line of conduct I may, in consequence, be induced to adopt, or recommend for adoption to the admiral and Major-General Spencer, upon whom much of the execution must necessarily depend.

I have the honour to be, &c. &c. &c.

(Signed)   H. W. Dalrymple,
                                                      Lieutenant-General.

The substance of the report of Mr. Viali has been given in the narrative.

(No. 2.)
To Major-General Spencer.

Headquarters, Gibraltar,
12th May, 1808.

Sir,

As I have not failed to inform you of the progress of events in Spain, and of the communications I have had with the Spanish general upon the measures he has it in contemplation to adopt, it is only necessary for me, at present, to put you officially in possession of my views in detaching your corps to join Admiral Purvis.

You may recollect that, to a proposal of mine, it was stated to Mr. Viali, in a conference he held with General Castaños's Private Secretary, that, in case of open war with France, the Spanish fleet, in Cadiz, would sail with part of the royal family to South America, either with or without a detachment of British ships; and, that then the Spanish batteries would co-operate with Admiral Purvis, in enabling the latter to take possession of the French squadron.

As this plan did not seem sufficiently digested, and depended on previous arrangements, which would probably create delay, and consequently failure, I have strongly urged the seizure of the French fleet, as the first act of hostility against France, without any direct or immediate reference to the plan of emigration, which, however, it would

83

eventually materially further: by this means, an important blow would be struck at the outset of the business, which could not fail to stamp a character of vigour upon the Spanish councils.

As I am not without hopes that this measure may be adopted; and as, in answer to a demand made by the Spanish general for troops, I informed him that such conjunct operations as could be undertaken by your corps, and Admiral Purvis's Fleet, for the purpose of making diversions in his favour, was all the aid I could offer, I think it may be essential that your corps should embark, and sail forthwith; for, although I could have wished to have come to a clearer understanding with General Castaños, before any step was taken, I agree with you, that it is still more important that advantage should be taken of the present favourable wind, to pass through the Streights, (*sic*) which opportunity, if lost, may not speedily recur.

I foresee no concurrence of circumstances, which, in the present situation of Spain, can justify any other than a conjunct operation between the troops and the ships of war, but I think it not impossible that, in seizing the French ships, even by the countenance and aid of the Spaniards, circumstances may arise to render the assistance of your corps necessary, exclusive of such further operations as you and the admiral may think proper to pursue.

(Signed)   H. W. Dalrymple.

(No. 3.)
To Admiral Purvis.

Gibraltar,
13th May.

Sir,

I have received notice from Spain, that the measures of security practised by Murat, and announced in the enclosed Proclamation, have had complete success; and that no further expectation remains of insurrection at Madrid.

When at first I wished to recommend the measures of securing the fleets of Spain and her foreign possessions for her lawful sovereign, should he ever be restored, I thought I was suggesting what might turn out materially to the advantage of His Majesty's service, as well as of the loyal part of the Spanish Nation; and I felt confident a spirit at that time existed in Spain, which might have given success to the attempt: instead of what I then hinted at, I was informed of the project of defence of which I have already furnished you with the details; the plan was bold and extensive, but seems, by a letter received last night from Spain, to have vanished from the mind that detailed it; and, in truth, some parts did bear the marks of wild and inconsiderate theory.

By your letter, just received, I am happy to find that a fermentation may possibly still exist at Cadiz, to which the appearance of a co-operative force may give consistence and effect. For this reason, I detach Major-General Spencer with the corps under his command, to join you, and the general will concert with you such measures as circumstances may recommend for the advantage of His Majesty's service.

Although my hopes of success are not sanguine, from the untoward state of affairs, and the ascendency the French have acquired in the Capital, I shall have at least the pleasure to reflect that nothing has been omitted to take advantage of any occasion, and that the execution is in such hands.

(Signed)   H. W. Dalrymple.

(No. 4.)

Exmo. Senor,

Muy Señor mio: En la Ciudad de Sevilla se ha erigido una Junta Suprema de Govierno de los quatro Reynos de Andalucia que Representando la Magestad del S^{or} De Fernando Septimo, nuestro unico y legitimo soverano, dicta quantas energicas providencia exigen las criticas circunstancias en que se halla la nacion Española y la justa causa de sa defensa. La misma Junta me ha comunicado sus superiores instrucciones, de que ha sido portador el Primer Secretario de ella el qual para a esa Placa acompañado de mi Primer Ayudante D^e Joaquin Navarro para tratar con V. E. a nombre de aquella Soberana autoridad aruntos de la mayor importancia en cuyo pronto y favorable acuerdo, espero encontrarán, en V.E. el apoyo que en distintas circunstancias me ha manifestado.

Reitero a V.E. mis respetos con los sinceros senti mientos que profeso a sa Persona Cuya vida guarde. Dios muchos años. Quartel General de Algeciras, 8° de Junio, de 1808.

E^{mo}. S^{or}.

B. L. M. de V. E. su mas,

Xavier de Castanos.

E^mo Sor General Dalrimple.

(No. 5.)
(Copy of Translation.)

Agreement made between the *Junta* of the city of Grenada, and the Supreme *Junta* of Seville, by the Commissioners of Grenada, Don

85

Rodriguez Riquelme, Regent of the Royal Chancelaria, and, on the other part, by His Excellency Señor Don Andrés Miñano, and the R^{mo} Pelho Manuel Gil, Auditors of the Supreme *Junta*. They agreed to the following:—

1st. That the army and its movements shall be directed by the general-in-chief, at Seville, who will form his arrangements, including the troops from Grenada who are placed under his orders, inasmuch as the kingdom of Seville is invaded and in danger, upon condition that, if Grenada or its kingdom be attacked, the commander-in-chief and Army of Seville shall act in the same manner for the protection and defence of Grenada.

2nd. That the *Junta Suprema* of Seville, being in the act of treating with the English, and having better means than any other province for this, Grenada accedes and consents to what this *Junta* may treat upon, being assured that it will watch over, and act for, the interest of this kingdom and the whole nation.

3rd. That Seville does not support its independence for its own particular interest, but for the general good in the defence of the country, which she believes useful and necessary. But this does not hinder the Supreme *Junta* from joining with Grenada in the defence of their king, inasmuch as they act for the same end.

4th. That what has been said is understood to last until our king and Lord Ferdinand VII. is restored to his throne, who, it is certain, will act for the general good of the nation, either by assembling the Cortez or by other means.

(Signed)

Andres Miñano.
Rod. Riquelmo.
Manuel Gil.

Seville, 11th June, 1808.

(A true Copy)

Juan Bautista Bardo,
Secretary.

Compared with the copy sent to this Provincial *Junta*, by the Supreme *Junta* of Seville.

(Signed)

Don Joaquin Pascal Baniga,
1st Secretary.
Don Rafael Anogo,
2nd Secretary.

Malaga, 16th June, 1808.

(Copy of Instruction's Given to Captain Dalrymple.)

The object of your mission to Seville is to communicate, confidentially, with the Spanish Government on all such matters as shall pertain to operations against the common enemy, and the consolidation of the power of the said Spanish Government, in as far as, under the circumstances of my want of instructions from His Majesty, I can take upon myself to act.

From your official situation, you are perfectly acquainted with all the communications I have made to His Majesty's Government on the subject of the late events in Spain; as, also, with the measures I have stated it to be my intention to adopt relative thereto. You will hold in mind the substance and spirit of those communications on all occasions where a reference thereto may be necessary.

Of the different requisitions stated in the note from the secretary to the Spanish Government, there is not one that seemed to me, upon the general principle, subject to objection; some of them depend upon the concurrence of the admirals commanding His Majesty's Fleets, particularly that off Cadiz.

You will, therefore, communicate with Admiral Purvis thereupon, that you may arrive at the seat of the Spanish Government fully aware of his intentions upon the subjects here alluded to.

Although I feel the strongest conviction that His Majesty will approve of every measure taken to forward the operations of the Spanish Government in hostility to that of France, some regard must be had to the possible consequences of any measure acceded to, in case of disaster, and the success of the French arms; as I should scarcely think myself justified in a temporary suspension of active hostility, and by that means relinquishing such military advantages as may have been gained, without a view to other advantages that might tend to the further prosecution of the war with success, should, unfortunately, the present struggle terminate unfavourably, and the power of France prevail in Spain.

Of this nature is the temporary occupation of the fortress of Ceuta, for King Ferdinand VII. or such other monarch as shall be acknowledged by the existing government of that kingdom, not recommended or supported by France.

This, as a temporary arrangement, must be of advantage to both nations, and will admit of the Spanish garrison of that fortress acting in the field.

With respect to the French ships at Cadiz, I am ignorant of the sentiments of the admiral on that subject, or what measures he has deemed it necessary to pursue; but, it appears to me, that some arrangement should be made, to preclude the possibility, under any unexpected or unfortunate change of circumstances, of all the ships of war in Cadiz falling under the power of France.

The mere possession of the ships, except for the purposes here hinted, it does not appear to me a great national object; and, perhaps, that end may, by other means, be still more effectually provided for.

The ships in Mahon are, it is to be presumed, safe whilst there; it is necessary, however, to remark, on the one hand, that the island is distressed for provisions; and, on the other hand, that Swiss or French troops are said to have been sent there by the pretended Board of Government at Madrid; it is, therefore, probable that the commander of His Majesty's Navy will be disposed to enforce a strict blockade of that island until the garrison shall be such as to ensure the possession of it and the fleet to the legitimate Government of Spain.

Should small arms and ammunition be required, you may safely say that, of the former, there are not more than is deemed necessary to replace the casualties of service; but that, of the latter, there may be some redundance, exclusive of what may be in the possession of the merchants; of course, every aid of that or any other sort, will be given that is compatible with the state of perfect preparation in which it is His Majesty's pleasure that this place should, at all times, be held.

Exclusive of your direct correspondence with me, relative to all matters which it may be necessary for me to know, and respecting which you may require more detailed instructions; you will not fail to communicate with Admiral Purvis on the objects of your mission; and, in any exigent case, when a speedy reference may be necessary to His Majesty's Government from that of Spain, you will send the despatch direct to the admiral, stating its tenor, that he may judge how far it may be necessary, for His Majesty's service, to send a vessel express. I need not add that this is a measure to: which it can very seldom be necessary or proper to recur.

(Signed)

H. W. Dalrymple,
Lieutenant-General.

(No 7.)
Extract of a Letter from the Right Honourable
Lord Castlereagh to Lieutenant-General Sir Hew Dalrymple.

Downing-street,
25th May, 1808.

Sir,

Your several confidential despatches, respecting the affairs of Spain, of the dates mentioned, (24, 26, 31 Mar., 8, 15, 28, 30 April, 7, 7 May), have been received, and laid before the king.

I am to convey to you, His Majesty's approbation of the conduct you have held in the correspondence which has been confidentially carried on with the Spanish general; and from advices, dated the 11th instant, which, together with yours of the 8th, were received from Cadiz this morning, it seems probable that the governor of Cadiz will act in concert with General Castaños, and that the standard of resistance to the French will have been raised in various parts.

The utmost exertions will be made to send out a reinforcement from hence, so as to enable His Majesty to afford the loyal party in Spain the assistance of 10,000 men, which General Castaños seems to require, including what can be spared from the garrison of Gibraltar. Should any requisition for troops have been already made to you, I doubt not that you have afforded it under such precautions as to ensure its communication with our fleet;—and certainly it would not be prudent for you to hazard so small a corps as you could spare from your garrison for any interior and mixed operations in the field.

The most useful manner in which such a corps could be employed seems to be the occupation of some garrison or post near the sea, which it is essential to occupy, and which would liberate an equal or a greater proportion of Spanish troops; and in this view, you will particularly direct your attention to Cadiz, as the point most important to the success of the exertions in Spain, or to the retreat to the colonies of those engaged, in case of failure.

As it has been stated, in the proposition made to you, that, in case the Royal Dynasty should be removed, measures will be taken to secure Spanish America, you will of course look to this contingency with the utmost anxiety, as it must be of the utmost importance that the resources of those opulent provinces should not fall into the hands of the French.

His Majesty entertains a full reliance upon your vigour and discretion, in the present juncture:—that as, on the one hand, you will not commit either the faith of his government, or the force under your command unnecessarily, or for an inadequate object, you will, on the other, act with determination and spirit, according to circumstances on the spot, relying upon the disposition of His Majesty's Government to give your exertions the fullest support.

I have the honour to be,

  (Signed)   Castlereagh.

N.B. This despatch was received by me the 8th, and the receipt acknowledged the 9th of June, in a letter of some length, in reference to the instructions I had received, and the actual state of things at the time.

Shortly after, further, or rather fresh, instructions, addressed to Rear Admiral Purvis, were forwarded to me, for my information and guidance.—To which the following was the reply.

To Lord Viscount Castlereagh.

(Extract.)

Gibraltar,
25th June, 1808.

My Lord,

I have to acknowledge the honour of your lordship's despatch, enclosing your instructions of the 4th June, addressed to Rear Admiral Purvis.

There was a moment of consternation and pause when my letter of the 13th May was written, but on the 31st, (the date of my last despatch,) the scene had completely changed; the hopes of every true Spaniard were exalted to the highest pitch, and the time was past for approaching those subjects which before had been, at least, patiently listened to.

The object became not only the expulsion of the French out of Spain, but even the total overthrow of Bonaparte's power; and whatever judgement might have been formed of the probability of ultimate success, it was, I think, evidently fruitless, as well as impolitic, to urge measures, which the Spanish rulers were prompted, perhaps constrained, by the temper of the people to refuse.

  (Signed)

W. H. Dalrymple,
Lieutenant-General.

To Lieutenant-General Sir Hew Dalrymple.

Seville,
15th June, 1808.

Sir,

According to the instructions (similar to Appendix, No. 6.) which I received from Your Excellency, I immediately waited on His Highness, the President of the Supreme Board of Government, on my arrival here yesterday, and delivered to him your letter, and, also, a packet from General Morla, the governor of Cadiz, enclosing letters for Lord Collingwood. I was received with much civility and attention; but His Highness declined opening the letters, or conversing with me on the objects of my mission, until a meeting of the board should take place. I, therefore, took my leave, and informed him where I was to be found whenever the board should intimate a desire to see me.

I called, this morning, on the Padre Gil, a member of the Board of Government, to whom I had letters of introduction. This man is, I understand, a very leading character in the *Junta*, and, as far as I am able to judge, he is a person of an enlightened and liberal mind, extremely zealous in the cause in which he is engaged, and possessing sufficient abilities to direct the proceedings of a party, which is evidently guided, in a great measure, by his opinions.

He acquainted me that it was the wish of the Board of Government that I should present myself at their meeting, at five o'clock this evening, which I accordingly did; and, having explained, in general terms, the objects of my mission, and the desire that was felt, on the part of the British Government, to co-operate with that of Spain in the prosecution of the great and glorious cause in which they were engaged, and to afford them such assistance as the circumstances of His Majesty's dominions would admit, I requested that an individual of the *Junta*, or some person properly authorised by them, might be appointed to correspond with me on those subjects; and that all propositions of the government should be made, through him, in writing, as considerable difficulties and inconvenience must necessarily arise from verbal communications.

This request was immediately complied with, and the Padre Gil was named as the person to communicate with me, on all occasions, in the name of the Spanish Government. Before I was to take my leave, the President informed me that the Supreme Board had determined to provide me with a house and establishment suitable to the important situation in which they conceived I was placed; and the Marquis de la Granina, a member of the *Junta*, who was present, made me the offer of his house, servants, and carriage; but all this I, of course, declined; and I shall endeavour, in the course of tomorrow, to hire a small house or lodging, where I may be more conveniently situated for business than at the inn where I am at present lodged.

I am to have a second interview with the Padre Gil tomorrow, and I shall make the result of our conference the subject of another despatch.

I have the honour to be, &c. &c.

(Signed)

William Cox,
Major, 61st Regiment.

To Lieutenant-General Sir Hew Dalrymple.

Seville,
16th June, 1808.

Sir,

In my letter of yesterday's date, I had the honour to inform Your Excellency of my presentation to the Supreme Board of Government, and what passed on that occasion. The interview between the Padre Gil and me, of which I spoke, took place this morning, and, in the course of our conversation, he explained to me the difficulties under which the newly formed government had to labour, through the disorganised state of their armies; their want of arms and clothing; and the necessity which they felt, under such circumstances, of imploring the assistance of the British Government.

He told me that they particularly required pecuniary aid, to meet the exigencies of the present moment, and he informed me of the letter, which had been written to Your Excellency, by General Herrera on that subject, and of his having sent an officer to Gibraltar to treat about the terms of a loan.

I here took occasion to observe that great delay and inconvenience must arise from such a mode of proceedings, and that I was confident Your Excellency would not enter into any treaty or correspondence with an individual who was not properly authorised to act in the name of the Spanish Government; that I was sent here to remain as the channel of communication between Your Excellency and them; and that I thought it would greatly expedite and facilitate the business, if he would write me a letter on the subject, stating to me fully what the wants and the wishes of the government were, in order that

I might transmit them regularly for your consideration; and that I was well assured Your Excellency would be disposed to meet their wishes to the utmost extent of your power.

This he has promised to do, and I expect to hear more from him on the subject this evening. He also informed me that he had written to Herrera, to apprise him of my arrival here, and the purpose of my mission; and, that it would, therefore, be unnecessary for him to hold any further correspondence with Your Excellency on those subjects, to which it relates. The *Junta* seem now to be satisfied with the present disposition of the British troops, under General Spencer; though I believe it was much their wish that they should have been marched into the interior.

Their landing at Ayamonte has had a good effect on the minds of the people, by convincing them, more clearly, of our determination to countenance and support their cause; and as it was the first request of our new Allies, I think it was highly proper that it should be complied with, but, otherwise, it does not appear to be a place of any importance for us to hold, particularly as the corps of French troops, which were supposed to be marching along the coast of Portugal, are known to have turned into the interior, with an intention of entering Spain by another route. I have had no opportunity, as yet, of touching on the occupation of Cadiz by our troops; and I feel it will be a difficult and delicate point to urge.

I shall, however, avail myself of the very first that offers to bring forward the subject, though I fear there has been, already, too much said upon it, in the negotiation which General Spencer has been carrying on with the governor of that place. The direct and repeated proposals which were made by him, on the subject of a landing, have, undoubtedly, excited the jealousy and alarm of the people, and it will, perhaps, be a matter of no small difficulty to allay their fears, and convince them of the honourable and disinterested motives which actuate the conduct of the British Government.

I have kept the despatch open until today (17th), that I might be enabled to accompany it with the enclosed letter from the Padre Gil, and the annexed propositions of the *Junta*, which I did not receive last might, as I expected: I also enclose my answer to the *padre*, by which Your Excellency will see that it is my intention to send the propositions of the Spanish Government directly to England, if Lord Collingwood shall think proper to forward them; but I shall not be able to pre pare copies of them for that purpose before tomorrow. I mean to enclose them to Lord Castlereagh, and I shall, at the same time, send His Lordship copies of the instructions which I have received from Your Excellency, and also of this, and my first despatch, for the information of His Majesty's Government.

I have the honour to be, &c. &c.

William Cox,
Major, 61st Regiment.

Note.—The four propositions enclosed in this letter related to—

The raising money as a loan to the Spanish Government at Gibraltar, to the extent of two or three millions of dollars.

The obtaining a subsidy from Great Britain, from 50 to 70,000 dollars.

The obtaining muskets, pistols, and other firearms from Gibraltar.

The obtaining ammunition and warlike stores from Gibraltar or the fleet.

(Enclosure.)
To His Excellency Father Manuel Gil.

Seville,
17th June, 1808.

Sir,

I have had the honour to receive Your Excellency's letter of this date with the accompanying propositions of the Spanish Government, upon which you desire my opinion.

As an individual placed here merely as the channel of communication between the Supreme Board and the commanders in chief of His Majesty's fleet and army, I can scarcely venture to offer my own sentiments upon subjects of such importance; but I shall feel it my duty, not only to transmit them immediately to those by whom I am deputed, but I shall also take upon myself to suggest to Lord Collingwood, who commands His Majesty's fleet off Cadiz, the expediency of sending a vessel express to England with copies of them, which I shall prepare for the purpose, addressed to His Majesty's ministers, in order that no time may be lost in making them acquainted with the wants and wishes of the Spanish Government, and that whatever succours they may be disposed to grant may be applied with as little delay as possible.

I am only authorised to say, generally, that it is the ardent wish of the British Government to second the exertions of the Spanish Nation in their glorious attempt to shake off the yoke of France, and to assist and establish their national independence; and that, for the attainment of that object, His Majesty is ever willing to forego any objects more immediately affecting the interests of his own dominions. I feel fully confident that not only Spain, but the whole world, will be convinced, by the generous conduct of Great Britain on this occasion, that she has ever been actuated by the most honourable and dis interested motives; and her views have ever been directed to the maintenance and support of legitimate sovereignty.

With respect to the money which it is proposed to draw from Gibraltar, I am sure that His Excellency the governor of that place will do all that lies in his power to facilitate the business, by making known to the merchants the desire of the British Government to assist that of Spain, and thereby encouraging them to enter into a loan, on such terms as may be agreed on, and I dare say it may be possible in this way to raise about two millions of *reals*, in addition to the sum which General Castaños has already drawn from the same source.

To expedite the arrangement of this business, I think it would be extremely desirable to send a proper person, who was conversant with commercial affairs, and authorised by the Supreme Board, to settle the conditions of the loan: the same I think should be done with respect to the money which is proposed to be raised by way of loan in England. As to small arms, ammunition, and the other military equipments which are mentioned in the third and fourth propositions of the Supreme Board, I am almost certain that none can be spared from Gibraltar; and that any supplies of that kind, which the British Government may be disposed to grant, must eventually come from England.

It will undoubtedly afford great satisfaction to His Majesty's commanders with whom I have the honour to correspond, and to whom I shall send copies of Your Excellency's letter, to hear that the ambassadors have been sent from hence to the Court of London to treat for peace, which must be a desirable object to both countries, and I am sure that they, as well as the British Government, will equally rejoice to hear of the general spirit which has called forth the exertions of the Spanish Nation in defence of their king and country, and of the state of preparation to which her armies have been brought in so short a time, to act against the common enemy.

With respect to the British troops which are already disembarked in this country, they are no doubt anxious to participate in the glory which there is every reason to hope will shortly crown the efforts of the Spanish Armies; but so small a corps, as they are at present, cannot be more usefully employed than in occupying an important place near the coast, particularly as the strength of the Spanish Armies, which is hourly increasing, is such as not to require their assistance in the interior.

I have the honour to be, &c. &c.

William Cox,
Major, 61st Regiment.

To General Sir Hew Dalrymple.

Seville,
22nd June, 1808.

Sir,

I have just been honoured with Your Excellency's letter of the 20th instant, and shall take care to pay particular attention to its contents. The idea of the junction of General Spencer's corps, with the Spanish army in the interior, seems now to be nearly at an end, particularly since my answer to Padre Gil's letter, (enclosed in my despatch, No. 2, 16th June, 1808,) the last paragraph of which evidently alludes to such an arrangement.

I believe that the proposal for the expedition to the Guadiana originated with Herrera, or the Governor of Cadiz, and was afterwards approved by General Castaños and the *Junta*. It was certainly undertaken by General Spencer in consequence of a request made to him in their name.

He wrote, on the 19th, to the Spanish General, informing him of his intention of proceeding to Lisbon; and this day, I understand, the *Junta* has received intelligence of his having actually landed at Ayamonte. There is such an apparent inconsistency in those two accounts, that I really know not how to reconcile them. When the Padre Gil shewed me General Spencer's letter, I asked him whether the measure proposed was approved by the *Junta*; and he assured me that it was entirely; as, however, I afterwards learned that the business was a good deal talked of, and that some strong expressions, respecting the conduct of the English, had been made use of by a member of the *Junta*, I thought it as well to ascertain, officially, what their sentiments were, and I, therefore, wrote this morning to Father Gil, the letter of which I enclose a copy. I have this moment received his answer, which I shall also subjoin.

I touched slightly upon the subject of occupying Cadiz by a British force, in a conversation which I had yesterday with the Padre Gil;

and I found, from him, that the question had already been discussed in the *Junta*, but was found to be totally inadmissible. He said that, even if they had approved of it, the jealousy of the people would never suffer it to take place.

I have frequently pressed the necessity of speedily adopting measures for the security of the South American Provinces, and have been every day assured that the matter was under discussion, and that no time should be lost in taking the necessary steps. I believe there has been much difference of opinion among the members of the *Junta*, with regard to the system that ought to be pursued; and I have reason to think that a plan which was formed is now entirely done away, and som thing quite different substituted in its stead.

Deputies are certainly named, and are now at Cadiz ready to sail; but I do not know whether they have yet received their final instructions, or what the nature of those instructions are; but I dare say they will be communicated to me. They carry out several copies of the enclosed manifesto, which I have obtained from Padre Gil, under an injunction of secrecy, *for the present*, as it is not to be published in Spain till after the departure of the deputies for America.

I have the honour to be,
(Signed)   William Cox,
Major, 61st Regiment.

P.S. The headquarters of the Spanish Army are, I understand, to be removed to Cordova. The first division, under General De Pedro, marched last night from Utrera; and the second, under General Pena, this day.

(Enclosure 1.)
His Excellency the Reverend Father Gil.
Seville,
June 22nd, 1808.

Sir,

By the letter from Major-General Spencer to the commander-in-chief of the British Army, which Your Excellency has done me the honour to communicate to me, it appears that the English general has it in contemplation to proceed, with the force under his command, to Lisbon, in consequence of information which he has received, of that place being left exposed by the march of a French corps from thence towards the Spanish frontier.

There can be no doubt but such a movement is likely to be attended with considerable advantages to the cause of Spain, by making a diversion on the coast of Portugal, which would oblige the enemy to draw back that part of his force which was destined to act against this country.

As, however, the corps under Major-General Spencer, and the reinforcements which are expected from England, are destined, by the British Government, to assist the loyal party in Spain, in their exertions to shake off the yoke of France, and establish the independence of their country; and, as this assistance has been afforded in consequence of the desire of that party, expressed through His Excellency General Castaños, it is of importance that the manner in which it is employed should, as far as possible, correspond with the wishes of his Excellency, and of the Supreme Board of Government, by which he is employed.

I have, therefore, to request that Your Excellency will have the goodness to communicate to me their sentiments on the subject, and acquaint me, whether the proposed measure meets with their approbation, that I may lose no time in informing his Excellency Sir Hew Dalrymple, (under whom Major-General Spencer acts,) and who will, in consequence, give such orders, respecting the future disposition of the British troops as he may judge necessary.

I have the honour to be, &c. &c.

(Signed)

William Cox,
Major, 61st Regiment.

(Enclosure 2.)

Sʳ Sargento Major Cox,

Muy Señor mio, contesto con mucho gusto à la muy estimable de V. de hoy.

Hay motivos para creer que el Señor Major-General Spencer ha desembarcado toda ó parte de su tropa Inglesa en Ayamonte; pero puedo asegurar a V. S. per documentos autenticos, y per Carta que dirije a dho General, el nro Don Francisco Xavier Castaños con fha de a Noche 21 que dexa al arbitrio del Mayor-Ge neral Spencer ó permanecer en Ayamonte, o pasar por mar a Setubal, y desembarcar alli, o acometer a la misma Lisboa, ó pasar mas al norte, como vea conviene al fin unico nuestro, y de la nacion Ynglesa, que es destruir à Junot, o impedirle que ataque a Estremadura, ó pretenda unirse al Escrito de Dupont, que retrocede de Cordova.

Añado que per la Ruta que sigue el ultimo, y por la situacion que tenía ya en Andajar, no parece que intenta pasar por la Sierra de Cordova a Estremadura, sino ver sí puede penetrar a la Mancha, lo que le será muy deficil.

Se tambien que despues que me vine de la Junta Suprema, ha recibido esta Posta, con aviso de haberse ganado ventajas considerables en el Algarve contra los Franceses aloque creo nos habrán ayerdado las tropos Inglesas, pues las Veteranos que teniemos en aquel punto, con cortas, y aun no podia haber llegado alli el Coronel Don Luis Pesino, que iba a mandorlas.

Nos ha embiado el Señor Gobernador de Gibraltar noticias hasto importantes: da todas los Fusilas que le es posible, y ha remitido al Puerto Utensilios de Campa mento, y todo prueba el Ardor con que se interesa en nuestra Causa, el que vemos y admiremos en toda la nacion Inglesa, por lo que le estamos sumamente reconocidos, y es general la satisfacion en ambas naciones.

Recuerdo a V. S. que no olvide el acelerar el convenio en que quedamos de acuerdo.

Dios gue a V. S. muchos años.

Quedo de V. S. con la mas perfecta consideracion su muy afecto y humilde siervo,

Manuel Gil, C. M.
Sevilla, y Janio 22nd, 1808.

His Excellency Sir Hew Dalrymple.

Seville,
24th June, 1808.

Sir,

Your Excellency's letter of the 17th did not reach me till yesterday morning, and I have since been honoured with both your letters of the 22nd instant, one of them arrived last night and the other this morning.

That of the 17th, which informs me of the authority which you had given to General Spencer, to proceed off Lisbon, accounts for the movements which he acquainted the *Junta* it was his intention to make; and which, in the absence of intelligence, occasioned by the delay of Your Excellency's letter, I was not able rightly to comprehend.

Captain Whittingham is just come over from Utrera; and I have conversed with him upon the points you desired. He assures me that General Castaños never encouraged the idea of a junction of the British troops with the main body of the Spanish Army in the interior; that it never was his wish that such a junction should take place; nor was it ever expected at Utrera: that all the general desired was, that General Spencer should disembark, and occupy the position of Xeres, in order to support the Spanish Army, in case of their being obliged to fall back, and to cover the important place of Cadiz, which it is of such consequence to defend. This plan, he says, was proposed to General Spencer, but, at once, peremptorily rejected.

Captain Whittingham is of opinion with me, that any proposition for the occupation of Cadiz would now be attended with the worst effects; and, he says, that, unless particularly desired to do so, he should not like even to mention the subject to General Castaños.

I do not find that the *Junta* have, as yet, taken any steps about the loan from Gibraltar, in consequence of my letter; and I even doubt whether the Deputies they have sent to England have been commissioned to treat for pecuniary supplies. There seems to be a great want of consistency in many of the measures of this Council; and I almost fear there is a want of unanimity amongst its members.

I have not heard anything from Lord Collingwood, nor has he mentioned a word of pecuniary supplies in a letter which I have seen from him to the *Junta*, written after he had received his last despatches from England.

I have the honour to be, &c. &c.
(Signed)
William Cox,
Major, 61st Regiment.

To His Excellency Lieutenant-General Sir Hew Dalrymple.

Seville,
28th June, 1808.

Sir,

I yesterday received a letter from Lieutenant-Colonel Tucker, of which I have the honour to enclose you a copy. Your Excellency may judge how much I was surprised to hear of General Spencer's return; particularly as I am left totally in the dark respecting the cause of it; and am equally ignorant of what his intentions now are. I have heard, but not officially, that he has written more fully to the *Junta*; and that he has informed them that the reason of his return from Lisbon was, that he found, on his arrival there, that the French were in much greater force than he expected; and that he did not think it prudent to risk a landing with so small a corps as that which he commands. I cannot help thinking it would have been better to have remained off the Tagus, even though his force was not, as yet, sufficient to attempt a landing; and have waited there for the expected reinforcements.

A diversion on the coast of Portugal seems, in the present moment, of infinite importance; and I very much fear that if the attention of the enemy, in that country, is not thus attracted, this part of Spain will be exposed to the most imminent danger.

An account is just arrived of a column of French troops, about 5,000 men, under General Belliard, being on the march to join Dupont; and there is every reason to think that they have, by this time, crossed the Sierra Morena, the passes of which, it now appears, are, by no means, so well-guarded as General Castaños and the Board of Government were led to suppose. The accounts hitherto received were that the Puerta del Rey and Despeña Perros were occupied by 1,000 regular troops and a large body of peasantry; and that the road was cut in such a manner as to render it totally impassable; it has, however, turned out that there are no regular troops there at all, and that the cut has not been made.

It is really quite melancholy to think that there should not be better information upon such essential points. This junction, which, if it has not already taken place, appears now impossible to prevent, will, of necessity, draw the whole of the force under General Castaños to a distant point; and this part of the country and the province of Estremadura will thus be left completely exposed to an incursion of the French from Portugal.

Under these circumstances, it appears to me of such consequence that General Spencer should again appear off the Tagus, that I shall write, this evening, both to him and Lord Collingwood, upon the subject, who will judge, from the information I give them, of the propriety of such a measure.

Captain Whittingham came over here yesterday from Utrera; he was accompanied by Mr. Gordon, of Xeres, who is come up to the *Junta*, to speak to them concerning the proposed loan from England. I fancy he is to be employed on this business, but the matter is not yet determined. Captain Whittingham returned to Utrera this evening, with the Count de Tilly, who, after he has consulted with General Castaños, is to go off express to Cordova, and from thence endeavour to pass round the rear of the French to the Puerto del Rey, in order to ascertain the true state of that part of the country, and the passes of the Sierra, and to secure them, if possible, in such a manner as to prevent the admission of any further reinforcements of the enemy, and cut off the retreat of those corps which have already passed.

I have the honour to be, &c. &c.

William Cox,
Major, 61st Regiment.

101

(Enclosure.)

H.M. Brig *Scout*, off Ayamonte,
25th June, 1808.

Sir,

I am directed to notify to you the arrival of Major-General Spencer, off the mouth of the Guadiana, and his intention to proceed on to Cadiz, at which place he requests you will transmit to him such particulars and information respecting the affairs in Spain as you may be in possession of, and consider necessary to impart to him, unless you should hear of his detention at Ayamonte.

I have the honour to be, &c. &c.

(Signed)

G. B. Tucker,
Lieutenant-Colonel, A. Adjutant-General.

Extract of a Letter from Major Cox to Sir Hew Dalrymple.

Seville,
30th June, 1808.

This conversation with Father Gil gave me an opportunity of introducing the question of occupying Ceuta, *pro tempore*, by a British force, which would liberate the Spanish troops at present doing duty in that garrison, and obviate the difficulty which now exists of supplying them with provisions: but this I find to be a most tender subject. Father Gil says, that he himself proposed the measure shortly after I came here; but that it was opposed by every member of the *Junta*, except the President; and he told me, in confidence, that the strong opposition met with was, in a great measure, to be attributed to the representations of Morla, the Governor of Cadiz, who had given it as his decided opinion that no Spanish fortress should be put in possession of the English.

Extract of a Letter from Sir Hew Dalrymple to Major Cox.

Gibraltar,
10th July, 1808.

I think, however, that Lord Collingwood would be more than justified by his instructions, did he lend every aid, and make every necessary advance, to refit the French and Spanish ships; provided arrangements were made that those ships, as soon as fit for sea, and manned with loyal subjects of Spain, should anchor out with the British Squadron, and be no longer under the fire of the land, and virtually a part of the place, and liable to the contingencies of the land-war. I think, for any *Junta* in Spain, that can give no national pledge, to object to arrangements by which Britain, being at all the expense, may share in the advantage with her ally, proves a jealousy so nearly bordering on *hostility*, that nothing further need be said about the matter; but, as I have already said, I leave the fate of the fleets to Lord Collingwood.

General Morla may complain of me for not redeeming General Spencer's pledge, (see Sir Hew Dalrymple's letter to Major-General Spencer, 4th July);—but what pledge has that officer given that he would keep the fleets in a state of preparation, for the mutual advantage of George III. and Ferdinand VII. and not for Napoleon the Great? What am I to understand of this same General Morla, who throws out insinuations to General Spencer that he shall want his corps for the defence of Cadiz, should any reverse befall the Spanish arms, (by that means thwarting the operations of General Spencer's corps, which are officially recommended by General Castaños,) although it is understood that this same general is the most strenuous opposer of our being admitted into any place?"

To His Excellency Lieutenant-General Sir Hew Dalrymple.

Seville,
16th July, 1808.

Sir,

Brigade-Major Stuart arrived here this morning, from Major-General Spencer, with a letter to me, enclosing one to His Highness the President of the *Junta*; and, by him, I have had the honour of receiving Your Excellency's letters of the 5th and 7th instant. As General Spencer's letter to His Highness was sent to me open, I have taken a copy of it, which is herewith enclosed; and the purport of the answer, with which Major Stuart returns this evening, is, that the Board cannot come to a final determination without consulting General Castaños, to whom the question is to be immediately referred by express; and that, whatever his opinion is, will be adopted by them, and the decision forwarded to the major-general.

From the letter which I have now received from General Spencer, I am led to suppose that he never made the offer which Father Gil speaks of in his letter, of which I sent Your Excellency a copy in my last despatch; and that the idea arose from General Morla's having mistaken something which he said in conversation; for he now tells me that he never had but one opinion upon the subject, which was "not to advance with his present force beyond Xeres." I believe it is very much the wish of the *Junta* that it should; and I am not yet quite certain, either from the wording of his letter to the President or that which he has written to me, whether he means to comply with their request or not.

The subjects mentioned in Your Excellency's letter of the 5th instant and its enclosures, have never been spoken of to me officially; but hints have been dropped, in private conversation, that it was imagined, amongst the members of the *Junta*, that there was not the most perfect understanding between Lord Collingwood and General Spencer; and that they considered the character and disposition of the latter as more open and liberal: that he had come forward in the most handsome manner, and not only made an unlimited offer of his services to the Spanish Government, but had also said that he would take upon himself to supply them with money; and this, I find, he really has done. Major Stuart informs me that he has already advanced 40,000 dollars; and that his intention is to supply them every fortnight with a like sum, until some other arrangement can be made.

Your Excellency's letter of the 7th instant, and its enclosure, (the proclamation from Murcia), relate to a subject which I consider of the very first magnitude, and it has, for some time past, occupied my most serious attention. The measure therein recommended is indispensable; and I am every day more and more convinced of its necessity. Your Excellency will see, by the enclosure No. 2, that I had anticipated your wishes in mentioning the subject to the *Junta*, and I had, before that, touched upon it in conversation, but the discussion was always evaded; and I never could obtain any other answer except that "the matter would be taken into consideration in its proper season; but that the time was not yet arrived." I have not yet received an answer to my letter; but, as soon as it comes, I shall send a copy of it to Your Excellency.

The proclamation of Florida Blanca was received here some time ago, but was carefully suppressed by this government; and I never could get a copy of it until that which Your Excellency has had the goodness to send me. It certainly speaks the language of strong sense and reason; but I fear there are not many here whose understandings are sufficiently enlarged to embrace the project which has been so wisely suggested, or to be convinced of its utility by the justness of the arguments which are adduced in its support.

I have the honour to be, &c. &c.

(Signed)

William Cox,
Major, 61st Regiment.

To His Highness the President of the *Junta*.
Puerto Santo Maria,
15th July, 1808.

Sir,

I have the honour to acquaint your Highness that I have this moment received a despatch from His Majesty's ministers, which induces me to send Major Stuart to wait on the *Junta*, to request the decision of the Spanish Government.

I shall, upon their decision, follow their wishes; and if they think the presence of the British troops is not indispensably requisite to the cause, and their departure will produce no unfavourable sensation, I shall obey the design I have the honour to communicate to your Highness, of proceeding to join Lieutenant-General Sir Arthur Wellesley off Portugal; or, if it is their opinion that the troops now here are not essentially necessary, they will have the goodness to express the same to me, and I will take upon myself to remain here until further orders.

I have the honour to be, &c. &c.

B. Spencer.

To His Excellency Lieutenant-General Sir Hew Dalrymple.
Seville,
27th July, 1808.

Sir,

I have the honour to enclose Your Excellency the copy of an official letter from General Castaños to the *Junta*, which accompanied the capitulation of General Dupont.

Father Gil promised to let me have a copy of this treaty yesterday, for the information of Lord Collingwood and Your Excellency; but as it has not been sent to me, I have this day written to ask for it officially: a copy of my letter is herewith enclosed.

Lord Collingwood does not appear to be perfectly satisfied with the terms granted to Bedel; and he asks me if I can assign a reason why this division should have been allowed to capitulate after the defeat and surrender of the enemy's principal force.

His Lordship observes that this division may, if they choose, be again within, or upon the frontiers of Spain, in a week after they are landed at Rochfort. I have informed him that the *Junta* are themselves by no means satisfied with that part of the treaty; and that they can assign no satisfactory reason for the favourable terms which have been granted.

My own opinion is that, as there was no Spanish force between Bedel and the Sierra Morena, General Castaños thought him in a situation to make his escape if he thought proper, and was, therefore, most probably glad to include him, on any terms, in the capitulation which was then pending, but not as yet concluded, with Dupont.

It appears now that this division of Bedel's, or rather Bedel's and Gobert's united, amounts to 9,000 men, instead of 6,000, as was at first imagined.

I have received Lord Collingwood's answer to my letter, enclosing him copies of the paper relating to the Morocco conspiracy; and I have communicated the substance of it to the *Junta*. As my letter on this occasion was in Spanish, and pretty nearly a translation of some paragraphs of His Lordship's to me, I shall send Your Excellency a copy of his letter, and the answer which has been returned to mine by the *Junta*.

I have not yet received an answer to my letter, of the 14th instant, to the Padre Gil. Your Excellency will see that I have reminded him of it, in that which I have written him today. Several letters, some with names and some without, have, I know, been written to the *Junta*, or to individual members of it, upon the same subject; and other publications, containing maxims similar to those inculcated by the proclamation of Florida Blanca, have appeared, but are all suppressed here with equal care. From one which has fallen in my hands, I shall send Your Excellency an extract, which appears to me to contain much good sense, though I do not approve of the last question proposed for discussion.

I have the honour to be,
> Sir,

> > Your Excellency's
> > > Most obedient and very humble servant,
> > > > William Cox,
> > > > Major, 61st Regiment.

P.S. An account has arrived here today which, though not official, is generally believed, that Cuesta has gained a complete victory over a French Army of 20,000 men, under the command of General Bessières, at Palencia, and has advanced towards Burgos: in consequence of which, King Joseph, who was at Vittoria, has thought prudent to return into France.

> > > > > W. Cox.

(Private.)

To Sir Hew Dalrymple.

Seville,

28th July, 1808.

My Dear Sir,

I have the honour to enclose you the copy of a letter (with its enclosure) which I have this day written to Lord Collingwood.

As I find, by Captain Dalrymple's letter of the 17th July, that you seem to think you cannot, with propriety, speak again to the *Junta* on any national subjects, I have refrained, though with extreme reluctance, from making use of your name in the same way which I formerly did in my official communications with the Board of Government.

At the same time, I feel most perfectly convinced that you are the person who ought to have the most leading part in everything which concerns the intercourse between Great Britain and this part of Spain, in the present day. No British officer can be so well-informed as you are of the state of affairs in this country; and no one has, or is likely to obtain the same unlimited confidence which you possess with those who are principally concerned in this wonderful revolution.

I have the honour to be, &c. &c.

William Cox,

Major, 61st Regiment.

To Major Cox.

Gibraltar,

2nd August, 1808.

Dear Sir,

I have just received your letter of the 28th past, marked *private*, with its enclosures, and think it strange that the *Junta* should submit to Lord Collingwood and myself, as a question, whether they should fulfil, or break through the terms of a convention, made by a general acting under their authority, and signed by one of their own body. To Lord Collingwood, in particular, I think the question is very singularly addressed, as His Lordship's opinion of the duty of the *Junta*, on this very question, may be very different from what he may consider as his own, being himself wholly unfettered by the provisions of the document in question. For my own individual share, my opinion exactly coincides with what must have been that of the Spanish and French generals, by whom the capitulation, or convention, was sanctioned, namely, that it is binding on the contracting parties, in as far as the means of carrying it into execution are in the power of each.

The laws of honour (and not the rule of political expediency) still continue, I hope, to govern the conduct of soldiers in solemn stipulations of the sort in question, and certainly the surrender of Wedel's corps can only be justified by the confidence he placed in that honour, which is the characteristic of the Spanish Nation. If the French have been the first to break the capitulation, it is very extraordinary indeed, and I think that fact should rest on something more striking and prominent than anything contained in No. 2, (this was an able paper, anonymous, but generally believed, or rather known, to be by Don Tomas Morla, Governor of Cadiz,) which seems to display more eagerness of research, than success in discovering plausible pretexts for a measure which the writer himself considers as standing in need of some justification.

The reputation of a government, particularly of one recently formed, is a valuable part of its property, and should not be lightly squandered; perhaps this question might be argued even on the grounds of expediency.

(Signed)

H. W. Dalrymple,
Lieut.-General.

His Excellency Lieutenant-General Sir Henry Dalrymple.

Seville,
3rd August, 1808.

Sir, I have the honour to enclose, herewith, the copy of a letter, which I have received from the Padre Gil, in answer to the last communications which I made to the *Junta* on the part of Your Excellency. It appears that they are not disposed to take any further steps in the business of Morocco; they seem to think it probable that the conspiracy no longer exists; and that they are, at all events, determined to let the matter sink into oblivion.

I was not honoured by Your Excellency's letter of the 21st *ult*, till this morning; and I at the same time received your despatch of the 28th. This was evidently owing to some neglect at the post-office, where I also found letters today of an old date, from Cadiz, and some others from Gibraltar.

It has been particularly unfortunate that Your Excellency's despatches, which were written the beginning of June, and also the arrival of the Andalusian deputies in England, should have been so long delayed;— and it is still more unfortunate that the *Pickle*, which was probably charged with despatches in answer to those, should have been lost, as she was approaching the Port of Cadiz. It is difficult to persuade the people here that those delays have been unavoidable; and I know that some are illiberal enough to throw out insinuations that the English are much more ready to promise than to perform.

Your Excellency will see, by the last paragraph of Padre Gil's letter, that we are likely soon to see the plan of this *Junta*, for a supreme and sole Government of Spain. I very much fear that many members of the board still cherish the flattering but illusory idea of possessing a superiority over the local governments of the other provinces; and I think it not improbable, that the plan which is about to be published may be tinctured by some such foolish and contracted notions. The recent successes of their army, the ostentatious reception of the conquerors, and the pompous celebration of these victories, are circumstances which, operating on weak minds, cannot fail to make a deep impression; and I am sure that they have tended much to strengthen the ideas conceived by the *Junta*, of their supposed superiority.

The longer these ideas are cherished, the more dangerous they will become; but they must in the end be done away with, and this shadowy grandeur resigned:—yet all who are acquainted with human nature know how difficult it is to relinquish power when once really possessed, or even to abandon the pleasing phantom of imaginary greatness. The present is certainly a momentous crisis; what the issue may be I shall not pretend to anticipate, but I freely confess that I cannot help feeling some degree of apprehension that this great and glorious cause may be ruined by the baneful effects of jealousy and disunion.

General Castaños and Don Tomas Morla both arrived here the day before yesterday; the former was received by all ranks of people with the strongest demonstrations of joy and gratitude. To avoid jealousy, the same compliments were paid to each of them on their arrival, and they were both met by a deputation from the *Junta* without the gates of the city. They were shut up the whole of yesterday morning, with the *Junta*, and I am inclined to think their debates were very serious, and touching points of much importance; but I am not yet acquainted with the result. I have reason to think that Morla is a strong advocate for breaking the treaty which has been made with Dupont, and that there are many of the *Junta* of the same way of thinking. Castaños would naturally be averse from such an act, which would so sensibly wound his honour. They all seem anxious to know the sentiments of Your Excellency and Lord Collingwood upon the subject.

I am sorry to say the reports we have had of advantages gained by General Cuesta over the French have proved to be false. I very much fear that he has been worsted in the engagements which took place on the 14th and following days of July; in consequence of which, he has been obliged to retreat; and, by the last accounts, his army occupied Salamanca and Ciudad Rodrigo.

An account has been received here, of a corps of 5,000 French troops having arrived at Evoramonte, in Portugal. It is supposed that they have been merely sent from Lisbon in search of provisions: but I can hardly think so large a body would be detached for that purpose, when an English force was on the coast. My own opinion is, that it is Junot's intention to evacuate Portugal, and endeavour to form a junction with the French Army under General Bessières.

I have the honour to be, &c. &c.

William Cox,
Major, 61st Regiment.

To Sir Hew Dalrymple.

Seville,
Saturday night, 6th August.

My Dear Sir,

I have written so much for this night's post, that I must beg of your goodness to excuse my not sending you a regular despatch; I shall, however, enclose the copy of a letter, which I have written to Lord Collingwood, with its several enclosures, which will give you every information which I could have communicated, had I written more formally.

I have again taken upon myself to address Lord Castlereagh directly, which I trust you will approve of. I have sent His Lordship copies of my last letters to you, No. 21, (3rd August) without its accompaniments; and the letter which I have now written to Lord Collingwood with all its enclosures.

To my astonishment, I have this day heard that the Count de Tylli, and the Assistente Hore (a creature of the Prince of Peace), are named the deputies from this *Junta* to the Central Board of Government. Miñano is to take the place of Tylli with the army.

I have the honour to be, &c. &c.

William Cox,
Major, 61st Regiment.

(Enclosure.)
To Lord Collingwood.

Seville,
5th August, 1808.

My Lord,

I have now the honour of sending your lordship a copy of the plan proposed by the *Junta* of Seville, for forming a Supreme Board of Government to represent the whole kingdom. I am happy to observe that it is divested of those sentiments with which I feared it might be contaminated. This public renunciation of all pretensions to supremacy appears to me a greater triumph, on the part of this government, than the glorious victories obtained by their armies in the field; and the plan which they here propose, if carried into effect, is likely to do more real service to the country at large, than the most brilliant military achievements, under the partial governments which at present exist.

That the *Junta* had other ideas than those now declared, and that they were cherished until very lately, I am perfectly certain; and I have great reason to suppose, that the Count de Tylli was a strong advocate for totally a different system. Your lordship asks me how this nobleman stands in the public estimation? of this, I can inform you in a very few words: his attachment to the king is very much suspected; his love for the country at large very doubtful; his general talents are moderate; his political knowledge extremely limited; and his private character by no means respectable. He is, however, what may be called a leading character in the *Junta*. He was very instrumental in its original formation; and has since distinguished himself a good deal, by his zeal, in the prosecution of their measures; at the same time, I am much inclined to doubt the purity of his intentions.

This party has, however, been over-ruled, and I hope this danger is now past and guarded against for ever, by this public declaration, which is ratified by the signature of all the members of the board. The man, who unquestionably possesses the greatest abilities in the *Junta*, and who takes the most decided lead in that Assembly, is the author of the enclosed publication, Padre Manuel Gil, the person who, as I have before informed your lordship, is appointed to correspond with me. He is a man of very uncommon endowments; and if he were a little less sensible of his superior talents, and not so tenacious of his own opinions, or impatient of listening to those of others, he would undoubtedly be a great character. Saavedra, the President, is a man of very tolerable abilities, good common sense, and some political knowledge. Your lordship will recollect that he was formerly a Minister of State, and was excluded from the Royal Councils, and banished with the unfortunate Jovellanos, through the influence of the Prince of Peace, for having advised his king to adopt measures which he conceived likely to conduce to the real interests of the nation.

An express arrived here the night before last, from Madrid, with a letter of a very extraordinary nature, ad dressed to General Castaños, from Grouchy, the French *commandant* of the metropolis, in which he states that the troops under his command being required for another service, he could wish the general would send part of his army to occupy the capital, in order to ensure its tranquillity, and protect the established French families, and the sick which might be left behind in the hospitals. He concludes his letter by a request, that whatever the general's determination may be, in consequence of this intimation, he would, at all events, send one of his officers to treat of matters which would probably be conducive to the interest of both nations. Major-General Mireno, the quartermaster-general of the Spanish Army, who is reckoned a man of very good abilities, has been sent off to Madrid on this business.

Two posts have since come in with intelligence, that the French Army have evacuated the Capital, and are marching towards Segovia; evidently to join Bessières, who is opposed to Cuesta. It is supposed here, that the French are panic-struck, and have resolved to quit the country altogether; but my own opinion is, that it is their intention to unite their whole force, and attack General Cuesta, who commands the armies of Castille and Gallicia; and, if they are successful in this enterprise, to turn their force upon those who may be induced, by their stratagems, to approach Madrid, incautiously, from this quarter, without the necessary combination of military movements with the other provinces, or being well assured of mutual support. Joseph Bonaparte has undoubtedly left Madrid, accompanied by several of the *grandees*, and all the ministers, except Cevallos. The inhabitants are in the greatest consternation, and are flying from the capital in great numbers, into this and the adjacent provinces as the only places of security; many persons of distinction have arrived here within the last two or three days.

I have written to the Padre Gil to acquaint him with your lordship's sentiments upon the Treaty with Dupont, and also to ask for information respecting the result of the conferences, which have lately taken place in the *Junta*, concerning the future operations of the army, and the destination of the French prisoners. I shall do myself the honour of enclosing your lordship a translation of my letter, and of the answer which I shall probably receive before this is closed.

As the recent events in this country have been of such vast importance, and the present state of things is so likely to produce some new, and possibly unexpected changes, it will, of course, be highly expedient that His Majesty's Ministers should be fully acquainted with what has happened, and is now passing. Your lordship will, no doubt, write fully upon those subjects, but, as I conceive that a case has again arisen, which authorises me, according to my original instructions, to address myself immediately to His Majesty's Government, I shall prepare a despatch for my Lord Castlereagh, which I beg your lordship will have the goodness to forward by the first opportunity.

I have the honour to be, &c. &c.

William Cox.

P.S. It is impossible to procure the maps and charts here, which your lordship has mentioned: I believe they are not to be had anywhere, except at Madrid. My letter to Lord Castlereagh contains a copy of the plan for forming a national government.

To Lord Viscount Castlereagh.

Seville,
6th August, 1808.

My Lord,

Your lordship has, no doubt, been fully informed, by Lord Collingwood and Sir Hew Dalrymple, of the recent events which have taken place in this part of Spain, of the victories gained by the army under General Castaños over the common enemy, and the consequent annihilation of the French Force in this province. These events, united with other circumstances which have occurred in different parts of Spain, have given a decided turn in favour of the loyal party, and have produced a state of things which must shortly bring about a still more important change. There seems now to be every probability that a general representation of the nation will speedily be formed to govern the country at large. The sentiments of the Supreme *Junta* of Seville upon this subject are at last made known, after repeated efforts to discover them; or, I might better say, this Assembly have now come to a final determination on points that were not before decided; and have published their resolution.

The necessity of a head to direct the affairs of the nation at large, and to rule and govern in the name of the whole kingdom, has long been apparent to all who were capable of reflecting seriously on the state of this country.

Several plans have been proposed, and many publications have appeared on the subject; some proposing to establish a military form of government; others to assemble the Cortes, according to the constitution of the country; and others, to appoint, at once, a viceroy, or lieutenant, of the kingdom. Perhaps the most simple plan of any which has appeared, the most easy to be effected, and the most likely to be adopted, is that which has just been published here by this government; and of which I shall do myself the honour of enclosing your lordship a copy.

I have thought it of so much importance that His Majesty's Government should, as soon as possible, be informed of what has happened, and is passing here, and also that it might be some satisfaction to receive this information from a person on the spot, that I have been induced to take the liberty to write directly to your lordship.

I only regret that there is not someone here more competent to the task: and I would, with great deference, beg leave to suggest the expediency of immediately sending out a person, invested with the necessary powers, and possessing sufficient abilities to direct the councils, and take that leading part in the affairs of the government which is likely to be established in this country, which Great Britain is entitled to act.

I cannot communicate the information which I propose to give your lordship better than by referring you to my last letters to Lord Collingwood and Sir Hew Dalrymple: I shall, therefore, do myself the honour of enclosing copies of them, and shall only beg leave to add that the demands of the government of this province for money and arms are repeated and urgent, and that I know their wants are great. They cannot be brought to believe that their propositions, which I had the honour to forward to your lordship on the 18th June, did not arrive in England time enough to have had an answer to them before this; and they most sensibly feel that, although their merits have been at least as great, they have not been so fortunate as other provinces, in obtaining the promised succours from Great Britain.

I have the honour to be, &c. &c.

(Signed)

William Cox.

To His Excellency Lieutenant-General Sir Hew Dalrymple.

Seville,
18th August, 1808.

Sir,

I have the honour to acknowledge the receipt of Your Excellency's letter of the 12th instant; the contents of which I have communicated, according to your orders, to the Supreme *Junta*. I shall do myself the honour of enclosing, herewith, copies of the letter which I wrote to Father Gil upon this occasion, and of his answer, which I have just received. I shall also send Your Excellency the copy of a letter which I wrote to him on the 14th instant, by Lord Collingwood's desire, respecting an application from Valencia and Catalonia for field-artillery; and in which I communicated to the *Junta* your coincidence in opinion with His Lordship on the subject of the Morocco conspiracy and the conduct of the Spanish agents at Tangier: to this I shall also annex Father Gil's reply.

On the 6th instant, I had the honour of sending Your Excellency the copy of a letter which I had written to Lord Collingwood, accompanied by the plan which has been proposed by this *Junta* for forming a General Government. I hope this may have reached Your Excellency before your departure from Gibraltar; but, in case it should not have been received, I shall put another copy under cover with this, together with a detailed account of the Battle of Baylen, which has just been published.

Count Tylli and Don Vicente Hore are the two members who have been elected, by ballot, to represent this *Junta* in the General Board of Government. The characters of these gentlemen are by no means respectable; and their nomination has caused a good deal of surprise and much dissatisfaction: it is said, and, I hope, with foundation, that they are likely to be changed.

The Council of Castile, it appears, have resumed their power and authority at Madrid, and are issuing orders and decrees as the Supreme Tribunal of the nation. This will, most probably, give rise to very serious disputes. Their authority may be acknowledged by some of the provinces, but will most certainly be opposed by many; and, amongst others, most decidedly by this. I very much fear the consequences of this variety of sentiment, which is so likely to prove an obstacle to the formation of the General *Junta*, and to produce those jealousies and divisions which are so much to be dreaded.

I have heard, with great astonishment, from Padre Gil, that a letter, addressed to Your Excellency from the Council of Castile, has been stopped at St. Roque, and a copy of it sent here (the letter, I am told, was not opened; but was accompanied by an unsealed copy), by the *commandant* of that place. I understand that the *Junta* have written to desire him to transmit the original letter to them, and that it will be given to me to forward to Your Excellency. These circumstances I learned from the *padre*, in a private and confidential conversation; but he told me that he was not authorised by the *Junta* to mention the subject. I could not help expressing fully what I thought of this very shameful and unwarrantable proceeding; and I told him that I was very certain Your Excellency would feel extremely indignant at hearing of such a palpable breach of that confidence which was supposed to exist between the two governments.

He seemed a good deal confused at finding that I took up the matter so warmly, and tried to excuse the conduct of the *commandant* of St. Roque, and the government which authorised it, by saying that there was a general order to stop all expresses which were not sanctioned by a passport from them; and that they also wished to save Your Excellency the embarrassment of being drawn into a correspondence with an assumed authority, which was not legitimate, and could not be acknowledged. To this I answered, that the superscription of a letter addressed to Your Excellency, from whomsoever it might come, ought to be considered as a sufficient passport; and that you were yourself the best judge of the propriety of the correspondence or the expediency of carrying it on.

I have the honour to be, &c. &c.

William Cox,
Major, 61st Regiment.

His Excellency Lieutenant-General Sir Hew Dalrymple.

Seville,
27th August, 1808.

Sir,

Since the letters which passed between the Padre Gil and me, of which I had the honour to enclose copies to Your Excellency in my despatch, No. 23, I have had no official communication with the *Junta*, though I occasionally hear what passes there, but not always through the same medium as formerly. The Padre Gil has not of late been so open and unreserved in his conversations with me as formerly, which I can only account for by supposing that the *Junta* are themselves ashamed of their own proceedings. The fact is, their attention has been, for some time past, so much occupied by vain and frivolous disputes, and by views of private interest and advantage, that they seem to have neglected entirely every concern of real importance, and almost to have lost sight of the general interest of the country.

Before General Castaños left this, it was determined that an additional force of 30,000 men should be raised in this province, and formed on the ground-work of five battalions of the line, which were left here for the purpose of training them. I have lately been informed, from good authority, that this business is entirely at a stand, and that, for the last fifteen days, the Board of Military Inspection, that have the management of this, as well as all matters relative to the pay, clothing, &c. of the army, have not been able to obtain an answer, or get back any of their official papers, which, according to the routine of office, they have been obliged to lay before the *Junta*, for their sanction and signature.

I think I mentioned to Your Excellency, in one of my letters, that Don Andrés Miñano, one of the members of the *Junta*, was appointed to accompany General Castaños, and remain with the army, in the room of Count Tylli, who, with Don Vicente Hore, were nominated as deputies from the *Junta* to the Central Board of Government. A salary of twelve thousand hard dollars a-year was assigned to Miñano, but, shortly after his departure, this scandalous misapplication of the public money, which was much talked of by the people, became a subject of discussion in the *Junta*; it was brought forward by the archbishop, who declared that he had always disapproved of the measure, and was only induced to lend his sanction to it, and sign the paper by which it was authorised, from a wish to avoid those dissensions to which he feared his refusal might give rise; a warm debate ensued, which ended in the order being rescinded.

About this time, Don Vicente Hore very prudently begged leave to decline his nomination as deputy to the Central *Junta*, and the archbishop was appointed in his place: he, probably, foresaw the likelihood of this Assembly being formed at, or, at all events, ultimately transferred to Madrid, and judged that so warm a friend, and decided partisan of the Prince of Peace, as he was formerly known to be, would not be well received in the metropolis. I understand that the Count de Tylli has, also, tendered his resignation, and that the Marquis de las Torres, a man of very respectable character, is likely to be appointed in his stead. Tylli is, also, too well known at Madrid to be very anxious to show himself there again; he was formerly obliged to fly from thence, under a strong suspicion of being concerned in a public robbery. I do not say this lightly; for I have heard it from many who were there at the time, and the fact has even been mentioned by a colleague of his own in the Supreme *Junta*.

I believe, however, that he would have gone, had he been able to gain the point of annexing a salary to the employment; but this was carried against him, by a great majority, a few days since, in the *Junta*. Part of the money which Mr. Duff has brought out from England, for the service of the country, arrived here today. I am ignorant of the terms on which this aid is granted by Great Britain, whether by way of loan or subsidy.

A million of dollars have, I understand, been sent out; and I am told by the *Junta* that their deputies in England have written to say that this sum is to be made up to a million of pounds sterling for Andalusia. Mr. Duff is, no doubt, furnished with full instructions as to the mode in which this money is to be delivered: it certainly would not be prudent to entrust so large a sum to the management of the temporary government of a particular province, without having a sufficient security for its proper application: my own opinion is, that the less money which is given to them the better, until the general government is formed.

This *Junta* have shown too evident signs of a wish to aggrandise themselves, and a disinclination to afford those aids to other provinces which they had it in their power to grant, not to afford just grounds of suspicion that their boasted loyalty and patriotism have, at times, been mixed with unworthy considerations of self-interest and personal advantage.

They are, every day, making promotions in the army without much attention to merit, and giving away employments of emolument which they really have no right to dispose of; they have even assumed the power of making canons of the church, a privilege belonging, exclusively, to the sovereign. Everything calls loudly for the formation of a Central *Junta*; and it will certainly be of the greatest consequence that an accredited agent of the British Government be sent out as soon as possible, to take a decided part in the government of their councils.

I have the honour to be, &c. &c.

(Signed)

William Cox,
Major, 61st Regiment.

To His Excellency Lieutenant-General Sir Hew Dalrymple.

Seville,
30th August, 1808.

Sir,

As my last letter to Your Excellency was sent, under cover, to Lord Collingwood, who, I since find, has left Cadiz for the Mediterranean, I think it probable that it may not reach you so soon as this; I, therefore, do myself the honour to enclose a duplicate of it. I, also, send herewith the letter which, in my despatch, No. 23, I informed Your Excellency was addressed to you by the Council of Castile, and had been stopped by the *commandant* of St. Roque. It is now upwards of a fortnight since I first heard of this shameful proceeding, and was told that the *Junta* had written, by express, to desire that the original letter, of which they had before received a copy, might be immediately sent here.

It was not, however, till yesterday that I received it, accompanied by a letter from Padre Gil, which I have, also, the honour to enclose. I have myself but little doubt that the letter has been opened, and that it had been detained here by the *Junta* until they thought its receipt, and the part which Your Excellency might, possibly, be induced to take in consequence, should no longer be likely to produce an effect contrary to their wishes.

Their great object was to prevent the other provinces of Spain from acknowledging the Council of Castile as the supreme tribunal of the kingdom, and, if possible, to annul its authority altogether; but in this they are not likely to succeed; they cannot, nor they ought not, to attempt to destroy a fundamental part of the constitution:—if any of the members, of which this branch of it is composed, have betrayed their country, or taken an active part with its enemies, let them be punished in the most exemplary manner:—both policy and justice require it; but the institution itself should remain untouched, and no attempt be made, for the present, either to alter or dissolve it. It has, after all, been determined that the Count de Tylli shall go as one of the deputies to the Central *Junta*. He is to be allowed five hundred dollars a month, to cover his expenses; and Minaño's salary, instead of being entirely done away, as I mentioned in my last letter to Your Excellency, is to be reduced to the same allowance. Tylli is, I understand, to set out this day for Ciudad Real, and the archbishop will follow shortly after.

An express arrived here, the evening before last, from Aroche, with intelligence that an account had been received there, from the *Junta* of Moura, of a victory obtained, on the 21st instant, by the combined

119

English and Portuguese Army, over the French, near Lisbon; in which it was stated the enemy had lost upwards of 3,000 men, and that Junot and the remainder of his army had surrendered prisoners of war. As there has since been no confirmation of this intelligence, and that Badajos letters, received here today, are silent on the subject, I should fear the news is untrue, or, at least, that the glorious event, which cannot now be far distant, has been anticipated.

General Castaños entered Madrid on the 23rd, with part of the army under his command, and was most joyfully received by all classes of the inhabitants. I think it probable that this night's post will bring some accounts from Captain Whittingham, who accompanied him; but they will be too late to go with this, which I mean to send to Mr. Duff, at Cadiz, to be forwarded to Your Excellency by the first opportunity.

I have the honour to be, &c. &c. &c.

William Cox,
Major, 61st Regiment.

(Enclosure, No. 1.)

Sevilla,
à 29 de Agosto, de 1808.

Muy Senor Mio,

Parö de orden de la Junta Suprema a V. S. el adjunto pliego para el Exmo. Señor Governador de Gibraltar queen este instante remite el Capitano General del Campo de San Roque y habia detenido por las ordenes generales de Policia que le habia dado esta Junta Suprema.

Dios guarde à V. S. muchos años,

B. L. M. de V. S.
Manuel Gil.

Senor Mayor Don Guillemno Cox.

Exmo. Senor,

La Divina Providencia acaba de libertar a esta corte de la opresion cruel en que ha yacido por espacio de quatro meses. Jose Napoleon, su comitiva y las Tropas Francesas que la circundaban han salido precipitadamente dirigiendose por Castilla la Vieja, esta prodigiosa emigracion al mismo tiempo que ha restituido a los corazones de sus habitantes la alegria y los con suelos que desaparacieron desde el momento de la agresion injusta de tan extraordinarios enemigos exige imperiosamente que el consijo de Castilla occurra por los medios mas prontos y efficaces a preparar una vigorosa defensa, y habiendo sabido el consejo con mucha satisfaccion que las provincias litorales de España han sido socor-

ridas en los presentes aconteci mientos por nacion Inglesa, con quantos auxilios han pedido y pendido de su posibilidad ha acordado que en su nombre y como su Gobernador interimo me dirija a V. S. por ser el Xefe de aquella potencia que reside con mayor inmediacion a España tributandole las mas expresivas gracias por tan generosas demonstraciones y que le manifieste al mismo tiempo nuestra actual situa cion y la necesidad urgentissima en que nos hallamos de acopiar trecientos mil fusiles con sus bayonetes y treinta mil pares de pistolas para armar un numeroso exercito que resista toda la fuerza que puede atentar nuevamente contra nuestra seguridad.

El consijo confia que continuando la buena correspondencia que han experimentado en esta occasion los Españoles de la nacion Inglesa se servira V.E. facilitarnos a la brevedad que la sea posible los trecientos mil fusiles y treinta mil pares de pistolas, de que tanto necesitamos, en la intelligencia de que su pago se harà como de una deuda nacional, (de que andarà el consijo y de que esta fineza le serà del mayor aprecio. Para no retardar la entrega de estos afectos ha comisionado el consejo al Comandante General del campo de San Roque que se presentarà a V.E. con este oficio y con la credencial correspondiente que le autorize para estos reciviendo baxo las formalidades y risquardos acostumbrados.

Dios guarde a V.E. muchos años.

     (Signed)   *Arias Mon.*

Madrid, 8 de Agosto, 1808.

To Lieutenant-General Sir, Hew Dalrymple.

Seville,
5th September, 1808.

Sir,

On the 31st *ultimo*, I had the honour of writing to Your Excellency by a courier, whom I despatched with a packet of letters, which I had received that day from Madrid, and which I was requested, by Captain Whittingham, in General Castaños's name, to forward to Your Excellency as soon as possible. I understand they have gone by the *Loire* frigate, which was to sail on the 22nd instant; and Mr. Duff informs me that he put my despatch, No. 26, which contained a duplicate of No. 25, on board the same ship.

The *Loire* brought out from England silver bars, to the amount of half a million of dollars, the whole of which has now arrived here, as well as that which came by the *Champion* and *Minorca*; and I understand that three transports are hourly expected at Cadiz, with nearly 40,000 stands of small arms, and a large quantity of ammunition.

Mr. Duff, who is charged with the delivery of those supplies, arrived here the day before yesterday, and I have had some conversation with him upon the business of his mission: I find that he is instructed to deliver the whole of the money and arms which have now come out under his care, to the provisional government of this province; from whom he is to take receipts, and who are to be entrusted with the sole management of them. It appears that it is the wish of the British Government that all the southern provinces of Spain should be supplied through the channel of this *Junta*, and a *hope* is expressed, in Mr. Canning's letter to the Andalusian Deputies, that the aids now granted may be considered as applicable to the general service of the country.

I cannot help expressing my regret that there should not have been some better security for the proper management of those supplies which Great Britain, with such a liberal and bountiful hand, has so generously bestowed; and that they should not have been placed at the disposal of Your Excellency, or Lord Collingwood, or some other person capable of judging, from circumstances on the spot, how they might best be applied for the general benefit of Spain. It appears, at least, the person entrusted with their care, should have had discretionary powers to dispose of them, as he should see most expedient, according to the state of things at the time of his arrival. By Mr. Duff's present instructions, he would have had no option, even though the iniquitous project of partition, which Your Excellency knows was once contemplated, were still in existence.

Whether the *Junta* of Seville may now think it necessary, according to the wish and intention of the British Government, to share the foreign aids which they have received, with the neighbouring Provinces, I know not; but it is very well known that when their brothers of Valencia and Catalonia were nobly defending the cause of their country, against the repeated and desperate attack of an incensed and inveterate enemy, almost bare-handed, and the brave Catalans were reduced to the extremity of substituting the trunks of trees, bored and hooped with iron, for cannon, that the patriots of this Province resisted their urgent solicitations for a supply of artillery, which they could have spared in abundance, from the well provided arsenals of Cadiz and Seville, although Lord Collingwood offered them the means of conveyance to any of the ports of Spain, where they might think necessary to send them.

Mr Duff informs me that the million and a half of dollars, which has now been sent out for Andalusia, is to be considered either as part of the money which this government, through their deputies, expressed a wish to borrow from Great Britain, or as a gratuitous subsidy, according as they may choose to accept of it; but the decision is not to be pressed for the present.

I have the honour to be, &c. &c.

William Cox,
Major, 61st Regiment.

To His Excellency Lieutenant General Sir Hew Dalrymple.

Seville,
7th September, 1808.

Sir,

I have been informed, in a conversation with Father Gil, that he has repeatedly received letters from Mr. Viali, and from the Vicar of Gibraltar, speaking in the most favourable terms of the young Neapolitan Prince, who still continues to reside there: praising his amiable qualities, and exalting his virtues in a manner which would seem to insinuate a wish to favour the speculation upon which His Royal Highness was sent from Sicily.

This conduct on the part of Mr. Viali in particular, who knows the disapprobation which the British Government have expressed of this intrigue, appears to me extremely indiscreet and improper; and I, therefore, think it my duty to make Your Excellency acquainted with it. Father Gil informs me that the letters which he has received from that quarter have not been answered, and he seems anxious to impress upon me that the views of Prince Leopold have not received any sort of encouragement from this *Junta*; and that, as a body, they had no part whatsoever in the invitation which brought him to Gibraltar; though he allows it is possible that Tylli, or some other individual of the *Junta*, may have been concerned in the business.

This, I think myself, there can scarcely be a doubt of; and indeed, I have some suspicion, though perhaps it may not be well founded, that there is still an idea cherished of making this prince either President of the Central *Junta*, or of appointing him regent of the kingdom. I am pretty sure that neither of these steps will take place, because I believe the general opinion is against it; but I should not be surprised to hear of the proposition being made.

I shall do myself the honour of enclosing herewith, to Your Excellency, a copy of an anonymous paper which Father Gil gave me some time ago, and which I did not think then of sufficient consequence to

123

trouble you with; but, as connected with the present subject, I think it right to send it. The original is in Mr. Viali's hand-writing; and though on a separate sheet of paper, appears to be a sort of postscript to another letter. Your Excellency will observe, that it is expressed in very ambiguous terms, and unconnected sentences, which are not perfectly intelligible at the first glance.

The short eulogium, at the commencement, is not without its meaning, and the observation that England wishes to assist Spain, generously leaving her perfectly free to make her own elections, is certainly meant to insinuate that Great Britain would not disapprove of Prince Leopold being elected to preside over the Spanish Government, though Mr. Viali very well knew the contrary to be the case. He then says, let what will happen, His Royal Highness has, at all events, been made fully acquainted with the individual conduct of the *Señorones*, as he is pleased to call them, of Granada. This relates to a dispute between the two *Juntas*, which had nearly been productive of the most serious consequences, and would probably have ended in open hostility, had it not been prevented by the moderate, but decided conduct of General Castaños.

★★★★★★

This happened immediately after the Battle of Baylen. Granada refused to acknowledge the supreme authority of Seville; a violent dispute ensued, and the Count de Tylli had the imprudence to propose, in the *Junta*, that a division of the Andalusian Army should be marched into Granada to reduce them to submission. General Castaños, who was present, got up, and, striking the table, said, "he should like to see the man who dared to order a division of the army under his command to march, without his authority; that he knew no distinction of provinces; he had the honour to be entrusted, he said, with the command of part of the Army of Spain, and he would never suffer it to become the vile instrument of Civil War!"

★★★★★★

Supposing the people of Granada to have been in the wrong on this occasion, what business had Mr. Viali to convince Prince Leopold of their misconduct, or even to speak to His Royal Highness upon the subject? It was certainly meddling and officious in the extreme.

I have the honour to be, &c. &c.

William Cox,
Major, 61st Regiment.

His Excellency Lieutenant-General Sir Hew Dalrymple.

Seville,
10th September, 1808.

Sir,

The day before yesterday I received a letter from Brigadier-General Doyle, of which I have the honour to enclose Your Excellency a copy. I am inclined to think there is some mistake in the date, as it came by an express, which brought despatches to the *Junta*, and I received, by the same conveyance, and upon the same subject, a letter of the 5th instant from Captain Whittingham.

I immediately had an interview with Father Gil, to whom I stated the substance of General Doyle's letter. I asked him whether General Castaños had written to the *Junta* upon the subject. He said that letters had been received from the general, in which he asked for a supply of money, but not at all in the pressing terms of General Doyle's letter; that the *Junta*, had in consequence, written to authorise him to draw for what he wanted, and that they had some time ago sent him 150,000 dollars. I observed that this sum would go but a very short way in the payment of so large a body of troops, and that, as there would be, probably, great difficulty in negotiating bills to any considerable amount, I thought it better that part of the money, which had been sent out from England, expressly for the purpose, should be immediately remitted to Madrid, for the use of the army.

Objections were made to this, the principal of which was, that the greater part of the silver, which they had received from England, had been sent out in bars; and was not yet coined. In short, the answer which I received was by no means satisfactory, and I, therefore, determined to address the *Junta*, in writing, upon the subject. I accordingly drew up the paper, of which I have the honour to enclose Your Excellency a copy, and I presented it yesterday, in person, to the *Junta*, having previously conversed with them on the principal points.

Your Excellency will observe, that I have made use of General Doyle's name only, as having written to me officially, though I have taken some facts, which I knew could be depended on, from Captain Whittingham's letter, in order to make my representation stronger.

I hope that Your Excellency will not think I have exceeded the bounds of my duty, in the step which I have taken on this occasion; and I trust that my conduct will not be disapproved of by His Majesty's Government, to whom I should write directly, if I knew any shorter channel than through the medium of Your Excellency.

I found myself peculiarly circumstanced, and felt it necessary at once to decide, called upon in the strong language of General Doyle's letter, who is acting under the immediate orders of government; and the still stronger expressions of Captain Whittingham, who, though he writes to me privately and confidentially, I must consider as the organ of General Castaños; and being myself aware of the critical situation of affairs, and the absolute necessity of the measure which they recommended, I thought it became my duty, though not invested with powers, which, under other circumstances, could authorise me to act as I have done, to speak decidedly, and assume a tone of firmness. In times like the present, and on such an occasion, it was necessary to do so. The safety of a nation is at stake, and I should conceive myself unpardonable, if I omitted any means of which in my poor judgement appeared likely to contribute to its salvation.

It was evidently the intention of His Majesty's ministers that the whole of the supplies afforded by Great Britain to this country, both of troops, arms, ammunition, and money, whatever may have been the manner in which they were given, or the channel through which they were sent, should be made use of in favour of the general cause of Spain, and with a view towards the grand objects of expelling the French from the country, and replacing the unfortunate Ferdinand VII. on the throne; and not for the establishment of any partial Government, or the aggrandisement of any particular province.

The Supreme *Junta* of Seville have lately manifested very different views, and I am sorry to say, they seem almost to have lost sight of the common cause, and to be wholly addicted to their particular interests. Instead of directing their efforts to the restoration of their legitimate sovereign, and the established form of National Government, they are seeking the means of fixing the permanency of their own, and endeavouring to separate its interests from those of the other parts of Spain.

To what other purpose can be attributed the order given to General Castaños, not to march on any account beyond Madrid? to what the instructions given to their Deputy Don Andres Miñano, to uphold the authority, and preserve the integrity of the *Junta* of Seville, to distinguish the army to which he is attached by the name of the Army of Andalusia, to preserve constantly that appellation, and not to receive any orders but what came directly from this government? and, above all, what other motive could induce the strong and decided measures of enforcing obedience to those orders, by withholding from General Castaños the means of maintaining his troops, in case of his refusing

126

to comply with them? If all the distant provinces of Spain, according to the example of this, had chosen to mark the limits, beyond which their armies should not pass, and had possessed this power of restraining them, the cause of the nation was totally ruined, and the triumph of its enemies the inevitable consequence.

What have been the late occupations of the *Junta* of Seville? Setting aside the plans, which were formed for augmenting the Spanish Army, in these provinces, and neglecting the consideration of those, which have been proposed in their stead, their attention has been taken up in the appointment of secretaries to the different departments, in disposing of places of emolument, in making promotions in the army; appointing canons of the church, and instituting orders of knighthood! such steps as these make their designs too evident, and I felt that my duty imperiously called upon me to declare, unequivocally, my sentiments, and to protest against such conduct.

I have this instant (9 at night) received the official answer of the *Junta*, and if I can possibly get it copied in time, shall send it this post by way of Badajos, and a duplicate tomorrow, by the way of Cadiz.

I have the honour to be, &c. &c.

William Cox.

(Enclosure.)
To Major Cox.

Madrid,
1st September, 1808.

Sir,

At the momentous crisis in which I write, the French, with their *united force*, pouring down upon Zaragosa, and our Army of Andalusia unable to move to its assistance for want of money, I feel it highly necessary to request that you do immediately, in the name of the British Government, call upon the *Junta* of Seville to send forward to this capital, without a moment's delay, the money brought out by Mr. Duff for the use of the army and the nation of Spain as may still remain in their hands.

I do not mean to enter into any discussion as to the intentions of His Majesty's Government, *quoad* the distribution of this money, at the moment it was sent from England; but I am confident it was intended to be employed according to *existing circumstances*, and for the benefit of the *cause of Spain*, and not for the use of *any individual Junta*. I do, therefore, thus solemnly protest, in the name of the government by which I am employed, against the appropriation of this money to any objects unconnected with the actual benefit of the army now in this neighbourhood and in presence of the enemy.

I have no doubt of your seeing the bearings of this question in the same light with me; and I have the fullest reliance upon your assistance to forward the money. I build upon your decision, and consequent prompt measures; then the object, which is at once so desirable and so imperiously necessary, will be produced; and towards the completion of which grand object all supplies, all troops, all monies which have been sent into this country, namely, the expulsion of the French.

I have the honour to be, &c. &c.

C. W. Doyle,
Brigadier-General,

(Enclosure.)

Paper addressed by Major Cox to the Supreme *Junta* of Seville.

Most Excellent Sirs,

By a letter which I have received from Brigadier-General Doyle, who is charged with a particular commission from the British Government, and at present resident at Madrid, from whence he writes, I am informed that the French, with their united force, are pouring down upon Zaragoza, that they have retaken the town of Tudela, and threaten an immediate attack upon the capital of Aragon.

Under these alarming circumstances, a meeting of the generals commanding the principal armies of Spain was held, at Madrid, on the 4th instant; and the result of their conference was an unanimous opinion that it was absolutely necessary for the troops under General Castaños to move forward immediately to Soria. It was, however, found that, notwithstanding the liberal supplies which Great Britain has so generously given for the service of this country, the Spanish Army was literally unable to move for want of money; and that the Supreme *Junta* of Seville had refused General Castaños the means of paying his troops, if he should presume to march beyond Madrid, which was contrary to their orders!

I could have scarcely thought it possible that the Supreme *Junta* of Seville, who have hitherto manifested so much zeal for the general cause of their country, and have done so much towards the attainment of the great object which the nation holds in view, could have been capable of those ideas of partial interest which are so clearly demonstrated in the orders to which I allude, or of withholding the means which the British Government, with such entire confidence, has entrusted to their care, for the general benefit of the Spanish Nation.

In the pressing exigency of the case, General Doyle was induced, upon his own responsibility, to negotiate bills upon England, and upon Mr. Duff, to the amount of 200,000 dollars; with which he has paid the army which takes its name from the province whose government has received a million and half from Great Britain, expressly for its support.

This has enabled General Castaños to put his army in motion, but it cannot last long in the payment of so large a body of troops, and the vast expenses attending their taking the field.

I therefore feel it my duty, both in conformity to the desire of General Doyle, the opinion of Mr. Duff, (whom I have consulted,) and my own view of the subject, to call peremptorily upon the *Junta* to send forward, without the least delay, a considerable portion of the money which is lately come out from England, for the use of the army and the general service of the country; and, at the same time, to protest, as I do solemnly, in the name of the British Government, against the appropriation of the money, or any part of it, to purposes unconnected with these objects.

(Signed)   William Cox,
                               Major, 61st Regiment.

Seville, 9th September, 1808.

(Enclosure.)

Reply of the *Junta* of Seville to Major Cox's Letter of the
9th September, 1808.

Contesta la Junta Suprema a la de V.S. de ayer 9, y no dexa de admirar su contenido.

Sabe muy bien per su General en Xefe la reunsion de las tropas Franceses en la Rioja, la fortificacion del Puento de Logrono, y los fines à que pueda dirigirse, y entre ellos baxa hacia Zaragoza y atacarla nueva mente.

El General en Xefe le ha escrito tambien la Junta de Generales celebrada en Madrid, y lo que se deter minó en ella.

Acaso podion faltarle algunos fundos para ponerse en marcha, porque era de creer, que la Mancha, y las demas Provincias, en cuya defensa se sacrifican muestras

tropas, las mantuviesen, y proveyesen à todos sus necesidades, à lo menos durante sa residencia en ellas, y las Andalusias habian hecho mas que ninguna otra Provincia de España, formando su Exercito, organisandole, preparendole, y dandole abundantemente quanto necesita esta gran maquiena, y haciendo gastos muy superiores à sus fuerzas y a su obligacion, lo que erigia tambien el agra-decimiente à lo que ha trabajado Andalusia, y las gloriosas, y unicas, hasta ahora, Victorias, que ha conseguido. El Señor Brigadier General Doyle, que no puede ignorar ningunas de estas Cosas hubiera manifestado su amor à España, persuadiendo à Madrid, al Consijo Real, y à las Provincias invadidas que aprontasen estos fondos, que ciertamente les tiraba de justicia.

Ademas que estos mismos gastos casi immensos à que ha tenido que atender Andalucia per si misma, y sola podien hacer que sin culpa, ni omision suya, se hubiesen detenido algun tanto los Socorros a su exercito que está en Castilla, y ciertamente no lo ha olvidado; son increibles las diligencias que hasta a hora ha hecho, para que nada le falta; ha prevenido à su General en Xefe, que si estrechará la necessidad, tome letras contra esta Junta Suprema, baxo la seguridad deque sezan pagadas punctualmente, tiene alli un vocal suyo en persona encargado ° di este destino, entre otros; ha enviado ya al General en Xefe algunos Millones, y advertidole continuera estas Remezas; en suma nada se ha emitido, ni si emitira para defensa de España en general, y sola Andalucia ha animado mas à las demas provincias ofrecidoles y dadoles Mayores auxilios que ninguna otra de la nacion, porque sabe esta Junta Suprema que fué creado para este fin, y que desempeñandolo, no hace mas que llenarlo.

No nos parece decoroso entrar à examinar por menor los Socorros que hemos debido à la generosidad Britanica, y que somos los primeros en publicar, alabar y a los quales hemos correspondido con una franqueza y buen fé que no son comunes, y que S. M. B. y sus ministros han sido los que mas lo han celebrado.

Tampoco conviene discursir sobre si estos Socorros han sido destinados para Andalusia solamente, y para provéer à los gastos considerables que ha hecho, sin recibir hasta ahora dinero de otra Provincia alguna y para pagar los deudos grandisimos que ha contrado, y a cuya satisfaccion es esta Junta responsable. Los Socorros han sido espresamente embiados à la Junta Suprema de Sevilla, como los enviados par la nacion Inglesa à Asturias y a Galicia, han sido para estas Provincias, que seguramente no podran mostrar ni tantos gastos hechos, como la Andalucia ha executado, ni haberlos repartido y auxiliado con ellas à otras Provincias con la abundancia y prontitud, que lo ha hecho esta Junta Suprema, olvidando alguna vez quizà aun sus propios interes es y defensa, y esto es una cosa demasiado publica y muy conocida de V. S. y de toda la nacion Inglesa, para que nos detengemos en ella.

El disenteres de esta Junta Suprema, y de todos sus vocales, el ardor con que se ha aplicado, y sostenido la causa comun de toda España, y las pruebas notorias que ha dado de estos dos hechos, no pueden, ni ocultarse à la penetracion de V. S. que tanto tiempo hace, los ver tan de cerca, ni a la nacion Britanica, que nos observa, y a quien V. S. habrá informado de ello, ni megarse aun par la misma embidia, aunque esta suela carece de Oyos.

Despeus de todo aunque nuestre General en Xefe nos escribe con la misma fecha 5 de Setiembre, aun que lo hace V. S. el Brigadier Doyle, y nada nos dice ni dedineros entregados per este, ni de letras que hayan librado, esta Junta Suprema sabia corresponder con honor à qualesquiera aviso del primero, ó aun sin el a qualesquiers letras que se nos presenten firmadas de sa nombre, tan alta es la confienza que tiene esta Junta Suprema de su General en Xefe y de «la nacion Britanica.

Esperemos que V. S. nos hará toda la justicia, que creemos no haber desmericido, y que estara persuadido, que para cumplir las obligaciones, que hemos contraido, no necessitamos mas que se nos manifiestan sencillamente.

Depues de escrita esta, se han recibido despachos de Inglaterra, y se contestará con la mayor brevedad, à nuestros deputados para que lo hayen al Sor Ministro Canning.

Dios gue à V. S. m^s a^s Real Alcazar de Sevilla, à 10 de Setiembre, 1808.

Fran^e de Saavedra.

To His Excellency Lieutenant-General Sir, Hew Dalrymple.

Seville,
September 14, 1808.

Sir,

By the last post I had the honour of sending Your Excellency the copy of a paper which I presented to the *Junta* on the 9th instant, in consequence of a representation which I received from Brigadier-General Doyle; I also sent the answer of the *Junta*, together with copies of Brigadier-General Doyle's letter, and of one which I received from Captain Whittingham upon the same subject. The following day, I had the honour to write to Your Excellency by the *Pluto*, and sent a duplicate of my despatch of the preceding day, and a copy of a letter which I thought it proper to write, at the same time, to Lord Castlereagh.

I have now the honour of sending Your Excellency the copy of a second letter, which I wrote to the *Junta* on the 11th instant, after I had closed my despatch to Your Excellency; but to this I have not received any reply. I understand that those letters have caused some sensation in the *Junta*; and I am in great hopes they have produced a good effect. Orders were given the evening I presented the first, to send off silver bars to the amount of 250,000 dollars, to Madrid, to be coined; but, having heard that the Mint of that capital has been destroyed, the *Junta* countermanded that order, and have sent 200,000 in money; they have also agreed to pay the money which General Doyle has drawn for, whenever his bills on Mr. Duff become due. Something was very necessary to be done, in order to bring them to reason; they are puffed up by vanity and folly, and their late proceedings have disgusted all classes of people, both in and out of Seville.

The Cabildo remonstrated strongly against their nomination to the vacant Canonries, which firmness they qualified with the name of rebellion, and threatened to use force in case of resistance. The Cabildo answered, that their only arms were reason and justice; and that if the *Junta* thought proper to make use of others, that they certainly were unprepared to oppose them. It is said, the Archbishop of Toledo has written to thank them for their conduct, and to protest against the appointments made by the *Junta*.

Those appointments have also created great dissatisfaction amongst the people: the vacancies have been left open for two or three years, in order that the rents might augment the public funds; and they say, with great reason, that, independent of the incompetency of the *Junta* to fill them up, in the present critical situation of affairs, when the necessity of money is so great, and they are straining every nerve to supply the deficiency, the revenues of those places would have been much better applied in support of the public cause than in augmenting the income of private individuals.

Since those appointments have taken place, and salaries have been annexed to the useless employments of some members of the *Junta*, and their secretaries, many people have withdrawn their monthly contributions, which they were before accustomed to pay.

A meeting of several of the deputies from the provincial *Juntas*, met a few days ago at Ocaña, and I understand it was determined that they should transfer their meeting to Madrid, as the properest place for the Central *Junta*. It is also said that they have resolved not to admit Count Tylli, as being an improper person, on account of his general bad character, and the particular stigma of being under sentence of a court of law, for being concerned in a public robbery! The folly of electing such a man to represent a great province is quite unaccountable!

The Council of Castile have published a most excellent justification of their conduct; but I still think that some of its members should be hanged. A copy of their letter to Your Excellency, together with many other papers and documents, is annexed to it, and it concludes by a sensible and well-written letter, addressed to the several provincial *Juntas*, which contains some observations, which appear decidedly aimed at the illiberal censure bestowed on them by this.

I could now, with great deference, submit to Your Excellency an humble opinion, that my further residence here, in an official capacity, can be of very little or no use;—the Central *Junta*, if not already assembled, must now very shortly be formed; in them all the power and authority of the nation will naturally reside, and from them all orders and regulations, of course, will emanate; if, therefore, my poor abilities can be of service anywhere, I should think that my residence near the seat of government, as a channel of communication between Your Excellency and them, might probably be the best situation; I am, however, far from thinking that I am a proper person for it, and I do not, by any means, wish to ask for an appointment to which I feel my abilities are inadequate.

I confess, however, that I am extremely anxious to see Madrid, and to have an opportunity of witnessing the interesting scenes that are passing, and I should be happy to make myself as useful as I could, even though I were not placed in an official capacity. Might I, therefore, presume to beg Your Excellency's permission to go there in any way, or in any situation you may think proper? if with an official appointment, Your Excellency may depend, at least, upon my zeal and attention, and, at all events, upon the most sincere gratitude for your kindness.

I have the honour to be, &c. &c.

William Cox,
Major, 61st Regiment.

(Enclosure.)
Seville,

11th September, 1808.
Sir,

I have received the answer of the *Junta* to the official paper, which I had the honour to present to them on the 9th inst.

It is not my wish, nor my object, to enter into minute discussions. I give the Supreme *Junta* every credit which is due for their great exertions in the common cause of their country. I have seen them with the highest admiration, and spoken of them with the greatest applause. I have seen a band of patriotic men unite for the purpose of repelling a perfidious enemy, of asserting the independence of their country, of restoring their unfortunate sovereign to his throne, and re-establishing the national form of government. I should like to see them pursue the same purpose steadily, and never look to anything beyond its accomplishment.

I make no doubt but the provinces which are still infested by the enemy, have contributed according to their means to the support of the war; but, even if they had been backward in this respect, Brigadier-General Doyle, whose love to the Spanish Nation can certainly not be doubted, had no power or authority which could oblige them, nor any influence which could persuade them to come forward, though reason and justice should require it.

He knew where funds were deposited by the government under which he was employed; he knew the intention of His Majesty's Ministers with respect to those funds; he knew that they were withheld, and that the general cause was suffering by it; and he knew *positively* that General Castaños had received orders, from the *Junta* of Seville, not to advance into Old Castile, and that they had refused to supply him with the means of disobeying those orders. Under these circumstances he felt the necessity of writing the strong letter to me, upon which I felt it my duty to make the representation, which I had the honour to address to the Supreme *Junta* on the 9th instant. I sincerely hope it may have the desired effect. My only object is to serve the Spanish Nation; and, in contributing to its welfare, I gratify my private inclination, at the same time that I fulfil my public duty. I must, however, speak plainly.

Whilst the enemy of Spain is in sight, it is no time to stand disputing whether this province or that province should maintain the army, upon which the safety of the whole depends. The cause of Navarre is the cause of Andalusia, and the cause of Catalonia is the cause of Galicia.

All their forces, all their means, all their efforts, should be directed to one grand object—the expulsion of the enemy, and the defence of their religion, their country, and their king, "*Que es la España toda.*" The whole of Spain is but one family; and when danger approaches its doors, it is not prudent to stand upon ceremony about which of its members shall get up to bar the entrance.

I still see the necessity of money being remitted immediately from hence to Madrid, for the use of the army; I am informed that there is little or no specie in that capital, and, therefore, think it probable that General Castaños would find great difficulty in negotiating bills to any considerable amount.

I have written fully today to His Majesty's Ministers upon all that has been done in this business, and I have sent them copies of the paper which I had the honour to present to the *Junta*, and the answer that has been returned.

I shall be truly happy to send one, which may be considered more satisfactory, and the Supreme *Junta* may rest assured that their compliance with the reasonable request which has been made to them will contribute much to induce Great Britain to send those further aids to Spain which I know she is yet inclined to afford.

I beg Your Excellency will have the goodness to lay this letter before the Supreme Board.

I have the honour to be, &c. &c.
(Signed)   William Cox.

(No. 9.)
To Sir Hew Dalrymple.

Cadiz,
10th June, 1808.

Sir,

I take the opportunity of a Spanish courier going to San Roque to give you an account of our operations hitherto.

On the 8th of June, a little before eleven, a. m. we arrived at Xeres. General Castaños, who had been previously appointed Captain-General of the Army of Andalusia, here received a despatch, calling him immediately to Seville. An affair had taken place, at Alcolea, near Cordova, in which the Spaniards had been worsted. Echavarri, a good partisan-leader, but no general, had occupied a position near Alcolea, his right defending the passage of the bridge, and his left extending into the plain.

General Dupont's division consisted of 17,000 men. Echavarri had with him 1,000 regular and about 10,000 new-raised men. The French advanced guard attacked the bridge, (which was defended with great gallantry,) whilst the main body crossed the Guadalquivir, at a pass, a short distance higher up, and took possession of the high ground upon the left of the Spanish Army, which Echavarri had neglected to occupy. The new-raised levies immediately gave way; but the few regulars conducted their retreat well, and lost only one piece of cannon, whose carriage broke down.

The French took possession of Cordova.

9th June. We arrived at Seville at five a.m. General Castaños, soon after, waited upon the President Saavedra. Upon his return, he expressed his wish that I should immediately go to Cadiz, and endeavour to prevail upon General Spencer to land, and advance, with his force, as far as Xeres, where General Castaños promised to meet him, and settle the plan of operations. At ten o'clock, General Castaños set off post for Carmona, where his headquarters are established, the advanced posts extending as far as Ecija. At 11, I went to the *Junta Suprema*, and received their despatches for the Marshal de Campo Don Eusebio Herrera, at Cadiz. This morning, about six o'clock, I landed here. I immediately delivered my despatches, *and found that things were far different to what I had been used to witness between you, Sir, and General Castanos.*

I, soon after, saw Sir George Smith, who desired me to wait upon General Spencer. Five hours' pulling against wind and tide brought me, at last, to the *Atlas*, on board which General Spencer was embarked. I delivered the message from Castaños, and told him of the extreme hurry in which the general had left Seville.

I, also, mentioned the despatch I had brought for Herrera. General Spencer said that he should wish to be acquainted with the contents of that despatch, and with the opinions of the Spanish generals to whom it was directed. That he could give no answer to anything I had to say, as it did not come in an official shape; and that, no doubt, General Castaños had not communicated to me his intended plan of operations. I returned to Cadiz, and got Don Tomas Morla and Don E. Herrera to write to General Spencer an account of the intelligence I had brought.

I am now waiting the answer, and shall return immediately to Castaños. General Castaños's Force does not, I am sorry to say, exceed, at the present moment, in regular troops, 5,000 men. He expects daily a reinforcement of 7,000 regulars, which he had sent on before he left Algeciras. He has under his command from 50,000 to 60,000 countrymen of the new-raised levies. I wish I could add that I entertain reasonable hopes of our success; but I really do not: and as, unfortunately, the people here have taken it into their heads that we could assist them if we would, we shall finish by being, at least, as much hated as the French.

The very moment General Spencer's answer arrives I shall set off for Carmona, and, I trust, I shall no more be forced to quit the honourable post you were pleased to assign to me.

I have the honour to be, &c. &c.

(Signed)   S. Whittingham.

To Sir Hew Dalrymple.

Headquarters, Utera,
17th June, 1808.

Sir,

I have the honour to inform you that I arrived at this place on the evening of the 15th; and it is General Castaños's particular order that I should express to you, Sir, how very grateful he feels for the kind and liberal manner in which you were pleased to meet his wishes at a moment which appeared so very critical!

During my absence, affairs have taken a very favourable turn.

General Castaños has got together, at this place, 8,000 regulars; and, having selected from the mass of peasantry the finest young men, he has regimented about 12,000 of them, and given them officers from the line. These new-raised corps are already tolerably dextrous in loading and firing. In Carmona we have between 3,000 and 4,000 regulars, and a strong body of peasants.

The regiment of the line, called *Voluntarios* of Arragon, supported by a considerable body of peasants, has taken possession of the passes of Sierra Morena, and particularly of Puerto del Rey. They are breaking up the roads, &c. &c. the more completely to cut off all communication between Madrid and Dupont's army.

Yesterday evening, General Castaños pushed on a detachment of 1,000 men, commanded by a brigadier, to Fuentos. The brigadier has under his command a body of light troops, who will patrol as far as Ecija.

On the right of this body is Colonel Valderaños, who has under his command so large a force of the new raised levies from the kingdom of Jaen that he solicited leave to attack the French in Cordova.

A considerable body of peasantry, commanded by officers of the line, has been sent to take possession of the passes of Estremadura, in case Dupont should attempt to retreat upon the Army of Portugal.

In a few days the whole of these dispositions will be consolidated, and we shall attack the French under very favourable circumstances. Should Fortune favour us, the victory must be complete, and the French Army annihilated. Should we be worsted, Dupont will hardly dare to follow up his advantage, surrounded, as he now is, on all sides, and his communication with Madrid cut off.

The last intercepted letter from Dupont to Murat is full of alarm.

It is reported, and some credit is given to the report, that General Cuesta, at the head of the Castilians, has intimated to Murat that he might retire from Madrid unmolested, provided he began his march towards Bayonne without delay; and threatened him with an immediate attack, in case his offer should not be accepted. That Murat had began to fortify the position of the Retiro.

That General Filangieri was at the head of an army of 16,000 regulars in Galicia; and that nothing could prevent his junction with General Cuesta, whose headquarters are at Valladolid.

Major Cox passed through this place on his way to Seville, and saw General Castaños.

I shall take the earliest opportunity of going to Seville, to see and communicate with the major.

I have the honour to be, &c. &c.

(Signed) S. Whittingham,
13th Light Dragoons.

I mentioned to General Castaños your idea of bringing the Spanish squadron at Mahon, together with the garrisons of Minorca and Majorca, to Cadiz.

The advantage of this reinforcement to the army, (at least 8,000 regulars,) and of the concentration of their naval force, was too evident not to strike General Castaños, and he appeared extremely pleased at your having suggested the idea. Of course, the garrisons might be replaced from the new-raised levies.

To Sir Hew Dalrymple.

Headquarters, Andujar,
25th July, 1808.

Sir,

I had the honour of writing to you on the 21st of this month. At four o'clock a. m. 23rd July, the troops of the third and fourth divisions were drawn up in line on each side of the high road, about two miles from the French camp, General Castaños and his suite, on the right, towards Baylen.

At seven o'clock, the head of the French column began to enter the street formed by the Spanish troops. The French Troops were in high order, and certainly amongst the finest I ever saw: 5,500 men, of which number 1,200 cavalry, followed by twenty pieces of cannon, filed off before the Spanish Army, and piled their arms at 800 *toises* distance.

It appears that the force of Dupont amounted, at the Battle of Baylen, to upwards of 9,000 men, *viz.*

5,500 prisoners of war.
2,600 killed and wounded in the action.
1,100 deserted after the action.
_____

9,200 total of the force of General Dupont's division.

General Reding had a nominal force of 15,000 men; but, of this number, the battalion of peasants (3,000 men) fled at the beginning of the action, and were seen no more; of the 12,000 men remaining, at least 5,000 were composed of the new-raised levies, inter mixed with the regular troops.

General Dupont made several partial and four general attacks upon the Spanish lines, and was constantly repulsed with great loss. The Spanish artillery performed wonders. In less than two hours they dismounted fourteen pieces of the enemy's cannon; and their well-timed discharge of grape upon the French line, as it advanced, produced the finest effect.

If we include the 400 men left sick at Cordova, and the great loss the French suffered at Mengibar and Villanueva, it is evident the division of General Dupont was at first composed of 12,000 men.

On the 24th July, at Baylen, at nine o'clock a.m. the division of General Wedel, consisting of 9,100 men, (of which 1,500 cavalry,) piled arms, and filed off towards Mengibar.

The cavalry of this division is in much better condition than that of Dupont. The infantry did not appear to me equally good. It is now forty days since General Castaños arrived at Carmona, where his whole army consisted of 3,000 regulars and about 15,000 runaway peasantry, who had disgraced themselves at the affair of the Bridge of Alcolea.

In this very short space of time his Excellency has organised a force, whose valour and discipline, directed by the talents of their general, have enabled them to beat 21,000 French, and reduce them to the ignominious necessity of laying down their arms. General Castaños returned to this place last night.

I have the honour to be, &c. &c.

(Signed)   S. Whittingham,
                                                      13th Light Dragoons.

P.S. You will have observed that the real numbers of the French have far exceeded what I supposed in my last.—S. W.

(No. 10.)

To Lieutenant-General Sir Hew Dalrymple.

Ocean, off Cadiz,
14th June, 1808.

My Dear Sir,

I received the favour of your letters of the 11th and 12th, the former acquainting me with the request made by General Castaños, the other enclosing the copy of a letter to General Spencer.

When your letter arrived, the troops were on the point of moving to the westward, towards Ayamonte, on the requisition which the Spanish governor had made to General Spencer, a day or two before, to meet, and prevent the approach to Seville of a detachment of the French Army, which was said to be marching by the coast from Portugal.

I stopped the sailing of the transport, until the general informed me of his resolution to proceed as originally intended; and the reasons which he assigned for not changing his destination, you will see in the letter which I enclose to you: and Colonel Bathurst, who brought it, entered more fully into the probable consequences of taking a position at Xeres; the principal of which was, that, on any disaster of the Spanish Army, an occurrence which made it necessary it should be reinforced, they would doubtless be called upon; completely engaging his corps in field service, for which it was not perfectly provided; identifying our army with theirs, in whatever might happen to it; and deviating from the line which His Majesty's Ministers, in their instructions, had provided.

I have heard that a degree of coolness, and perhaps a little jealousy, had shown itself, whenever there was any mention or allusion to our putting a garrison into Cadiz; and I believe the appearance of the troops before the port, and the application which had been made for pilots to carry the ships into harbour, to have been the sole cause of it; and I very much suspect that the application to General Spencer to proceed with his corps towards Ayamonte, was more for the purpose of removing them from before Cadiz, than any apprehension they had from an enemy in that quarter; for, yesterday, two gentlemen, (a member of the Supreme Council and a rear-admiral,) who were deputed to come to me, informed me that the accounts they had from that quarter were vague—they came from a suspicious quarter—and that they themselves did not believe the French were advancing, as had been stated.

If that is the case, that they show doubts and apprehensions from

140

our army, I would submit to you, Sir, in the event of their not finding anything to engage their service where they are gone to, whether they had not better be at Gibraltar, until it is determined to what point they should proceed; for, hovering upon the coast, they will consume their water and provisions, and, perhaps, when wanted to proceed, have to return to port to complete.

The Spaniards having completed their batteries against the French ships, and ready to open upon them, they surrendered this morning, and are now under Spanish colours; there has been much care taken to do them no injury, which the Spaniards say was to preserve them fit to go to America, should that be necessary.

Your despatches, which I brought out, went to England yesterday by the cutter *Alphea*; and I hope today the deputies to the Court of London will go in the *Alceste*. The admiral being one of them, it was not convenient that he should go before the surrender of the French ships.

I have the honour to be,
 Dear Sir,
   With the highest esteem and regard,
    Your faithful and most obedient servant,
 (Signed)   Collingwood.
Everything the Spaniards propose is "*por Mañana;*" but I have just been informed the plenipotentiaries will not be ready for two days.

(Enclosure.)

H. M. S. Atlas,
12th June, 1808.

My Lord,

I am just honoured with your lordship's letter, in answer to which I beg to submit to you the impropriety of my corps taking up a position in the interior, subjecting myself to be called upon to join the Spanish Army, perhaps at Seville, unequipped as my corps is to take the field, and which I conceive so contrary to the wishes of His Majesty's Ministers.

I am, therefore, still anxious to proceed off Ayamonte as soon as possible.

  I have the honour to be, &c.
   (Signed)   B. Spencer,
              Major-General,

The Right Hon. Lord Collingwood.

Ocean,
20th June, 1808.

My Dear Sir,

The moment I received your letter of the 17th, I despatched a ship with yours to General Spencer, and gave directions to Captain Boyles, that whenever the general determined to go, (which I understood from Captain Boyles's letter he had resolved,) to send a sufficient convoy to the Tagus.

To the major-general, who had done me the honour to ask my opinion, I observed, on one hand, that where the troops then were, they were doing nothing, nor was there any immediate prospect of their having anything to do; they were expending their provisions and water, without means of replenishing them; that the Spaniards had shown much jealousy when they were near Cadiz, and did not seem at all urgent for their landing anywhere: that, on the other hand, the French force in Portugal was reduced to a small number; that amongst the several forts they were much divided; in every point to the southward the French forces were in embarrassing and critical situations; that the population of the country was, without exception, adverse to them; and that the object to be obtained there, by opening the river to the squadron, was of the first magnitude; leaving him with those observations to make his own decision.

I informed him, that the moment I knew that he was gone there, I should send a frigate to the north-west of Cape Roxent, to cruise for the reinforcements expected from England, and inform the commanding officer where he was. Major-General Spencer, in his letter of the 18th, informs me of his intention; if he should not go to Lisbon, which he had not yet determined upon, nor received Your Excellency's letter, he should, in a few days, return to Cadiz.

I am sorry he had so resolved, because I am sure the Spaniards felt uncomfortable at the presence of the army here, and it will embarrass them; they have resolved they shall not come into the town, and every appearance of urging it distresses them. I would rather recommend that (if they are not gone to the Tagus) they should return to Gibraltar, and, completing their water and provisions, be held ready to go to that point where it is intended they should act.

I mentioned to General Spencer that I concluded he maintained a correspondence with General Castaños on the subject of his movements.

At Minorca and Majorca they describe themselves to be strong, and having nothing to apprehend; however, they made the proposal for entering into a convention with us for their defence; and, in the course of it, demanded money, arms, and the protection of the fleet; when, in return for these, it was required that their fleet should be given to us, to be held for their king Ferdinand, or that a part of them should join our squadron against the enemy; or, lastly, that they should be laid up, part at Minorca, part at Malta, to prevent their passing over to the enemy.

They rejected all these proposals; so that whatever we did for them, was to be solely for the honour of having their friendship. A paper that was sent, by the governor, to Admiral Thornbrough, contained an account of what had lately happened at Barcelona. The proclamation of the Spanish governor, recommending good order, and submission to the French, had given great disgust to the Spaniards, who quitted the town, and assembled at Mataro, and the neighbouring towns, and considerable numbers of *cuirassiers* and other troops, being reinforced by others from Barcelona, amounting in all to about six thousand; the people, on having notice of this assemblage of troops, rang the bell, called *Sameten*, and they were soon joined by a multitude, to the amount of 16,000 armed men.

On the night of the 5th, they passed a bridge, and then cut it down, and, charging the French, fought all night. On the 6th and 7th, there was fighting, but at intervals. On the 8th, and until the morning of the 9th, there was continued battle, which was not over when the vessel sailed which brought the account to Minorca; but, in the port, he saw the families of the French officers embarking in small vessels to go to France. This all happened without the town, to which many of the wounded were brought. The exterior French Army was reinforced from Monjuick, the garrison, and citadel, so that not more than two thousand were left in those fortresses.

It is very extraordinary that the Spaniards will not send any despatches to their colonies—there is not a vessel of any kind gone from them; but I have sent to Barbadoes and to Jamaica, by the *Flying Fish* Schooner, and by her, sent many letters which the merchants wrote to their correspondents at the Havannah and La Vera Cruz, with some of the edicts of the government. By that schooner I received instructions from Lord Castlereagh to spare no exertion or expense in supporting the Spaniards: but there can never be order until there is one generally acknowledged Council of Government, formed by deputies from all the several Provincial Councils with whom Foreign States may treat. The want of this, I believe to be the reason why there is yet no instructions given to the colonies in the West Indies;—for Seville represents but a small part of Spain.

I am ever, my dear general,
Your faithful and most humble servant,

Collingwood.

His Excellency Sir Hew Dalrymple.

Ocean,
23rd June, 1808.

My Dear Sir,

I have been exceedingly hurried to get my letters ready for the fleet off Toulon and Malta. Yesterday the *Windsor Castle* arrived from Ayamonte, and by her I learnt the convoy with the troops had sailed. I think there is the chance of their doing some good; if the French are found to be weak, and few, as represented by Sir Charles Cotton—and the Portuguese as ready to make head against them as they say they are, the troops with General Spencer may compel them to confine themselves to the Citadel; and if the river is opened by the occupation of St Julian's, it is impossible to say how advantageous the result may be.

Should it be otherwise, and they are found in too great force, for I do not think that reports received in the way Sir Charles Cotton got his information, should have much confidence in the truth of them—the appearance of the army there will embarrass the French, and make them call in the troops they have at Elvas, or Badajos, leaving that part of the country open to the operations of the Spaniards. This is the only thing that presented for them to do, except lying at Ayamonte, where there was nothing for them, and I believe their return to this anchorage would have caused a renewal of that jealousy with which the Spaniards viewed them when they were here before. If they do not succeed at Lisbon, it will be necessary to return to Gibraltar to replenish their provisions and water, as they have not been in any place where they could be supplied.

The governor last night sent me a paper, containing an account of the battle they had fought at Barcelona, in which it is stated that the French threw down their arms and surrendered; but no quarter was given them, they were put to the sword; and the Spaniards advanced within two leagues of Barcelona, where they formed a line of 20,000 men, to cut off the communication of Barcelona with the country. The whole province of Catalonia was in insurrection.

The Supreme Council have yet despatched no person nor vessel to the West Indies, nor do they seem to have any anxiety on that subject. I cannot account for what seems so great an omission, except that themselves have not sufficient light into their affairs to enable them. to give any instructions, or that this Council of Seville do not consider themselves to have authority to give them.

The governor has sent a request that they may be supplied from England with a large quantity of clothing for their army, and linen for shirts, which I will transmit to England, when I have a ship for the purpose. I hear nothing of the movements of their army, nor that of the French; but if they do not something, like Barcelona, they will let their enemy increase in strength. The business there seems to have been conducted with science: the roads were filled with timber-trees and abatis, and the fields and narrower ways deeply trenched, so that the cavalry could not act; a squadron of frigates have made their escape from Toulon, and, I suspect, either gone to Naples, where the queen has sent a little expedition against Procita; or more East, to the Adriatic, to join the Russians at Trieste, and bring them down to Toulon.

I have the honour to be, &c. &c.

Collingwood.

His Excellency Lieutenant-General Sir Hew Dalrymple.

Ocean, off Cadiz,
25th June, 1808.

My Dear Sir,

When I wrote to General Spencer, on receiving the information from Sir Charles Cotton, I do not recollect I gave any opinion upon the subject, but told him I had forwarded Sir Charles Cotton's letter to you, and that I concluded he maintained a correspondence with General Castaños on the subject of his movements. A letter I received from Captain Boyles informed me, that the general had asked for a convoy to go to Lisbon, to which I made no reply until your letter came to me, which seemed to approve of the measure; I was glad of it, and gave orders for the convoy whenever General Spencer wished it.

At Ayamonte they had nothing to do; there were in that quarter a very few French, whom the Portuguese (encouraged by the appearance of our troops) were very eager to reduce. They were eating the provisions and drinking the water where it could not be replenished; and their return to Cadiz I thought of as you do; for I understand, while they continued here, they caused extreme jealousy, and doubt of our good intentions. I have since heard, from Mr. Gordon, of Xeres, that they were continually increasing their force in the garrison, and had at last 10,000 men in it, which, on the departure of the troops, were all marched off, and there only remains now five battalions of militia, amounting to about 2,500 men.

I am sending an officer to Barbary, to endeavour to get the emperor's permission to purchase horses; whether that can be accomplished, I do not know. I have understood there always was a great objection to the exporting horses from thence. I remember a Moor telling me that the emperor gave horses as presents, but that it was contrary to their religion to sell them.

I have just received a letter from Sir Charles Cotton on the subject of the troops: he seems to be sanguine in his expectations; I am not; but think that in every case they will do good: and if the Portuguese are as ripe for revolt as they say they are, it is impossible to foresee how much good may result from the unexpected appearance of a British force, whose actual strength is unknown, and, as is common in such cases, may be much exaggerated. There is a letter for you, also, which I must beg your pardon for having torn, and was very near opening, before I looked, as I ought to have done, at the direction.

There is nothing more disagreeable to me, and that I can worse direct, than purchases; perhaps it is known at Gibraltar whether the Moors will sell their horses, and what is the common price of ordinary ones. If you can, my dear Sir, give me any information that will direct me, I will be very thankful to you.

The *Orestes*, in coming out with despatches, captured a vessel from St. Sebastian, bound to the Caraccas with despatches from Murat to that governor, they were sent to England; but the crew of her, and a number of letters were brought here, which I have sent to the Spaniards for examination; they have now got passports for the Rio Plata, and La Vera Cruz, and their first despatches are about to sail.

I believe the French, in all the southern provinces, will very soon be annihilated. The state of Barcelona was most doubtful, but they are supposed to have been reduced to great extremity there, by the battle with the peasantry. How they are in the north, I believe, is little known; and I suspect, that in Biscay the armament is not very forward.

If the Spaniards keep close to the French Army, always annoying, never fighting them in any numbers, they must surrender here.

I am, &c. &c.

Collingwood.

To His Excellency Sir Hew Dalrymple.

Ocean,
7th July, 1808.

My Dear Sir,

I am much obliged to you for your letters of the 1st and 4th. You will have received, from Major Cox, the account how the proposal to garrison Ceuta was received; and I am quite convinced, that every proposal, which can be construed, as proceeding from interested motives, will increase their doubts and jealousy, of which they appear at present to have a good share. Besides, there is another consideration, which will prevent the *Junta* from acceding to such proposals, which is the danger of having their authority questioned.

I hear that when it was proposed to send the French prisoners to Ceuta, the governor of that fortress objected, stating that the resentment against them was such, that he could not be answerable for their lives; in short, he did not choose to have them there.

Before I received Morla's answer to the letter I had written to him on the subject of the ships, I sent Captain Legge to him, to represent the danger of placing the ships where they were going to; that, on any reverse of fortune with the army, which would enable the French to come here, they would fall into their hands. Captain Legge was also to mention to him the subject of my letter, which stated the probability of the French sending a squadron to the West Indies, to support those plans, which their emissaries had doubtless formed there; and the necessity of their having a force to counteract them, or, at least, to co-operate with the English, in defending their provinces.

On the last subject, he said they had no doubts; they were quite confident (I wish it may be well founded) in the integrity of the colonies. On the former, that the ships were moved to a place of more security, from winds and weather; for, as all their own resources, as well as what England could supply them with, would be required to maintain their army, it was impossible to apply any of their funds to their navy.

Captain Legge (as I had directed him) observed that, as their means were confined, probably the English Government would maintain the captured ships for Fernando VII. and hold them for his service; but Morla evaded the subject, not thinking it necessary to give a reply to it, but assured Captain Legge, that I might have no anxiety about the ships, for both French and Spanish, and Arsenal, should be burnt, whenever there was a chance of the enemy penetrating to this quarter.

Last night I received a letter from him, with a copy or letters intercepted, from Junot, at Lisbon, to Bonaparte and Murat; he describes himself as entirely cut off from all communication either with France, Murat, or Dupont;—of 12,000 men, that part of them are with him at Lisbon, and the rest in the defences near him. He describes the insurrections at Oporto, and the general disaffection of the people. He is in danger of being attacked by the English, and when he is, he will do, what his (Bonaparte's) generals ought to do. It is odd, that, in the state of the country he describes, those letters should not be written in cypher.

I am much obliged for what you tell me of Mr. Baker, and of the possibility of getting horses; but I have great doubts, notwithstanding the abundance, that we shall get any. The emperor was gone with his army. I have not heard from him, but Slowey says, he will use his influence for granting them, in his own way; that the emperor will inform me, on what terms we may have both horses, mules, and whatever else Barbary produces; that neither England nor Spain shall pay for them; that it will not be necessary to send any person to select, or to purchase them, they will do that themselves. Now, all this can only have Ceuta in view; give him Ceuta, and we shall have anything; without it, nothing. So that business, I fear, will end. There is no power in Spain to which a Foreign State can address itself.

I received a letter yesterday, from General Castaños, enclosing the copy of a letter he had written to General Spencer. I enclose a translation of it. In the evening, and before General Spencer could have received Castaños's letter, I had a note from General Nightingale, to say, General Spencer, with a part of the troops, were about to proceed to Xeres. Is not it very extraordinary, that Castaños has not known the state of the passes before, and now only imperfectly? The convoy, from England, is in sight, and now, changes may take place.

I am ever, my dear Sir, &c. &c. &c.

(Signed)   Collingwood.

Enclosure from The Honourable Captain Legge to Lord Collingwood.

Repulse, off Cadiz,
5th July, 1808.

My Lord,

In compliance with your lordship's directions, which I received yesterday evening, I waited upon General Morla this morning. He informs me, he had written to your lordship, by the lieutenant of the

Confounder, in answer to the questions I was directed to put to him. He does not seem apprehensive that the French are likely to send a squadron to their colonies, in South America; and, when I stated to him the necessity of keeping up a Spanish Force, in case they should, to co-operate with a British Force, and by way of ensuring a friendly reception for that British force, in the Spanish Colonies, he stated a total want of money to pay the sailors, and that he hoped the South Americans already knew the state of affairs between the two countries at home.

He informs me, however, that he has ordered the dismantling the ships to be put a stop to, till he hears from the *Junta* at Seville, in consequence of your lordship's letter to him.

When I mentioned that, in case of any want of stores, some of the ships might possibly be repaired in the English dockyards, for Ferdinand VII. he did not seem disposed to enter much upon the subject, but hinted that at present there was no treaty between the two countries, or even a signed armistice, which he seemed to regret, as the English privateers still distressed the Spanish trade.

He expressed himself strongly against any jealousy subsisting between the two countries, and that he hoped, as soon as a treaty was concluded, the war would be carried on with mutual good faith against the common enemy; that the war was not like any former war; that we were not fighting for a colony, or an island, but for the liberty of the two countries themselves.

He objects to mooring the ships below the Puntal, from their distance from the Arsenal, and from their not being safe there with strong easterly winds; and as to any danger of their falling into the enemy's hands where they now lay, he begs me to assure your Lord ship that should the enemy come down in force, while he commands at Cadiz, every ship should be burnt, with the Arsenal, sooner than that they should get into the possession of Napoleon.

General Morla expressed, in general, a strong desire to meet your lordship's wishes, as far as he himself was concerned, on every point. He mentioned an intention of fitting out the *St. Anna,* as soon as they had the means, but at present they had not "*un sous,*"—such was his expression.

There is a report today of the Spaniards having taken a convoy of ammunition and provisions, going to Dupont's army, with a reinforcement of 1300 men. I have enclosed the *Mercury's* report of Guard, who yesterday boarded a small vessel from Villa Nueva, who told the officer that accounts had arrived there of the surrender of Junot to the Portuguese.

General Morla had received your lordship's letter respecting the horses from Morocco. I have now stated, as fully as I am able, what passed between General Morla and myself; but I make no doubt, your lordship has received a more full and satisfactory answer in his reply of yesterday to you, and as he speaks French but indistinctly, it is not easy to understand him in conversation without an interpreter.

I remain, &c. &c.

(Signed)

A. K. Legge.

(Enclosure.)

Translation of the Copy of a Letter from General Castaños to Major-General Spencer.

Most Excellent Sir,

Since I have transmitted to Your Excellency the communication of my plans, almost in every manner conformable to those proposed by Your Excellency in your last letters from Ayamonte and Cadiz, of the 25th and 27th June, events have occurred, which oblige me at present to alter them, of which I hasten to give you notice.

The enemy, (although I have not heard it officially,) I am assured, have forced the posts of Puerto del Rey and Despeñaperros, in Sierra-Morena, not because they have beaten us, but because one of our best battalions of light troops, and which has been distinguished in Campaign, called the First Volunteers of Arragon, have abandoned that point. I do not know whether they are gone to Arragon, their country, or whether their chief has been gained over by the enemy:—an event which astonishes me, as it is the first of the kind amongst the Spanish troops.

The enemies reinforce; it is, therefore, necessary to attack them immediately; but, as the chances of war are various, it appears to me indispensable that Your Excellency should disembark at Port St. Mary, and remain at Xeres, where, in case of defeat, you will be a point of support in our retreat; and, favoured by this position, we may have it in our power to attempt new enterprises. If Your Excellency approves of this proposal, the competent orders are given at the port and at Xeres.

If, as I promise myself, we beat the enemy, Your Excellency may re-embark, and follow new projects in the Tagus, with this difference, that I do not approve of a disembarkation at Ayamonte, because the present circumstances of the Algarves are distinct from the times when we embraced this system;—at present there are no enemies in that quarter; you can, therefore, be dispensed with. We have some forces there, under the direction of Colonel Contreras, a skilful soldier, who will organise them in a short time. If Your Excellency disembarks at Ayamonte, it will be to call the attention of the French dedicated to Lisbon.

If I destroy Dupont, it will be the moment for Your Excellency to threaten Lisbon, indistinctly, right or left, as, in that case, if they attempt to abandon Portugal, to assist their army here, Your Excellency may then enter Portugal, be master of the country, and even harass them in their retreat. This is my opinion, which I believe is in combination with the actual state of the country, and which I should wish Your Excellency to adopt, if it merits your approbation, and I shall constantly transmit my informations.

I enclose to Your Excellency the signature of Don Joaquim Rodriquiz, Commissary of War, that you may know it, in case of your having occasion to write to him, requiring assistance.

I remain, with the highest consideration, &c. &c.

Headquarters, Cordova,

3rd July, 1808.

To His Excellency Lieutenant-General Sir Hew Dalrymple,
Commander in-Chief.

Ocean, off Cadiz,
26th July, 1808.

Sir,

I have received the honour of Your Excellency's letter of the 24th instant, enclosing a detail of the circumstances which led to the victory obtained by the Spanish forces, which is so glorious to the army that achieved it, and so highly beneficial to their country,—on which happy event I beg to congratulate Your Excellency.

The despatches you have sent to me for England, and Sir Arthur Wellesley, I will forward by the earliest conveyance. The handsome manner in which General Castaños acknowledges the merit and services of Captain Whittingham gives me very great pleasure.

I informed Your Excellency that I had received a letter from General Spencer, desiring that the transport, with artillery, might remain here until I heard from you; but, as from your former letter, I concluded you had made your determination respecting them, and as here they were reducing their water and provisions, I thought the

151

sooner they arrived at Gibraltar, the sooner any new disposition of them would be made, and they can now depart from thence in number what you propose, and completed in whatever they may want.

They left this on Sunday, for Gibraltar, and whenever such part of them as you propose should proceed to Lisbon come here, I will immediately forward them with a convoy. I return to Your Excellency the letter addressed to Lieutenant-Colonel Ramsay.

I have the honour to be, &c. &c.

(Signed)   Collingwood.

(No. 11.)

Letter from Right Honourable Lord Castlereagh to Lieutenant-General Sir Hew Dalrymple, Communicating the Appointment of Sir A. Wellesley.

Downing-Street,
6th July, 1808.

Sir,

Your despatches of the dates stated, (2 & 4 June), have been received, and laid before the king: and I am to convey to you His Majesty's approbation of the line of conduct which you have so judiciously pursued in your communications with General Castaños, and in sending Major-General Spencer's corps off Cadiz. His Majesty's Speech and Order in Council, which I have transmitted to you separately, will fully disclose the feelings of His Majesty towards the patriotic efforts of the Spanish Nation. It must be evident that, if this noble spirit which has burst forth, and which seems to be universal through the provinces of Spain, can be maintained for any considerable time, the most beneficial results may take place, not only to Spain itself, but to Europe and the world.

If, on the contrary, the effort shall turn out to be merely momentary, and shall languish or cease upon conflict or ill success, not only the servitude of Spain, but that of Europe, may be, for a long period, irrevocably fixed. I am, therefore, to desire you will neglect no means in your power for encouraging the spirit, and assisting the efforts of the Spanish Nation, and take every opportunity of expressing the disinterested wishes of Great Britain in their favour, as well as His Majesty's determination to afford them every means of assistance he can supply. I take this opportunity to inform you that Lieutenant-General Sir A. Wellesley has been ordered to sail from Cork, with a corps of near 10,000 men, and is appointed to rendezvous off the Tagus; where it is hoped, according to the advices received from Vice-Admiral Sir Charles Cotton, his expedition will be attended with immediate success. He has been instructed to send to Cadiz for the corps under Major-General Spencer, unless it shall be at the time employed in that quarter upon an object of greater consequence to the common cause. He will, of course, take care that his proceedings shall be communicated to you.

I have desired you, in my separate letter, to transmit the most recent state of events in Spain to Sir John Stewart, in Sicily, and Sir Alexander Ball, at Malta; and I trust you will not neglect any occasion of informing them, particularly the former, of the progress of events: and you will pursue the same line in respect to Lord Collingwood.

I thus write to you under the impression of the intelligence received from Major-General Spencer, dated off Cadiz, the 6th June; at which time, preparations were making for taking possession of the French squadron: and our commanders were waiting for a ratification, by the *Junta* of Seville, of the conditions proposed by them for their co-operation. The despatches of the admiral and general leave us little room to doubt that their propositions have been, in the main, acceded to, and that His Majesty's forces are acting in alliance with the *Junta* of Seville. The promptness with which the merchants of Gibraltar advanced a loan for the aid of the Spanish Army under General Castaños has afforded His Majesty much satisfaction.

I have the honour to be, &c. &c.

(Signed)   Castlereagh.

To Lieutenant General the Honourable Sir Arthur Wellesley.

Gibraltar,
16th July, 1808.

Sir,

Having received directions from Lord Castlereagh to forward to you all possible information respecting the state and progress of events, in the southern parts of Spain, I lose no time in communicating the substance of what I have had opportunities of learning upon those points, as also the observations I have made thereupon.

The latter end of May the insurrection was I believe general in every province and subdivision of the kingdom, not actually kept down by the presence of the French Armies, and the clergy in general; and the populace have displayed a degree of revolutionary and fanatical fury which I understand to exceed even what appeared during the

French Revolution; but, as the motives (loyalty and religion) were very different from those in France, there has been of course a difference in the results.

In almost every considerable place there is formed a *Junta Suprema de Gobierno*; that of Seville (with which we have hitherto communicated most) evidently betrays the wish to assume the character of the National Government, a pretension that will produce bad consequences, if not checked in time. I must add, that every *Junta* acts in the name of Ferdinand VII. towards whom the popular enthusiasm is at present principally directed. Although General Spencer proceeded to join Admiral Purvis, off Cadiz, by my authority, I think it necessary to state that I had no part in the negotiations that were carried on between that officer and Admiral Purvis on the one part, and Governor Morla and General Herrera on the other.

I am confident that it is decided at the *Junta* at Seville, by a very large majority of the members, that our troops are not to be admitted, as a garrison, into any place of strength. I am also informed, from good authority, that General Morla, the Governor of Cadiz, is the most strenuous supporter of this resolution: this fact I think it my duty to state, as General Spencer seems to be persuaded that this General Morla looks to his corps for the defence of Cadiz, should any reverse befall the Spanish Armies.

I have an officer of the Sicilian quartermaster-general's staff (Captain Whittingham) at present with General Castaños's army; him I shall direct to communicate with you in future, and I beg to recommend him to you as a man of great zeal and activity, and a perfect Spaniard. I have also an officer, Major Cox, of the 61st Regiment, at Seville, through whom Lord Collingwood and myself have communicated with the *Junta*: this officer I also beg leave to recommend to your attention, he has displayed considerable talents in the Mission upon which he has been employed.

I enclose an extract from one of Major Cox's despatches, as to the subject of our being allowed to occupy Cadiz, by which you will judge of the grounds upon which my opinion is formed. (Cox's Correspondence, June 30th). Probably, before this despatch can reach you, General Castaños will have fought Dupont. In case of disaster, he wished General Spencer to occupy a position at Xeres: the general meant to advance with a part of his force, keeping something afloat to afford assistance to General Morla for the defence of Cadiz. He also meant to have a detachment at Port St Mary's.

At Valencia the Supreme *Junta* was formed some days earlier than at Seville; and the proceedings of the populace (by whom everywhere the governments were formed) were, at Valencia, marked with peculiar violence; and above 300 French traders were, at the beginning, put to death. Since that, it is pretty clear that the populace of the town of Valencia have checked, if not entirely defeated, Moncey's division, which had reached that place by overpowering and, after a desperate action, nearly annihilating a Swiss and another regular regiment, at a pass called the Cabrillas, and evading another corps the Valencians had in the field: they believe, in Valencia, that this last corps had cut off Moncey's retreat, and destroyed his corps. I do not assert the accuracy of any of these particulars; but entertain no doubt that, upon the whole, the French were baffled there.

Barcelona is in the hands of the French; and our accounts from Catalonia are vague and uncertain. Arragon is in arms, certainly; and we have official notice of a defeat the French have sustained at Saragossa, with immense loss: there seems somewhat fabulous in the narrative, though generally credited in Spain, where it is attributed to N^a S^{ra} la V. del Pillar. Such are the ideas of the people at this moment.

Next to the support General Castaños hoped to derive, in case of disaster, from the position he wished Major-General Spencer to take at Xeres, the strongest opinion he has lately given touching the employment of the British Force, is to act upon the Tagus: but I conceive this likely to originate from the jealousy of our intentions with respect to Cadiz. I have found the Spaniards shrink from any proposal that tends to place at our disposal their fleets or their fortresses; and I think a large force off Cadiz would cause a garrison to be sent there, even from the army opposed to Dupont.

I transmit a publication from the *Junta* at Murcia, (to which the name of Florida Blanca is affixed,) that paints, in warm and true colours, the present peril of Spain. Of Bonaparte we hear nothing: his armies seem to be left to their fate.

I have received deputations from Seville, Jaen, Granada, Valencia, Cartagena, the Balearick Islands, and most of the towns on the coast of the Mediterranean between the Straits and Catalonia, and even from Tortosa, in that province: all speak the same sentiments, and all make the same demands,—money, arms, and ammunition.

I have the honour to be, &c. &c.

(Signed)   H. W. Dalrymple,
                                                    Lieutenant-General.

(Enclosure—Translation.)

Murcia,
22nd June, 1808.

Provinces and cities of Spain! We are all of one way of thinking: our will has declared itself in a wonderful and most unequivocal manner. We are all anxious to defend our country, and to maintain the august rights of our amiable and wished-for Ferdinand VII. Let us dread a complete disorganisation, if discord should prevail; let no other words be heard throughout the Peninsula but words of union, fraternity, and defence. Let us be truly great, and rise above the insignificant considerations which take up the attention of weak minds. Let us not individually affect supremacy. Let a solid and central government be established, consisting of provinces, which shall have power to issue orders and laws in the name of Ferdinand VII.

The General Cortes, held in 1789, solemnly acknowledged our present worthy monarch as prince of the Asturias, and heir to the crown. The deputies of that assembly, and King Charles IV. respectively swore, upon the Gospel, to maintain the privileges, rights, laws, usages, and customs of the kingdom. The *grandees* and lords did homage to the king agreeably to the laws and usages of Spain. By this mutual oath, the subjects are bound to pay the obedience which they have sworn, and the sovereign to fulfil his solemn promise to maintain the laws, usages, and customs of the nation.

The first, and perhaps the most essential, is the succession to the crown settled in our great code, called *Las Partidas*, the laws of which evince the most ancient mode of succession in Spain. This mode the nation ever refused to alter; and, accordingly, when King Philip V. wanted to introduce the French Salique Law, by which women are excluded, (an attempt which was renewed at the above-mentioned reciting in 1789,) the members unanimously declared that:

His Majesty had it not in his power to alter the Spanish Settlement which he had sworn to maintain, and that, therefore, the Princess Charlotte of Brazil was to inherit the crown, in failure of her brothers.

In consequence of this convention, by which the subjects bound themselves to allegiance, and the sovereigns to the performance of their sworn promises, it is submitted to the consideration of the nation. The resignations and abdications of King Charles IV. and Ferdinand VII. in favour of the Emperor of the French, have been positively and notoriously null and void; being made in favour of an individual who does not belong to the family appointed by the *Cortes*, in conformity to the laws, rights, usages, and customs of Spain; and contrary to the solemn and reciprocal oath taken by the king and his subjects at a solemn meeting of the said assembly.

Besides this nullity, which releases us from the obligation of acknowledging the emperor of the French as our sovereign, there is, further, the compulsion under which they were made, and the circumstance that the individual appointed was with a powerful army on the spot where the resignation took place, and whither the prince, who had been solemnly acknowledged, and proclaimed king by the nation, was drawn by deceit and treachery.

King Francis I. of France, refused to fulfil the treaty made with the Emperor Charles V., and by virtue of which he had recovered his freedom, under pretence that he was a prisoner when he signed it. Let nations compare the two facts: Francis I. had been taken at the famous Battle of Pavia, in the course of an open and just war; and Ferdinand VII. has been taken at Bayonne, when he fancied that he was going to embrace an intimate ally, who invited him there to consolidate and draw closer the bands of peace and union, and to heighten the glory of the two nations.

The cession and abandonment of a fortress, or even of a province may be tolerated, if it brings a bloody and cruel war to a conclusion; but the unheard of and surprising resignation of a great monarchy in time of peace, and without any farther communication to the nation, or consent of the respective kingdoms, than to have extorted it from a monarch in confinement, or even perhaps printed it, without its ever having taken place, is so violent and extraordinary a proceeding, that no other instance of the kind is to be found among the usurpers of crowns in the annals of the whole world.

The French newspapers censured the conduct of England, when her forces made themselves masters of our frigates, and of the Royal Navy of Denmark; what will they say, then, upon the black attempt of disposing of the whole monarchy of Spain, under the cloak of friendship and alliance? The powerful Charlemagne, with disciplined armies, and an immense empire, attempted to assert certain claims upon this kingdom; but the chaste Alphonsus made him sensible, at Roncesvalles, that even petty sovereigns, like that of Leon, could destroy those, who, like Nebuchadnezzar, trust only in their own forces.

He who has justice on his side is under the protection of God! and if God be with us, they set up in vain who assail and persecute us. Cities which have a right to vote in the *Cortes'* let us unite, let us form a body, let us form a council which shall, in the name of Ferdinand VII., organise all the civil dispositions, and let us avert the evil with which we are threatened, namely, *division*.

The report, really dreadful, that, in each capital, the Board of Government deems itself *supreme*, would create anarchy, desolation, and the ruin of all; and we, who united should prove invincible, shall, through *division*, afford the common enemy the satisfaction of seeing us in the most melancholy state. Let Spain shed tears if such should be her fate.

Ferdinand VII. is invested with the supreme power; the *Cortes* acknowledge him as hereditary prince; the nation has proclaimed him king; Seville, Granada, Valencia, Saragossa, celebrated cities, now come forward, unite, adopt this plan; appoint a place and day for the meeting of the representatives of the people, make them known, and, for the present, act for the noble cities of Burgos and Toledo, which, being in a state of subjection, cannot express their sentiments. Captains general, renowned general officers, patronise this proposal, which will save your country. Worthy Herves! you ought to be formed into a military council, vested with the power of issuing orders to the commanders of our armies; and, being thoroughly acquainted with all the resources of the country, and the movements of the enemy, it will be for you to direct their operations, and to send assistance, whenever it may be requisite, and where essential service may be rendered to the nation.

This city is confident that this last remedy is the only one that can save us. A Central, a Supreme Government is absolutely necessary; Ferdinand VII. requires it; Ferdinand cannot be restored to his throne without this union and sovereignty.

Whenever all the provinces are united by means of their representatives, there is no rivalry for superiority, the formidable arms of disunion and intrigue are effectually wrested from the hands of the enemy, and foreign powers know with whom they are to treat of peace or war. In short, by acknowledging an universal government in Spain, the monarchy will be preserved, whole and entire, for its lawful and beloved sovereign.

This city expects to be favoured with an answer from you, for her information and satisfaction.

(Signed)

Clemente di Campos.—Josef, Bishop of Cartagena.—Count de

Florida Blanca.—Joachim de Elquita.—Julien Josef Retamosa,—M. Marquis de Espiñardo y Aquilar.—The Archdeacon of Villena Vicente Heyeta.—Count de Campo Hermoso.—Ant°. Fontes Abal, Marquis del Villar.—Ant°. Fernandez de St. Domingo.—Viscount de Huerta.—Louis St. Jago Bado.—Francisco Lopez de Aquilar.—Josef Herrarijes,

Agreeably to the Resolution of the Board,

(Signed) Anto. Josef Calahorra.

To Sir Arthur Wellesley.

Gibraltar,
24th July, 1808.

Sir,

Major General Spencer having strongly urged the detaching a part of the artillery officers and men, belonging to the garrison, to join the corps under your orders, I have requested Lord Collingwood to furnish the means of sending, to Lisbon, one company of artillery, and two 5½ inch howitzers: the heavy 12 pounders, which encumbered General Spencer's corps, not having suitable equipments for field service, I have ordered back, as also the other company of artillery, which I cannot spare from hence, and which I am confident you cannot stand much in need of, as the supply of your force, with an adequate proportion of artillery, could never be calculated to depend on a supply from hence, which was not ordered, and could not have been in contemplation the end of last month.

If a veteran battalion, which I am promised, arrives here, I can afford you the temporary service of an effective battalion, by the same tonnage, provided directions that may arrive from England, at the same time, do not interfere with the arrangement. I congratulate you upon the victory, of which I enclose the details.

(Signed) H. W. Dalrymple,
Lieutenant-General.

To Sir Arthur Wellesley.

Gibraltar,
27th September, 1808.

Sir,

Adverting to my letter of the 24th instant, I have now the honour to acquaint you that before Lord Collingwood received the letter I addressed to him, on the subject of the artillery, His Lordship had directed the transport, with the two companies on board, to return to this place, and they, in consequence, arrived here yesterday.

I shall now wait, until I hear from you, or receive orders from England, before I make any further detachments from this garrison.

(Signed)   H. W. Dalrymple,
                                                                        Lieutenant-General.

(No. 12.)
To Major-General Spencer.

Gibraltar,
9th June, 1808.

Sir,

As a corps of British troops is already before Cadiz, I think it expedient that no time should be lost in rendering it as respectable as possible. I, therefore, now send you the 6th Regiment and the detachment of artillery I promised. You will find that the latter wants many equipments; for which, it is to be hoped, the country will be able to supply substitutes, in case of a landing.

As it is evidently the intention of His Majesty's Government to furnish troops upon the requisition of that of Spain; and, as the promised corps, amounting in all to ten thousand men, is given in consequence of General Castaños having, in his communications with me seemed to require that number, it is of importance that no proposal upon the subject of landing should, at the present moment, originate with you; or that you should even, too eagerly, grasp at any such proposition from an individual officer, however flattering it may be, without being sure he acts by the authority acknowledged at Seville, within which the fortress of Cadiz is placed.

That unjust and injurious sentiment of the British character, which is displayed in the striking paragraph of the Marquis of Soccorro's last unfortunate manifesto that alludes to the combined army and fleet then off Cadiz, has been diligently propagated by the enemy, particularly in the vicinity of Cadiz, where so many have suffered by the war; I feel that to counter act that prejudice will be a delicate, but certainly a most important consideration; and I cannot but rejoice that the sentiments expressed in my private and confidential communications with His Majesty's Government enable me boldly to hold a language that will speak home to the enlightened and liberal mind of General Castaños, to whom, as also to the Board of Government at Seville, I shall send a despatch, relative to the landing of the forces, as soon as I have had the necessary communications with Lord Collingwood, whom I am to see this morning.

Of course, nothing that is here said is to interfere with the exercise of your own judgement, in case of the actual appearance of an enemy, or the fortress of Cadiz being placed in a state of danger; but even then, in discussing the measure, it would be extremely desirable that no form should be used, and certainly not persisted in, which the jealousy of the Spanish officer in command could construe into the language of dictation or superiority.

As the idea of a diversion in Portugal, first proposed, does not seem to meet with your approbation, I deem it not impossible that it may be proposed that a position should be taken to cover Cadiz. Instead of, in the first instance, occupying the place, it may be stated that such a movement would, probably, produce the most beneficial effects. Your corps is, from time to time, receiving reinforcements; its original strength is, probably, very little known, and the strength of all bodies of troops that assume an attitude of apparent boldness is, generally, exaggerated.

As this language would be wise or otherwise, according to local circumstances, and the nature of the country, I should be very glad if you would favour me with the necessary information upon these essential points; that, should the measure be proposed, I may judge of the value of the reasons urged in its support.

At present, the Spanish Nation is unanimous; and the combined effort, at the same moment, and in nearly the same form, proves that there is somewhere a power that actuates the whole.

But these separate Boards of Government, constitutionally formed, but, also, constitutionally independent of each other, without any man, or body of men, to whom foreign nations can look, may produce several inconveniences and some difficulty; at present, the best way is, certainly, to follow the current; to direct it when possible; but never to sanction the assumed power of any men, or body of men, although usurped for the best and the most patriotic motives. I have here daily opportunities of seeing effects of the present ferment, which afford me this useful lesson.

(Signed)   H. W. Dalrymple.

I have enclosed the copy of my late despatch from the Secretary of State.

To Major-General Spencer.

Convent,
10th June, 1808.

Dear General,

I Enclose the translation of an extraordinary requisition which I received last night, and to which I saw no cause to wait for your opinion, to give a decided negative. I never made the offer alluded to, and I should never have thought of authorising the movement proposed, particularly on the call of two individuals, speaking in their own name, and giving no account of the actual state or situation of either the Spanish or French Armies, or what plan of operations either seems about to pursue. This will be given you by Major Cox, who proceeds to Seville, to communicate with the government there, on all those points which it may be necessary to discuss, as I am tired out with the applications that are made to me from all quarters; and several times, I fear, I have given displeasure by not entering into the detail of difficulties which I have it not in my power to relieve.

In case of any direct proposal for the disposition of the corps under your orders, I shall desire Major Cox to transmit it to you forthwith, that I may, as early as possible, be favoured with your sentiments thereupon; if the case is of an urgent nature, and the operation will not remove you too far from the fleet, you will, of course, exercise your own judgement without waiting for mine; but, in such case, you will, naturally and of course, communicate with Lord Collingwood, without whose approbation I do not think any measure should be adopted. In answering the enclosed, I proposed the occupation of some fortress on the coast, by which an equal or a greater number of Spanish troops might be liberated for the field.

(Signed)

H. W. Dalrymple.

Major-General Spencer.

Gibraltar,
12th June, 1808.

Sir,

Thinking it expedient to have a confidential officer at the headquarters of Don F. Xavier de Castaños, Captain-General of the Army of Andalusia, I have to acquaint you, that I have selected Captain Whittingham for that service, who has directions to communicate with you as circumstances require.

(Signed)

H. W. Dalrymple,
Lieutenant-General.

Major-General Spencer.

Gibraltar,
12th June, 1808.

Sir,

Should you have thought it expedient to comply with General Castaños's requisition, and have proceeded to Xeres, you will consider yourself as fully authorised to acquiesce with him in any further movements which your own judgement and military experience may approve.

General Castaños, and the members of the New Spanish Government, can have no interests distinct from those of Britain in the present contest: and:

> The first principle which His Majesty's Ministers wish to be observed, is a fair and honourable co-operation with the Spanish Nation, in any attempt they may make to throw off the yoke of France.

Should those endeavours prove fruitless, it becomes the next object to secure a retreat for those who *wish to fly from tyranny, and to impede the extension of that tyranny over South America.* Holding those objects in view, it seems essential to ensure a communication with, and the means of falling back upon, Cadiz, which I should conceive to be the point to which the French corps, under General Dupont, is to direct its operations.

As I have it in command, on the one hand, not to commit the force under my directions unnecessarily, or for an inadequate object, and on the other to act with determination and spirit, according to circumstances on the spot, I conceive that I fulfil His Majesty's commands in taking upon my own responsibility, in the present case, any measures your experience and judgement may suggest.

H. W. Dalrymple,
Lieutenant-General.

(Signed)

Major-General Spencer,

Gibraltar,
15th June, 1808.

Sir,

I have received the honour of your letter of the 10th instant, informing me of the proceedings at Cadiz up to that date.

As I signified to you, when you were about to sail from hence, that the advices I had recently received from the interior of Spain discouraged the expectation of any of that co-operation upon which the measure of detaching your corps to join Admiral Purvis was first grounded, I feel no surprise at the difficulties you have met with, particularly as to taking possession of Cadiz. Captain Whittingham has reported to me, in detail, the result of his mission, by General Castaños's desire. Whether you should advance to Xeres or not, could only be decided by your own experience and judgement; this might, perhaps, have been only an experiment, to prove what sort of aid the Spaniards were to expect from the British Force before Cadiz.

I have reason to think, from my latest communications, that neither General Castaños nor the Government at Seville have any immediate wish that you should land, particularly until you are reinforced. When the time comes that they may think such a measure advisable, General Castaños will feel the propriety of communicating to you his plan of operations. You will then decide according to your own judgement and military experience, holding in mind the considerations detailed in my letter of the 12th instant, (communicating with Lord Collingwood and acting in concert with him).

Captain Whittingham, as I have already signified to you, is with General Castaños, by my orders; and any communications he shall make to you, you are to consider as official.

The nature of Captain Bradford's mission to Seville must be, of course, perfectly of a private nature, as you would, otherwise, have alluded to it in your letter. I think it will, however, be better for that officer to join you forthwith, as Major Cox, whom I have sent there, is fully instructed with the intentions of His Majesty's Government. Don Eusebio de Herrera is the gentleman, I believe, who addressed to me, by Sir George Smith's desire, a very extraordinary requisition for the march of troops; I have transmitted his letter to General Castaños, hoping that, notwithstanding the present state of Spain, the *Junta* at Seville will see the necessity of not allowing official communications in their name to pass through so many channels.

(Signed)
H. W. Dalrymple,
Lieutenant-General.

To Major-General Spencer.

Gibraltar,
17th June, 1808.

Sir,

I have to acknowledge the honour of your despatch of the 12th, and entirely agree with you in opinion as to the inexpediency of your advancing to Xeres, if you had reason to believe, by so doing, you would be drawn into more extended operations in the field; for such, your corps is certainly not equipped.

I have received a letter from Sir Charles Cotton, dated the 12th, from Lisbon, requesting the co-operation of your corps; with the assistance of which, if it amounts to 5,000 or 6,000 men, he does not seem to doubt of being able to take possession of the whole of the maritime means now collected in that river.

I have to request that you will communicate with Lord Collingwood upon the expediency of this measure at the present time; and if no objection arises from the local circumstances at Cadiz, I think it should be immediately adopted.

Should any reason, which I cannot foresee, operate against this determination, I shall be glad to know it. In the state of things in Spain when I received my last advices from thence, your remaining off Cadiz seemed altogether inexpedient; and I was about to request your return to this Port until the reinforcements should arrive, and the further instructions promised by His Majesty's Ministers be received.

To act in Spain will, of course, be considered as the ultimate design of your corps.

(Signed)   H. W. Dalrymple.

P.S. Your corps nearly amounts to 5,000 men; if not quite, the deficiency may be supplied, perhaps, by Sir C. Cotton from the fleet, by landing marines. I have not the means of sending anything at this moment.

Major-General Spencer to Lieutenant-General Sir Hew Dalrymple.
Cadiz,
July, 1808.

Sir,

I have the honour to transmit to Your Excellency a letter from Sir George Smith upon an urgent demand made for an immediate supply of money, of which the *Junta* is in such want as to have chosen the dismantling the fleet from the 15th instant, as a less evil than sacrificing the rising hopes of the country by disbanding the army. Under these circumstances, I have taken upon me, in the name of the British Government, to assure General Morla, until I hear from Your Excellency, that the money absolutely required for the use of the fleet shall be granted; and I further his request; that a sum, independent of what may be advanced to the *Junta* of Seville, may be furnished to him, to repair the French ships of war and put their fleets in order, which they must keep in view as a last resource.

I have directed two regiments to land, tomorrow, at Puerto St. Maria; and, as barracks can be procured, I shall cause the rest of the force to land: but I do not think it prudent, at this season of the year, to put the men under canvass, unless absolutely requisite; as it is to this force General Morla looks for the defence of Cadiz, should any reverse befall the Spanish Arms.

I have the honour to acknowledge the receipt of Your Excellency's letter; and, by the first opportunity, shall direct Colonel Bowes, of the 6th Regiment, to proceed to Gibraltar.

I have thought the situation of affairs, with regard to the Spanish resources for supplying their immediate expenditure, so critical, that I send Captain Bradford as the bearer of this despatch to Your Excellency: he can give any further information you may require upon this important subject; in which is so deeply interested the honour of the existing Government, and the safety of South America.

I have the honour to be, &c. &c.

(Signed)

B. Spencer,
Major-General.

(Enclosure.)
Sir George Smith to Major-General Spencer.

Cadiz,
2nd July, 1808.
Sir,

The Spanish sailors of the squadron in the harbour of Cadiz being about to be discharged, I waited upon General Morla, who told me it proceeded entirely from the want of money; that he had but just enough to pay the soldiers, and supply the most urgent demands; that the *Junta* of Seville had ordered him, in consequence of these distresses, to discharge the sailors.

I took it upon myself to assure him that the means of paying the sailors should be immediately afforded him; on which condition, he most readily agreed to give immediate orders to stop the discharging the sailors. He will not require money for that purpose till the 15th instant; when he will give in a statement of the money required for a fortnight's pay; and continue doing so twice every month until other measures are determined upon. He also offers, that if the British Government would advance money, to proceed, without loss of time, to repair the ships taken from the French, and fit them for sea. He says nothing could afford him more satisfaction than that part of the Spanish squadron was united with the English upon any service that might be required.

(Signed)   George Smith,
                                                        Lieutenant-Colonel.

Lieutenant-General Sir Hew Dalrymple to Major-General Spencer.
                                                              Gibraltar,
                                                          4th July, 1808.

Sir,

As Lord Collingwood is in possession of full instructions from His Majesty's Government upon the subject to which your letter alludes, I have transmitted that, with its enclosure, to His Lordship. I am ignorant by what authority Sir George Smith offered himself as a negotiator upon this occasion, or in whose name he contracted the engagement he mentions; but if he intended that I should fulfil what he promised, I fear his indiscretion may have created some inconvenience, exclusive of that which must necessarily result from the doubts that the Spaniards cannot fail from thence to entertain, through what channel the real intentions of the British Government is, in point of fact, to be conveyed, or by whom its intentions are to be fulfilled.

(Signed)   H. W. Dalrymple,
                                                        Lieutenant-General.

Lieutenant-General Sir Hew Dalrymple to Major-General Spencer.
                                                              Gibraltar,
                                                          5th July, 1808.

Sir,

In reply to your letter which I received yesterday, by Captain Bradford, I only adverted to the subject upon which you principally dwelt; there are, however, other points that you incidentally touched upon, which I feel I cannot consistently pass over.

After having informed me that you are landing your troops at Port St. Mary's, you add, by way of accounting for your placing them in barracks, that you do not think it prudent at this season of the year to put the men under canvass, unless absolutely requisite, *as it is to this force General Morla looks for the defence of Cadiz, should any reverse befall the Spanish Arms.* I think it now incumbent on me to ask what arrangements you have made with General Morla for the purpose you

167

mention? In the first place, I think I can assure you that *it was once* determined, in the *Junta*, (and of that determination General Morla was one of the warmest partisans,) that you should not be put in possession of any one fortress whatsoever, particularly Cadiz.

In the next place, should a reverse happen to the Spanish Arms, it is to be presumed that General Castaños's army will not be exterminated, but that he will be able to take a position, perhaps, at Xeres, perhaps even to cover Seville. Under such a circumstance, I think you would find yourself reduced, without an option, to pursue those measures of which you before disapproved; indeed, you have already said:

> With regard to any position in the outside of the Island of Leon for the British Troops to occupy, you thought you could not, in honour, place your corps in such a situation, without having made up your mind to advance into the interior, should the Spaniards urge you to that measure for the defence of Seville, or any important point.

I have already told you, from good intelligence, what has been General Morla's real disposition as to the admitting you into Cadiz; were you to urge the expediency of your entering that place after having received intelligence at Port St. Mary's of any reverse having befallen the Spanish Arms, General Morla would, I think, again be enabled, and with truth, to say to you that he could not reconcile the people to the measure of your admittance.

I beg to observe that I do not here advance as an opinion of my own that, being at Port St. Mary's, you would be bound, in honour, to advance in the interior as far as Seville; on the contrary, I should never sanction, by my approbation, such a measure: neither do I object to your occupying, even joined to a beaten Spanish Army, a position to cover Cadiz; and I think it would be absolutely necessary, now you are landed outside the island, so to do.

But as you have adopted the measure without my previous knowledge, and contrary to an opinion I suggested in my letter of the 17th *ult.* I think I should neglect a duty which I am commanded to perform, which I shall not delegate, but which I shall be extremely glad to be relieved from, did I not call for the explanation I now request.

(Signed)   H. W. Dalrymple,
                                                    Lieutenant-General.

Major-General Spencer to Lieutenant-General Sir Hew Dalrymple.
Puerto San Maria,
7th July, 1808.

I have mentioned to Lord Collingwood my intention of proceeding to Xeres with Brigadier-General Nightingale's brigade, the light infantry, and four guns and horses, as soon as the means of conveying them can be procured; the expense of which must be defrayed by the British Government; and will, with the utmost economy, average one thousand pounds a week: but it is absolutely necessary that the horses, and peasantry to conduct them, be on the spot.

Nor can I trust to contingencies for the removal of my guns; without which, I could not attempt anything, nor could I afford them any assistance: this indispensable expense I shall take on myself, to meet the views of the Spanish Government. *Nor shall I neglect the design repeatedly expressed by General Morla to Brigadier-General Nightingale, Sir George Smith, and me, to trust the defence of Cadiz to the British Forces, if any reverse befall the Spanish Arms.*

(Signed)
B. Spencer,
Major-General.

Lieutenant-General Sir Hew Dalrymple To Major-General Spencer.
Gibraltar,
10th July, 1808.

Sir,

I have just received the honour of your letter of the 7th, and am glad you have acquiesced in General Castanos's requisition; but it is my opinion that you should collect your whole Force at Xeres, as, when divided, I think it useless for any valuable purpose whatever. I can add nothing to what I have already said relative to the suggestions thrown out by General Morla, as to his trusting the defence of Cadiz to the British Forces, until you send me some official document from that officer to prove that he is in earnest, which I have very substantial reasons to doubt.

The movements of a British Army must, of course, be at the expense of Britain; and there can be no doubt that your deficiency of equipment for the field will require some arrangement, and must enhance expense.

I conceive, however, that the instructions which authorise your corps to act on shore, and the authority I have already given you to accede to any proposal from General Castaños to proceed to Xeres, necessarily conveys to you a sanction to defray and charge the incidental contingent expense attending that or any other movement equally authorised. I have never received any official notice of Colonel Bowes being placed on the staff of this garrison, as brigadier general, and have not, of course, put him in orders as such.

(Signed)
H.W. Dalrymple,
Lieutenant-General.

Lieutenant-General Sir Hew Dalrymple to Major-General Spencer.

Gibraltar,
17th July, 1808.

Sir,

I have received a despatch from Lord Castlereagh, dated 28th June, in which is contained a copy of His Lordship's letter to you of the same date. I find, from the tenor of those letters, that no communication from me had reached His Lordship subsequent to the revolutions against the French in the southern provinces of Spain.

As the troops under your orders are to be considered as a part of the force commanded by Lieutenant-General Sir A. Wellesley, it is only necessary for me to request that the detachment of artillery and the engineer officers, together with the guns and howitzers which I attached to your corps from hence, be returned, as soon as possible, to this garrison.

The 6th Regiment will continue under your command; but not having received any notice from the Horse Guards of Colonel Bowes's being placed upon the staff of this garrison, as brigadier-general, I can only say that I think he had better return here than continue to serve as colonel in an army to which he is not regularly attached; for doing which, he has my full authority.

This letter is written under the impression that none of the artillery officers or men belonging to this garrison are absolutely necessary for any operations you may have undertaken in the field in front of Cadiz; for which, the detachment belonging to your corps will, I conjecture, be amply sufficient: should, however, the contrary be the case, you are at liberty to retain whatever officers and men may be necessary to complete your detachment to the number so employed until the service is over. I have written to Lord Collingwood to request that a convoy may be appointed for the artillery transport.

(Signed)
H.W. Dalrymple,
Lieutenant-General.

(No. 13.)
To His Excellency Sir Hew Dalrymple.

Palermo,
24th July, 1808.

Dear Sir,

This letter will be delivered to you by His Royal Highness Don Leopold, second son to the King of the two Sicilies. This prince goes to Gibraltar to communicate immediately with the loyal Spaniards, and to notify to them that his father will accept the regency, if they desire it, until his nephew Ferdinand VII., King of Spain, be liberated from captivity.

Don Leopold, and his cousin, the Duke of Orleans, will offer themselves as soldiers to the Spaniards, and will take such situations as may be given to them, suitable to their illustrious rank. If their visit should not be acceptable to the Spaniards, Don Leopold will return to Sicily, and His Serene Highness the Duke of Orleans will proceed to England.

Being of opinion that the appearance of an infant of Spain may be of the greatest utility at the present crisis, and in all events can hardly be productive of harm, I have urged His Sicilian Majesty to determine upon this measure, which I conceive to be required at his hands, in consequence of the manifesto of Palafox, which you have probably seen.

At the distance of a thousand miles, however, we cannot be supposed to be accurately informed here of many circumstances, with which you, probably, may be intimately acquainted. Prince Leopold, therefore, will be directed to consult with you, and to follow your advice, which I have no doubt you will readily and cheerfully give him. I take the liberty at the same time of recommending him to your care and protection.

I have the honour to be, &c. &c.
(Signed)   W. Drummond.

To the Right Honourable William Drummond.

Gibraltar,
11th August, 1808.

Dear Sir,

I must confess that nothing could, in my opinion, happen more out of season than the arrival of the Duke of Orleans and Prince Leopold, at this exact time.

The French have been beaten, and have laid down their arms to Spanish generals and Spanish soldiers, and greater skill and gallantry have never been displayed than by these troops; the several *Juntas* of government have in all parts, not immediately under the pressure of the French Armies, exercised a wise authority, which has been universally acquiesced in with in their limits; and the only difficulty that seemed to threaten, was from the *Junta* of Seville, which was suspected to entertain a design to engross more than their share of power. Luckily I think for Spain, (but certainly the contrary for the views of any royal visitants,) this *Junta* did not know of a volunteer regent so near, or (if the suspicion I have mentioned was well founded) they would, through his means, have perhaps assumed an authority that would have distracted Spain, and perhaps ruined the great cause which is now at issue.

It has come to pass, however, that this *Junta* has published an address, recommending the formation of a Central Government to direct the helm of the State during the captivity of their lawful sovereign; but, above all things, Spain is enjoined to steer clear of the question of succession, as that would divide their opinions, create animosity, and ruin their cause.

This recommendation is probably suggested by an address from Murcia, recommending a National Government, but sustaining the claim of the Princess Charlotte of Brazils. I believe the people at Seville once thought of the House of Sicily, but they have just deprecated the question themselves.

My own opinion is, that our government cannot, consistently with the most solemn assurances, become a party to this business, and I am confident they are anxious to avoid any such appearance; I have, therefore, felt myself constrained to disavow the arrangement though made by you, as I am at the eve of my departure to take the command of a considerable army assembling in Portugal, which circumstance the ill designing might so couple with the arrival of these persons, as to authorise any disagreeable conclusions.

After some hesitation, I have consented that Prince Leopold should be received here under certain restrictions, but the Duke of Orleans proceeds to England forthwith.

I have the honour to be, &c, &c.

(Signed)

H. W. Dalrymple.

172

(No. 14.)
Lieutenant-General Sir. H. Dalrymple.

Malta,
12th July, 1808.

Sir,

I beg leave to address you on a subject of importance, respecting the Duke of Orleans. His Highness has been encouraged by their Sicilian Majesties and Mr. Drummond to go into Spain, conceiving that the appearance of a member of the House of Bourbon will be acceptable to the Spaniards. I enclose copies of my correspondence with His Highness and Mr. Drummond on this subject. I must confess to you, Sir, that I was surprised at reading the two lines that follow Mr. Drummond's signature, as I do not perceive any reason for simulation, and I cannot but conceive that it would have been more becoming a minister to have expressed fully his doubts and real sentiments on such an occasion.

I am directed, by Lord Castlereagh, to order the Duke of Orleans a passage to England, in any of His Majesty's ships bound there. His Highness was to have embarked on board of His Majesty's ship *Thames*, which will sail from hence, with the convoy, the first of next month; but, as the *Thunderer* will go sooner, I have directed Captain Talbot to receive His Highness. I have written a private letter to the duke, recommending him to go to England, for I do not conceive that he can be allowed to go to Spain without the sanction of His Majesty's Ministers, more especially as I have reason to believe that the Archduke Charles is now on his way for that country.

The Spaniards evince a character worthy of their brave ancestors. They have passed the Rubicon; and their cause is now that of almost all Europe. I hope that our conduct on this memorable occasion will be so generous and liberal as will convince them that we have not any selfish views in our offers of assistance and interposition. The confederate powers who join us should take warning by the fatal disasters which resulted from their operations in the late wars against the French Government, in which they evidently betrayed great jealousy of each other, and showed that they were not fighting the cause of the Bourbon family, but taking advantage of the misfortunes of France to aggrandise their own dominions.

I have not time to send copies of my correspondence with the Duke of Orleans and Mr. Drummond to Lord Collingwood; I must, therefore, request you (should you judge it necessary) to send them to him.

173

I have the honour to be, &c. &c.

(Signed)   Alexander. J. Ball.

(The four following letters were enclosed in the preceding.)

To His Excellency Sir Alexander Ball.

Palermo,
4th July, 1808.

My Dear Sir,

His Highness the Duke of Orleans has applied to me to write to you on a subject about which he appears to be extremely interested. I take it for granted that you are acquainted with all the events which have lately happened in Spain. The duke thinks that the appearance of a Member of the House of Bourbon in that Country might be acceptable to the Spaniards, and of great service to the common cause. In this I perfectly concur with His Highness, and if you be of the same opinion, you will, probably, have no objection to send a ship here to carry His Highness to Gibraltar. He himself is exceedingly sanguine. We have letters from London down to the 7th of June.

Portugal has followed the example of Spain, and Lisbon is, probably, now in other hands. An invitation has been sent to Sir Charles Cotton.

I have the honour to be, &c. &c.

(Signed)   W. Drummond.

Weigh well what is said here,
Written at the side of the person.

To Sir Alexander Ball.

Palermo,
4th July, 1808.

My Dear Sir Alexander,

I now apply to you with confidence to do me a great service, and one which may, perhaps, be of some use to the general cause, and to that of England in particular. You have heard the delightful news from Spain, and the glories, the wonderful exertions of the Spanish Nation, for their king, their government, their religion, and their independence. You cannot wonder that, being a Bourbon, and so very near the spot where my services may be of some use, I should be most anxious to make a tender of them; and, setting aside all personal considerations, I must own that I am persuaded my presence and services, at this critical juncture, might be of use in giving impulse to the generous efforts of the Spaniards, and lead them there where a deadly blow may be struck at the usurper, and upset his odious empire.

My name and my presence may have great effect on the French Troops in Spain and upon the French in France; but no time is to be lost, and I know you well enough to be certain that you need not be put in mind *qu'il faut battre le fer pendant qu'il est chaud*. I know you would do for me alone what I ask of you for public considerations of such magnitude. What I wish is, that you might send me any ship to convey me from hence to Gibraltar. Mr. Drummond sends you this express, and writes to you to request it from you, as he heartily concurs in my wishes to see me conveyed there, where both duty, honour, and gratitude to the country who so generously supported me imperiously calls me.

This court are, also, informed of my intention, and are very anxious that I might be enabled to repair to Spain with the greatest despatch. I cannot give you an idea of the effusion of affection with which I have been honoured, by the queen and by Her Majesty's sons when (about an hour ago) I communicated my resolution to them. It was a scene never to be forgotten. If you can send me a frigate, so much the better; but a brig, a sloop, or cutter, anything; I don't care what, provided I can be conveyed immediately to Gibraltar, from whence I will shape my course, by other means, where my presence may be judged most useful. I entreat it of you in the most pressing manner.

I remain, &c. &c.

(Signed)   Louis Phillipe d'Orleans.

To His Excellency the Right Hon. W. Drummond.

Malta,
9th July, 1808.

My Dear Sir,

I am honoured with your letter of the 4th instant, acquainting me that His Highness the Duke of Orleans has expressed a desire to proceed immediately to Gibraltar, with a view of going into Spain; conceiving, as you do, that the appearance of a Member of the House of Bourbon might be acceptable to the Spaniards, and expressing a hope that, should my opinion accord with that of His Highness and Your Excellency, I shall despatch a ship of war to convey him down, I have, in consequence, ordered His Majesty's ship *Thunderer* to call at Palermo, for the accommodation of His Highness; but I beg leave, with great deference, to observe, that the subject is of so great importance and delicacy that it can only be finally decided upon at Gibraltar, where His Highness will receive such information and advice as will guide his future proceedings. Possibly, indeed, the posture of affairs may be such as to induce His Highness to wait for the opinion of His Majesty's Ministers.

It is reported that the Spaniards have invited the Archduke Charles to accept of the regency, and that he is now on his way to Spain. If, therefore, the Duke of Orleans were to interfere, it might afford great umbrage to the archduke, and occasion jealousies that might hurt the cause.

I have the honour to be, &c. &c.

(Signed)

Alexander John Ball.

To His Serene Highness the Duke of Orleans.

Malta,
9th July, 1808.

Sir,

I am honoured with your Highness's letter of the 4th instant, expressive of your desire to proceed to Gibraltar, with a view of going into Spain, conceiving that the appearance of a Member of the House of Bourbon might be acceptable to the Spaniards.

I have, in consequence, ordered His Majesty's ship *Thunderer* to call at Palermo, for the accommodation of your Highness to Gibraltar, where, on your arrival, you will receive such information as will guide your future proceedings, and may, possibly, induce Your Highness to wait for the opinion of His Majesty's Ministers.

I have the honour to be, &c. &c.

(Signed)

Alexander John Ball.

(No. 15.)
His Royal Highness Prince Leopold.

Headquarters, Gibraltar,
11th August, 1808.

Sir,

Your Royal Highness will, I hope, pardon the inconvenience to which you have been exposed, from the infinite delicacy of the situation in which I find myself placed from the sudden and unexpected arrival of your Royal Highness, for an avowed purpose, respecting which I have not received the commands of my sovereign, and which involves considerations of the first moment, at the present crisis.

To relieve your Royal Highness from this state of inconvenience and doubt, I presume to *suppose* what may be acceptable to the king, my master, and to act in consequence; confiding in His Majesty's indulgence to the goodness of my motive should I act amiss.

I shall give orders for the reception of your Royal Highness into this garrison, with all the honours due to your rank and character, as soon as the necessary arrangements can be made for that purpose, and such accommodation be prepared for your Royal Highness, and your attendants and family, as the limited means of this garrison will allow. For this purpose, I presume to request that your Royal Highness will give orders that a list of the names of all persons attached to your person be given in to the major-general, who will, in my absence, command the place.

During your Royal Highness's residence here, (or until His Majesty's pleasure shall be known,) every facility shall be given to those noble Spaniards, who may be desirous of paying their respects; subject only to such regulations as the major-general commanding the fortress may see cause to establish, for the purposes of police and the security of the place.

The Provisional Government of Andalusia, which has acquired great weight by the talents of its members, the wisdom of its proceedings, and the brilliant successes attained by the generals and troops acting under its orders, has publicly proclaimed the necessity of establishing a National Government; and has, in its declaration, sanctioned some leading principles, which, I think, the British Government will highly approve.

Without presuming to judge what effects that publication may produce upon the objects of your Royal Highness's voyage, it is only necessary for me to say, that, as it will follow, of course, if your Royal Highness be named Regent of the Kingdom, that a fit deputation will be sent from the Spanish Nation, to attend your Royal Highness, I shall direct that the persons composing it, be received here as attached to Your Royal Highness's retinue, and proceed with you to Spain. But no such deputation from any local or provisional government will be so considered. Such, Sir, are the terms which I humbly presume to propose, should your Royal Highness still retain the design of establishing yourself here for the present.

I have the honour to be, with sentiments of high consideration and respect,

(Signed)   W. H. Dalrymple,
                                                          Lieutenant-General.

177

(Copy.)

S. E. Sig. Generale Sir Hew Dalrymple.
Gov. Com. Gen. della Piazza di Gibilterra.

Eccellenza,

Ho ricevuto con molto gradimento il foglio di V. E. della data di questo stesso giorno, e mentre le manifesto di rimanere pienamente soddisfatto de suoi sentimenti, le assicuro che mi adatteró, é faró ubbedire la Gente del mio Seguito alle sagge misure, che ha creduto di enunciarmi nel mentovato foglio per la mia dimora in cotesta Piazza, desiderando, che l'E. V. sia certa della mia premura nell' uniformarmi a tutto cio, che possa incontrare il piacere di S. M. Britannica, e sia analogo alle attime disposizioni colle quali si regolano le guernigioni de suoi Reali Dominii, ed alle particolari providenze relative a questo assunto.

Ho ordinato che dal Maggiordomo Maggiore, Principe di Cassero, sia rimessa al Maggior Generale, Comandante di Cotesta Piazza, la nota di tutta la gente del mio Seguito. E contestandole i sentimenti della mia riconoscenza, sono collo maggior considerazione.

Di V. E. Rada di Gibilterra, 11 Agusto, 1808.

    (Signed)   *Affecionatissimo,*
                                                 Leopoldo.

To Lieutenant-General Sir Hew Dalrymple.

                                          Downing-Street,
                                          4th November, 1808.
Sir,

I have to acknowledge the receipt of your letter of the 31st October, with the accompanying papers therein referred to; also, your letter of the 2nd instant, with its enclosures. Your despatches from Gibraltar, to assume the command of the army in Portugal, immediately after your letters were written, announcing the unexpected arrival of Prince Leopold and the Duke of Orleans at that place, and acquainting me with the measures you had taken thereupon, will, I trust, explain why I did not address you on a subject, the conduct of which had, from this circumstance, passed, together with the command of that garrison, into other hands. I have great pleasure, however, in assuring you that the measures pursued by you, on that delicate and important subject, received His Majesty's entire approbation.

    I have the honour to be, &c. &c.
    (Signed)   Castlereagh.

(No. 16.)

To the General Commanding the British Army in Portugal.

Oporto,
18th August, 1808.

Sir,

The Bishop of Oporto having expressed to me his wish to see me in private, in order to make me an important communication, which he desired to be kept secret, I went to his palace last night at a late hour. The bishop told me, that he had taken the government of Portugal in his hands, to satisfy the wish of the people, but with the intention to re-establish the government of his lawful sovereign, and he hoped that His Majesty, the King of Great Britain, had no other point of view in sending troops to this country. After having given him all possible assurance on that head, the bishop continued:—that as the prince regent, on leaving Portugal, had established a regency, for the government of this country, during his absence, he considered it his duty to resign the government into the hands of that regency as soon as possible.

My answer was, that I had no instructions from my government on that head, but that I begged him to consider whether the cause of his sovereign would not be hurt in resigning the government into the hands of a regency, which, from its having acted under the influence of the French, had lost the confidence of the nation; and whether it would not be more advisable for him to keep the government, until the pleasure of the prince regent was known.

The bishop allowed that the regency, appointed by the prince regent, did not possess the confidence of the people; that several members of it had acted in such a manner as to shew themselves as friends and partisans of the French, and that, at all events, all the members of the late regency could not be re-established in their former power, but, he was afraid, that the provinces of Estremadura, Alemtejo, and Algarva, would not acknowledge his authority, if the British Government did not interfere.

After a very long conversation, it was agreed that I should inform our ministers, with what the bishop had communicated to me, and, in order to lose no time in waiting for an answer, the bishop desired me to communicate the same to you, expressing a wish that you would be pleased to write to him an official letter, in order to express your desire that he might continue the government, until the pleasure of his sovereign was known, for the sake of the operations of the British and Portuguese troops under your command.

The secretary of the bishop, who acted as interpreter, told me afterwards, in private, that the utmost confusion would arise from the bishop resigning the government at this moment, or associating with people, who were neither liked nor esteemed by the nation.

I beg leave to add, that although the bishop expressed the contrary, yet it appeared to me that he was not averse to his keeping the government in his hands, if it could be done by the interference of our government.

(Signed)   Frederick V'decken,
                                                          Brigadier-General,

To the General Commanding the Army in Portugal.

Oporto,
22nd August, 1808.

Sir,

Your Excellency will have received the secret letter, which I had the honour to send you by Brigadier-General Stewart, (later Marquis of Londonderry), on the 18th, respecting the communication of his Excellency the Bishop of Oporto, relative to his resignation of the government into the hands of the regency, established by the prince regent. In addition to what I have had the honour to state upon that subject, I beg leave to add that his Excellency the bishop has this day desired me to make Your Excellency aware, in case it might be wished that he should keep the government in his hands until the pleasure of the prince regent may be known, that he could not leave Oporto, and the seat of government must, in that case, necessarily remain in this town. His Excellency the bishop thinks it his duty to inform you of this circumstance as soon as possible, as he foresees that the City of Lisbon will be preferred for the seat of government as soon as the British Army have got possession of it.

If the seat of the temporary government should remain at Oporto, the best method to adopt, with respect to the other provinces of Portugal, appears to be to cause them to send deputies to that place, for the purpose of transacting business relative to their own provinces; in the same manner as the provinces of Entre Douro, and Tras las Montes now send their representatives.

One of the principal reasons why his Excellency the bishop can only accede to continue at the head of the government, under the condition of remaining at Oporto, is, because he is persuaded that the inhabitants of this town will not permit him to leave it, unless by order of the prince regent.

It might also be advisable to keep the seat of government at Oporto, as it may be supposed that Lisbon will be in a state of great confusion for the first two months after the French have left it.

(Signed)   Frederick V'Decken.

To Lieutenant-General Sir Hew Dalrymple.

Oporto,
28th August, 1808.

Sir,

Your Excellency will have received my secret letter of the 18th and 22nd instant, relative to the temporary government of this kingdom. His Excellency the Bishop of Oporto has received, lately, deputies from the province of Alemtejo; and the kingdom of Algarve, part of Estremadura, *viz.* the town of Leira, has also submitted to his authority; and it may be, therefore, said that the whole kingdom of Portugal has acknowledged the authority of the temporary government, of which the Bishop of Oporto is at the head, with the exception of the city of Lisbon and the town of Setubal (or St. Ubes).

Although the reasons why these towns have not yet acknowledged the authority of the temporary government may be explained by their being in possession of the French, yet the bishop is convinced that the inhabitants of Lisbon will refuse to submit to the temporary government of Oporto, in which they will be strongly supported by the members of the former regency established by the prince regent, who, of course, will be very anxious to resume their former power.

The bishop, in assuming the temporary government, complied only with the wishes of the people; he was sure that it was the only means of saving the country; but, having had no interests of his own in view, he is willing to resign the authority, which he has accepted with reluctance, as soon as he is convinced that it can be done without hurting the cause of his sovereign, and throwing the country into confusion.

There is every reason to apprehend that the inhabitants of the three northern provinces of Portugal will never permit the bishop to resign the government and submit to the former regency; they feel extremely proud of having first taken to arms, and consider themselves as the deliverers and saviours of their country. And as the inhabitants of Lisbon will be as much disinclined to submit to the temporary government of Oporto, a division of the provinces, which will excite interior commotion, will naturally follow, if not supported by Your Excellency.

It has appeared to me that the best way to reconcile these opposite parties, would be in endeavouring to unite the present government at Oporto with such of the members of the former regency, who have not forfeited, by their conduct, the confidence of the people. And, having opened my idea to the bishop, his answer was, that he would not object to it if proposed by you.

I, therefore, take the liberty of suggesting that the difficulty above mentioned would be in a great degree removed, if Your Excellency would be pleased to make it known, after Lisbon has surrendered, that, until the pleasure of the prince regent was known, you would consider the temporary government established at Oporto as the lawful government, with the addition of the four members of the late regency, who have been pointed out to me by the bishop as such who have behaved faithfully to their sovereign and country, *viz*:—

D. Francisco Noronha,

Francisco da Cunha,

The Monteiro Mor, and

The Principal Castro.

These members to be placed at the head of the different departments, and to consider the bishop as the President, whose directions they are to follow; a plan which will meet with the less difficulty, as the President of the former regency, named by the prince regent, has quitted Portugal, and is now in France.

The circumstance that Lisbon is now in a state of the greatest confusion will furnish a fair pretence for fixing the seat of the temporary government in the first in stance at Oporto, to which place the gentlemen above mentioned would be ordered to repair without loss of time, and to report themselves to the bishop.

Independent of the reasons which I had the honour of stating to Your Excellency in my letter of the 22nd instant, why it is impossible for the bishop to leave Oporto, I must beg leave to add that, from what I understand, the greater part of the inhabitants of Lisbon. are in the French interest, and that it will require a garrison of British troops to keep that city in order. The Bishop of Oporto, although convinced of the necessity of considering Lisbon at present as a military station and of placing a British *commandant* and a British garrison there, yet, from a desire that the feelings of the inhabitants might be wounded as little as possible, wishes that you would be pleased to put, also, some Portuguese troops in garrison at Lisbon, together with a Portuguese *commandant*, who, though entirely under the orders of the British governor, might direct the police in that town, or at least be charged with putting into execution such orders as he may receive from the British governor under that head.

If Your Excellency should be pleased to approve of this proposal, the bishop thinks Brigadier Antonio Pinto Bacelas to be the properest officer of those who are now with the Portuguese Army, to be stationed at Lisbon, and who might also be directed to organise the military force of the province of Estremadura. The bishop is fully convinced that the temporary government of the country cannot exist without the support of British troops; he hopes that our government will leave a corps of 6,000 men in Portugal after the French have been subdued, until the Portuguese troops may be sufficiently organised and disciplined to be able to protect their own government.

I have the honour to be, &c. &c.

(Signed)   Frederick Von Decken,
                                                     Brigadier-General.

To Brigadier-General Decken.
                                        Headquarters, Ramalhall,
                                              August 24th, 1808.

Sir,

I have to acknowledge the honour of your letter of the 18th instant, and am much surprised to understand thereby that the Bishop of Oporto has taken the government of Portugal into his hands, as that is a measure of considerable delicacy and importance, and which I by no means understood to have taken place.

What steps it may be advisable to take in consequence of this event, I cannot at this moment determine, particularly without having communication with Sir Charles Cotton thereupon, who will not, however, I conjecture (any more than myself) entirely approve of the strong step you have taken, in recommending it to the bishop to retain an authority which I cannot conceive to have been conferred by the unanimous voice of the Portuguese Nation.

And I must request that, in future, you will hold no language which may be interpreted as being expressive of the sentiments of His Majesty's Government, or of those of the officers, commanders-in-chief of the British Army and Fleet, without having received distinct authority and instructions for so doing, in order that the sanction of Britain may not be cited for different and, perhaps, opposite measures.

(Signed)   H. W. Dalrymple.

To His Excellency Lieutenant General Sir Hew Dalrymple.

Oporto,
1st September, 1808.

Sir,

I am very sorry to see, by Your Excellency's letter of the 24th last, which I had the honour to receive last night, I have had the misfortune of having excited your displeasure, and I lose no time to beg you will be convinced that your direction shall be most strictly obeyed; and that, even in case instructions should reach me from government, I intend not to act upon them until I have received your orders.

The Bishop of Oporto knows that I have received no instruction, neither from you or from government. All that has passed between him and me, on the subject of his resignation, has been only considered as private, although, on the part of the bishop, as a means to convey his ideas to you. If, in the letters which I have had the honour to write to you, there are proposals which have not been stated as made by the bishop, it is owing to his desire not to mention his name where it might be suspected that he wished to remain at the head of the government; but the fact is, that all proposals and remarks have been suggested either by himself or his secretary: and Your Excellency may be sure that the bishop has not received from me any hint whatsoever as to give him hopes that you or our government wish him to remain at the head of the temporary government.

It is true that (as I had the honour of stating in my letter of the 18th of August) I had no instruction to return in answer to the first communication of the bishop: he might take into consideration whether it would be advisable to resign at the present moment; but I was then convinced that the bishop was the only man who had some influence over the mind of this uncultivated people, which was in a state of revolution; and I considered that even the appearance as if the government was to be taken away from the man they had chosen for their leader, might be of the most fatal consequence for the common cause.

I had every reason to endeavour to gain the confidence of the bishop, and could, therefore, not object to convey to you his wishes; and the more as from my assuming no authority whatsoever, it remained entirely in your hands to act according to your pleasure. The brilliant achievements of the army under Your Excellency's command have made a great change in the state of affairs. Order might now easily be restored; whilst it would have been difficult as long as the country was the theatre of war, and the necessity of complying, at least, apparently, with the wishes of the people, who have taken arms, is certainly removed in a great measure.

The declaration of the bishop, that he cannot leave Oporto, and, therefore, take no part in the government, if the seat of it is not transferred to this town, will leave it entirely in the hands of Your Excellency to take a fair pretence from thence, to exclude the bishop from the government; and to give it to the former regency; or to such member of them as you will think proper.

I beg leave to add that, since a few days, the bishop appears to be aware that the seat of government will not be transferred to this town, and that he, consequently, must resign. Although I do not know him sufficiently to form a decided opinion, yet I dare say he is too much attached to the interest of his sovereign to use his great influence against the government Your Excellency will think proper to appoint, with the exception of several members of the late regency, whom he accuses of being in the French party.

Frederick Von Decken,
Brigadier-General.

To His Excellency the President of the Supreme Board of Council
at Oporto.

Headquarters, Torres Vedras,
1st September, 1808.

(This letter was dated 31st August; but the copy sent to Lord Castlereagh, from Portugal, was dated 1st September.)

Sir,

I have the honour to inform Your Excellency that the French Army will soon quit Portugal, in consequence of a convention concluded for that purpose between the French commander-in-chief on the one side, and the admiral commanding His Majesty's fleet off the Tagus and myself on the other. The ratifications of this convention are not yet exchanged, and I have not an accurate copy of the treaty at this moment in my possession, to transmit to Your Excellency; but I think it essential that you should have the earliest possible notice of the fact: in the meantime, I have ordered the substance of the several articles to be communicated to Major Ayres Pinto de Souza, who is here on the part of General Bernadine Friere.

As soon as Portugal is relieved from the oppression of that power by which the authority of the lawful prince, and the regency, which, on his departure, he established, was suspended, it might naturally be supposed to ensue that everything should revert into the channel from which it was diverted by foreign force; but as some members of the regency appointed by the prince seem to have abandoned his cause, and adhered to the enemy, and have consequently rendered themselves incapable of resuming their former functions, some delicacy certainly becomes necessary in re-establishing a government which the Portuguese Nation will be inclined to avow.

On this point, I have read, since I took the command of this army, the papers addressed by the Supreme Board of Government at Oporto to Sir Charles Cotton, in the beginning of August, together with his answer thereto. It would be presumption in me, so early after my arrival in the country, and unacquainted as I am with the circumstances of the case, to offer any opinion on the means proposed to accomplish an end which I do not hesitate to acknowledge has my most perfect approbation: and it seems evident that, next to the expulsion of the French from Portugal, no object can be so important as to take early precautions against those evils which might arise to the people from local or any source of jealousy.

(Signed)   H. W. Dalrymple.

To His Excellency the Most Illustrious the Bishop of Oporto.
                                                    Headquarters, Cintra,
                                                    5th September, 1808.
Sir,

As effectual measures are taking for the speedy embarkation of the French troops, Portugal will soon be relieved from the foreign force by which it has been oppressed. The prince regent will then be reinstated in all his rights; and, were there no just ground of objection, the Council of Regency, which he appointed, would resume the exercise of their functions of course.

As, however, a number of the members composing this council are strongly suspected of being closely connected with the French interest, I feel myself authorised to state that, however desirous the king, my sovereign, may be to interfere as little as possible in the internal affairs of Portugal, it will be impossible for His Majesty, under the peculiar circumstances of the case, to acquiesce in the return of those persons to power. An arrangement of this nature His Majesty apprehends would be equally inconsistent with the stability of the government, the restoration of public confidence, or, perhaps, even the safety of the individuals themselves.

In regard to those members of the regency who kept aloof from the interests of the enemy, and retained their fidelity to their lawful sovereign and the confidence of the nation, it will, I think, be admitted that such persons (and, doubtless, there are such) have an unquestionable claim to the situation in which they were placed by the prince, if at present in Portugal.

His Majesty deeming it necessary for the peace of Lisbon, and highly conducive to the interests of the prince regent, that a regency should be established in Lisbon, with the same powers that were delegated by the prince regent on his leaving Portugal, I have it in command (upon communication with such leading individuals in Portugal as may have given undoubted proofs of their fidelity to their lawful sovereign) to take measures for forming a Council of Regency as soon as possible, composed of such persons of rank, character, and talent, as may be found ready to undertake and qualified to discharge so important a trust; but with as limited a change of persons left in authority by the prince regent (particularly in the subordinate departments) as may be compatible with the public interests.

I need not mention that the persons to be selected and appointed are merely to act in their several capacities and functions till the pleasure of the prince regent shall be known. In fulfilling the duty thus imposed upon me, I naturally address myself, for assistance, to Your Excellency and the members of the Provisional Board of Government over which you preside.

You have already turned your thoughts to the great question now at issue, and are doubtless prepared to propose measures so to complete the Council of Regency, according to the views above developed, as to merit the confidence of the nation, and to prevent any just cause of discontent in any other Provisional Government, or other respectable description of the people. For my own part, I have only been able, from the information I have received since my arrival in Portugal, to form one decided opinion on the subject, which is, the infinite importance to the public welfare that Your Excellency should yourself hold a distinguished place in the proposed Council of Regency.

From the devotion Your Excellency has already shewn to the cause of your country, I am induced to indulge the hope that you will complete the great work you have begun, by giving Portugal a regency, faithful to the prince, and possessing the confidence of the people, and I need not urge any arguments to prove the indispensable necessity that this should be accomplished without delay.

(Signed)   H. W. Dalrymple, L. G.
                              Commander of the British Forces, in Portugal.

To Lieutenant-General Sir Hew Dalrymple.

Oporto,
16th September, 1808.

Sir,

I have the honour to acquaint you that I arrived here yesterday afternoon, and, having waited on the bishop in the evening, am happy to say that his answer to the communication I was directed to make to him, is such as you will, I hope, consider favourable. He consents to repair to Lisbon, for the purpose of being placed at the head of the regency, and the only reservation made, is in regard to the mode of his appointment to that situation.

On this point, his Excellency has directed me to explain that, of the members of regency originally appointed, whose conduct is unimpeached, there are, at present, in Lisbon, *viz.* D. Francisco de Noronha; D. Francisco de Cunha, and the Principal Castro. Count Monteiro Mor is understood to be with the army, in the Alemtejo. The bishop, therefore, thinks that the most regular and legal proceeding will be to assemble the three members of the regency, who are in Lisbon, and cause them to proceed, as their first step, to the election of a president, which your influence will secure to himself.

A letter should then be written to him, by the regency, announcing his election, and requiring his immediate presence in Lisbon; with which summons he will immediately comply. This his Excellency considers as the only course by which the forms of the government will not be violated: any other would render questionable the authority of the regency, in general, and his own, in particular; and might expose him to the displeasure of the prince, whom he would, on no account, offend. In short, his mind appeared to be made up on the point, and I hardly think he will be prevailed on to accept the situation under any other circumstances.

You will observe that the name of the Principal Castro, mentioned by the bishop as eligible for the new regency, does not, I believe, appear in the project of government proposed, by the *Junta* of Oporto, to

Sir Charles Cotton. The Bishop says the Principal Castro was obliged to accept the office of Minister of Laws and Religious Worship, under the French, which he could not at the moment decline, without great personal risk, but that he resigned very soon, under pretence of bad health: he is brother to the bishop.

The bishop is anxious that his intentions should not be known here until the moment of his departure, as he apprehends some opposition on the part of the people. Baron Decken is the only person to whom I have mentioned them; and I requested him to remain here, even if recalled, which he daily expects, in order to receive your farther commands, and prevent delay on the part of the bishop, after my departure.

There will be no difficulty, in regard to the Portuguese garrison for Almeida, as a considerable body of troops are near the place. I shall proceed thither by Tuesday or Wednesday at furthest, or earlier, if the march of the troops shall appear to require it.

I have the honour to be, &c. &c.

(Signed)   Robert Anstruther,
Brigadier-General.

To Lieutenant-General Sir Hew Dalrymple.

Lisbon,
9th September, 1808.

Dear Sir,

I had, yesterday, the honour of receiving your orders, conveyed by the adjutant-general's letter of the 7th, directing me to repair to Lisbon, to arrange with the French general different points relative to the occupation of the town, by the British troops. As also, your communication of the steps that have been taken by the existing government of Oporto.

I have not yet been able to communicate with the officers named to arrange with me the time and mode of occupation by the troops, but I hope, in the course of this day, to be able to make a communication to you upon the subject.

After having reflected maturely upon the several topics which you did me the honour to communicate, I shall take the liberty of submitting to you my ideas, with that diffidence, however, which I ought to feel upon a subject, in great measure, new to me, and respecting which there has hardly yet been sufficient time for me to acquire the requisite information.

Whether the apparent jealousy entertained by the leaders of the Portuguese Army could have been avoided or not, it is not now material to inquire. It is totally unfounded, and is as childish as it is groundless. Nor is it probable that any additional umbrage they can take, will have any material influence in the final settlement of the country, when it shall be seen that it is the *bona fide* intention of the commander of the British Forces, in execution of the instructions of their government, to replace the Portuguese monarchy on the footing on which it stood, previous to the irruption of the French Army. The following principles appear to me such as it would be desirable to establish, *viz.*

That the ancient and original regency, as far as it may be prudent, should be established, with the addition of the Bishop of Oporto, and such other members as may be agreeable to him. That this regency should be proclaimed the moment the French are completely embarked. That, if the consent of the bishop cannot be had in time, his name should, nevertheless, stand at the head of the government, leaving it to him to decline hereafter if he sees fit. That the residence of the regency should be peremptorily fixed in Lisbon, there being no probability that the people of the capital will submit to the species of controlling influence, which it seems to be the wish of some to throw into the hands of the Provincial Government of Oporto; and there being reason to apprehend that the most serious evil consequences might be expected to result from pursuing an opposite line of conduct.

It is extremely natural for the bishop, and those who are his advisers, to conceive that, by fixing themselves at Oporto, supported by that popularity and reverence which late events and local circumstances throw round their government; holding in their hands the resources of the Northern Provinces; retaining that degree of influence which the nomination of a regency would give them; and withdrawn from any immediate contact with the British Power; they will gain, in real and substantial influence, infinitely more than they seem to lose in *éclat* and ostensible place.

Such a proposition I should, however, hold to be altogether incompatible with the future welfare of the country. Similar reasons, I think, make it extremely desirable that the nomination of the regency should be the act, not of the government of Oporto, but of the British commanders; and that, in the execution of this act, they should seem only to re-establish the government left by the prince regent, upon his removal to Brazil.

It seems to me perfectly clear that the restoration of that government is as much the effect of the efforts made by Great Britain, as much the result of the success that has attended her arms in Portugal, as any other event whatever that has marked our progress in this country; and that neither the Portuguese Government nor any individual whatever can reasonably object to any step, however strong, which the British commander may deem necessary to take, in order to complete the re-establishment of everything upon the basis which was fixed by the Prince of Portugal, subject always to his future pleasure.

It, moreover, seems to me to be entirely in conformity to the Instructions which you did me the honour to communicate, to proceed to the arrangement of the government, without any reference whatever to existing local interests; and this principle is carried so far, that, if I mistake not, you are, under circumstances, empowered to assume the government of the country into your own hands, until further instructions from Britain can be received.

Without having recourse to this last extremity, it is fortunate that an opening is given for arranging such a government as will be agreeable to the leading authorities acting in the northern parts of Portugal; by including the names of the four members of the original *Junta*, who have remained faithful to the interests of the monarchy; placing at their head the bishop as President; and adding such other names as it may be found, after communication with his agent, Don Louis de Figueira, are likely to be acceptable to him.

In the above view of things, I cannot help deeming it of the highest importance that the admiral and yourself should, from this moment, consider all interference on the part of the Portuguese, in the affairs of government, beyond what it may be necessary to leave in the hands of inferior magistrates, inadmissible, until after the regency is fully established; that the establishment of that body should be entirely your act; that it should be fairly avowed that the liberation of the country from a foreign army, and the opportunity of restoring the Portuguese monarchy that now presents itself, having been conquered by the British sword, it is the right of the British Government, and the duty of the British commanders, to place the government in such hands as to them seem most likely to preserve the peace of the capital; to insure the prosperity of the country at large; and to possess the confidence of the prince.

That, in carrying these measures into effect, they are actuated by no other interests than such as are purely Portuguese. That the moment the regency is established, all military interference will become unnecessary, and will cease; but until that moment arrives, and until the peace and subsistence of the capital can be secured, the most effectual and prompt measures will be taken to insure tranquillity by military means, and all offenders against the public peace will be proceeded against with most rigorous severity.

As a consequence of the above idea, I would further suggest, that, until the final embarkation of the French troops, no part of the Portuguese Army should be permitted to enter Lisbon, and that all remonstrances on that, or any other subject connected with our present relative situation, that may be made by the leaders of that army, should be met with the most decided resolution, not to give way on subjects so materially affecting the welfare of this country and the honour of the British Army.

In order to convey my ideas in a more precise form, I have drawn up a draft of a proclamation, which should certainly run in name of yourself and the admiral.

Whatever proclamation is adopted should be immediately prepared and transmitted by some confidential person, and printed ready for circulation the instant the French march out; and I am of opinion it should be such as could be communicated to them for their concurrence, which, if it can be obtained, would give great facility in the preparation. It should be accompanied by another, and third, to be issued in the name of the officer commanding the troops, which should contain regulations of police, and such details relative to the preservation of good order as it may be necessary to introduce into the more general proclamations.

I must here observe that there seems to be a great want of persons whose principles are known to be well affected, with whom to communicate, and through whose agency to prepare these preliminary steps; for I apprehend some of the persons, named in the paper you yesterday communicated to me, will not make their appearance till the French are gone. If you can give me any information on this subject, I should be extremely obliged to you.

It only remains that I should apologise for taking up so much of your time, on a subject respecting which I must acknowledge I am a very inadequate judge.

I have the honour to be, &c. &c.
(Signed)   John Hope,
                                                              Lieutenant-General.

(Translation.)

To His Excellency General Sir Hew Dalrymple,

Most Illustrious and Most Excellent Sir,

After having completed the glorious restoration of the regency in the capital, agreeable to the decree of our august prince regent, Your Excellency desired to reward my labours by promoting my nomination to a situation in the regency. Supposing that some recompense might be offered for my endeavours to be useful to my country, and being fully persuaded that the best rewards for services done to religion and our country are new occasions to render them still greater, and knowing, by the force of reason and experience, the importance of my remaining in my present situation, I thought that, for the service of God and the prince, I ought not to resign it.

However, as I wish to comply with the desires of Your Excellency, and from a consideration for the governors of the kingdom, who now inform me of my nomination, I shall have to go to Lisbon, agreeable to my promise to General Anstruther, and I can assure Your Excellency that my intentions embrace no other object than the interests of religion and of my country.

Animated with the sincerest sentiments of respect and gratitude, I am, &c. &c.

(Signed)   Bishop of Oporto,
                                             Governor.

Without a date, but received the 30th September at Lisbon.

                                             H. W. Dalrymple,
                                             Lieutenant-General.

To Lieutenant-General Sir Hew Dalrymple.

                                             Downing-Street,
                                             4th November, 1808.

Sir,

I have the honour to acknowledge the receipt of your letter of the 2nd instant.

Your proceedings, for establishing the regency in Portugal, having been only reported to me in your letter of the 20th September, written on the eve of your departure from thence on your return to England, it was not possible for me officially to transmit to you, previous to your arrival in England, an answer to that letter.

In the first interview I had with you, I, however, intimated to you, that the arrangements made with respect to the regency, under the instructions which you had received, had been approved by His Majesty, as the most suitable, under all the circumstances, to the dignity and interests of the prince regent.

(Signed)

Castlereagh.

(No 17.)
To General Friere.

Headquarters, Ramalhall,
23rd August, 1808.

Sir,

I have the honour to enclose, for Your Excellency's information, a copy of the suspension of arms, agreed upon yesterday, and signed by Sir A. Wellesley and General Kellerman. It may be necessary to explain to Your Excellency, that what is mentioned about the Portuguese Army relates to some corps in the part of the country mentioned in the article; but that the army serving under Your Excellency's immediate command, united with the British troops, is comprised under the same head with them.

(Signed)

H. W. Dalrymple.

Major Ayres Pinto da Souza.

Headquarters, Cintra,
2nd September, 1808.

Sir,

I reply to your letter of yesterday's date, with which I am just now honoured, and beg to remind you, that, on the 23rd of last month, I enclosed, to General Bernardine Friere, a copy of the articles of the agreement for a suspension of hostilities between the hostile armies, which were to serve as a basis for the proposed convention for the evacuation of Portugal by the French Army. In reply to the letter which adverted to these articles of agreement, the general might, as a matter of course, have made any observations, or recommended any stipulations he thought proper; and I am sure you will do me the justice to assure the general and the Portuguese Government (if necessary) that I advised and even urged you to recommend it to his Excellency to favour me fully with his sentiments on the subject, whilst the negotiations were in progress.

As my wishes on this point were never acceded to, and as I never received one word of comment from General Friere relative to the basis on which the present convention is founded, I hope I shall be excused in expressing some surprise at this late expostulation on terms fixed and agreed upon, and to which the honour of the commanders of the British Army and Fleet is pledged, in as far as their influence or power can be supposed to extend, by the common known laws of war.

(Signed)   H. W. Dalrymple.

To His Excellency General Friere, Commander of the Portuguese Troops.

Headquarters, Cintra,
2nd September, 1808.

Sir,

I had the honour to transmit to Your Excellency, on the 23rd of last month, the several articles agreed upon as the basis of a convention for the evacuation of Portugal by the French Army, and I now enclose a copy of the convention itself, as ratified by the French general-in-chief. I received the original of this paper the day before yesterday, at an early hour; but, as the French general had accidentally omitted to affix his signature to the convention itself, (it being only at the end of the additional articles), I was obliged to send it back, in order to have that error rectified, which put it out of my power to transmit you the enclosed authenticated copy so early as I could have wished; I, however lost no time in causing Lieutenant-Colonel Murray to make a confidential communication of the substance of the whole to Major Ayres Pinto da Souza, who, doubtless, lost no time in communicating the same to Your Excellency.

I shall be anxious to receive a communication from Your Excellency as to the position you wish the Portuguese Army to occupy until the embarkation of the French troops; and there are now many details of importance to arrange, which I should be happy to confer with Your Excellency upon, when it may suit your convenience.

(Signed)   H. W. Dalrymple.

(No. 18.)

Translation of a Despatch received by the Chev. de Souza from the Bishop and President of the Supreme *Junta* of Oporto.

(Extracts.)

Porto,
28th August, 1808.

I have had the honour of receiving Your Excellency's despatches, &c.

Thirty-two thousand English troops have landed in this kingdom, according to their own account; they have already had some actions

195

with the French, in which they were always victorious. The accounts received here are not as yet authenticated in all their circumstances; for which reason I do not, at present, send Your Excellency an official relation: it is, however, certain that the English attacked the enemy with incredible valour, and always conquered them. Finally, the French offered to capitulate, which the English consented to, and framed the preliminary articles, of which I send you a copy, and upon which the Supreme *Junta* has made the following observations.

1st. That our general was not called to assist at the convention, but only informed of it after the articles were formed.

2nd. That this Supreme Government, representing His Royal Highness, was not consulted.

3rd. No declaration whatever was made respecting the manner the French Army was to retire; being clear that, in consequence of the offensive and defensive treaty, entered into by us, with the province of Gallicia, we can never consent that twelve thousand armed enemies should pass through Spain on their evacuating this country.

4th. The line of demarcation established for the two combined armies obliges a part of our force, (the Army of Observation, commanded by General Baccelar,) which is at Santarem, to retire much further from Lisbon, which ought not to be permitted.

Lastly. That, by these articles, the French are allowed to take with them whatever Portuguese property they may think proper, that they may embark them on board the Russian squadron; and that all persons attached to the French are at perfect liberty to depart with them.

The Supreme *Junta* has thought fit to make these representations to the English general.

   (Signed)   Bishop and President.

P.S. With regard to the Russian squadron, in order to avoid any reprisals, I have sent the enclosed despatch to the commander of the said squadron, having first communicated it to the English general, that he might know our intentions in this respect.

(A faithful translation,)

   (Signed)   De Souza Couttinho.

Note.—This despatch ought to have been enclosed to me, but was omitted. The despatch to the Russian admiral was to announce to him the neutrality of the Tagus to his squadron. I was not the English general to whom the bishop alludes.—H. W. D.

(Two days after the preceding despatch, the following was addressed, by the same person, the Bishop of Oporto, to Sir. H. Dalrymple.)

(Translation.)
The Bishop of Oporto to Lieutenant General Sir Hew Dalrymple.

Porto,
30th August, 1808.

Most Illustrious and Most Excellent Sir,

Having been informed of the arrival of Your Excellency, to continue to us the protection for which we have hitherto been indebted to the most illustrious and most excellent General Sir Arthur Wellesley, I, with the greatest satisfaction, present myself to Your Excellency, congratulating myself on your safe arrival, and begging of Your Excellency the good offices of your protection; at the same time, assuring you of my respect and gratitude.

I have the honour to be, &c. &c. &c.
(Signed)   Bishop and President,
                                   Governor.

(No. 19.)
Lord Viscount Castlereagh to the Lord Mayor of London.

My Lord,

I have the honour to acquaint your lordship that Captain Campbell arrived, this evening, with despatches from Lieutenant-General Sir Arthur Wellesley, dated Vimiera, the 22nd *ultimo*, giving an account of two victories obtained over the French Army, in Portugal; the first, on the 17th, at Zambria, over the advanced corps of the French, consisting of 6,000 men, commanded by Generals Laborde and Brennier; in which the French were defeated, with the loss of 1,500 men, in killed, wounded, and prisoners; the second, over the whole of the French Army in Portugal, consisting of 14,000 men, commanded by General Junot; wherein the French were completely defeated, with the loss of thirteen pieces of cannon, twenty-three tumbrils of ammunition, and about 3,500 men, killed, wounded, and prisoners.

In consequence of this action, General Kellerman arrived, with a flag of truce, at headquarters, on the 22nd, to treat for terms.

Lieutenant-General Burrard landed, and arrived in the field of action, after the battle had commenced, on the 21st *ultimo*; but he generously declined taking the command from Sir Arthur Wellesley. On the 22nd, Lieutenant-General Sir Hew Dalrymple landed, and took the command.

    I have the honour to be, &c. &c. &c.

       (Signed)   Castlereagh.

      To General Sir Hew Dalrymple.

                                   Almeida,
                        21st November, 1808.

My Dear Sir Hew,

    In consequence of the remoteness of this place, and the almost incredible delays and difficulties attending all communication with it, I did not learn, till very lately, not, in fact, until the arrival of Sir John Moore here, the extent and violence of the frenzy which has seized John Bull on the subject of the convention for the evacuation of Portugal. It is very obvious by what persons, and by what unworthy means, the public opinion has been misled, and the passions of the multitude inflamed on this subject; and, under such circumstances, I really rejoice to find that your conduct (with which that of the whole army in Portugal may be said to be identified) is about to be brought before a tribunal, capable, I trust, of judging the merit of the case, and of doing you and us that justice which a set of profligate politicians attempt to deprive us of.

    In looking over my papers, the other day, I found the enclosed original, which you gave me at my departure for Oporto. You may, perhaps, wish to produce it, and I hope it may reach you in time.

    You will learn, from other sources, the state of affairs in Spain. I consider them as very critical; but think that Sir John Moore will now be able to unite all, or nearly all, the British Forces, and to collect on them such part of the Spanish as may have sense enough to avoid general actions with the French at the present moment. Such has not been the case with Blake, nor with the corps of Galluzzo. I hope Castaños will be more prudent.

    I expect, every hour, to be permitted to join my brigade. Having, from hence, been employed to manage the advance of the army, Sir John Moore has thought it fair to keep me to bring up the rear: this is now very near accomplished, the Buffs and Sixth alone remaining behind. I have no notion of our intended movements, and will not speculate upon them.

    I beg you will have the goodness to present, &c. &c.

       (Signed)   Robert Anstruther,
                                      Brigadier-General.

To Lieutenant-General Sir Hew Dalrymple.

Madrid,
18th October, 1808.

Sir,

I learn, both from my private letters and from the newspapers, that no public measure ever received the same universal disapprobation, in England, as the convention made by you with the French Army in Portugal. Under these circumstances, I trust that the unsolicited offer of my opinion and evidence will be attributed to the sole motives which occasion it—a sense of justice; and of that duty which exists between man and man. For the correctness of my opinion I dare not answer, but for its impartiality I may. With the convention I had no concern. With all its conditions I was not acquainted till after it was sent to England; and between us there existed no friendship which might give a bias to my feelings.

Of the principally obnoxious article, which allows the return of the French to France, my opinion at the time was that it was highly advantageous. It seemed to me that, if this was not granted to them, the French could not avoid defending themselves to the last. A resolution to this effect, though it might, ultimately, have ended in their unconditional surrender, would, in the meantime, have occupied our army for a great length of time, and might have exposed it to great distress, from the uncertainty of the communication with the fleet, and from the non-existence of any magazines or preparation for a campaign ashore. An inevitable consequence must have been that the efficacy and numbers of the army for future operations, would have been materially impaired.

Believing, also, as was then supposed, that the enemy's force did not amount to more than 16,000 men, the disadvantage of the distant junction of this reinforcement to the French Army in Spain, bore no comparison, in my judgement, to the advantages of the more immediate union of double the number of highly-disciplined British Troops to the newly-recruited Spanish Armies. Such were the reasons, at the time, which made me approve this article. I have since been in Spain, and am better enabled to judge of the value of this reasoning; and my decided opinion now is that the speediest union of the largest British Army that can be collected with that of Spain is indispensable to the welfare of the common cause.

The Spanish Government have pressed, in the strongest manner, the arrival of our army; and, let it be observed, that the necessity that has occasioned these urgent demands, while it has no connexion with the objection to this article of the convention, entirely supports the reason for which it was made. With respect to the other articles, I must, with the same truth, declare that I do not approve of some of them; but, as they are of minor consequence, and do not seem to be much objected to, I need not advert to them.

I do not just wish this opinion to be put in the public papers; but, in any other manner, you are authorised to make what use of it you please.

I have the honour to be, &c. &c.

(Signed)   William Bentinck.

LEONAUR

ALSO FROM LEONAUR
AVAILABLE IN SOFTCOVER OR HARDCOVER WITH DUST JACKET

THE FALL OF THE MOGHUL EMPIRE OF HINDUSTAN *by H. G. Keene*—By the beginning of the nineteenth century, as British and Indian armies under Lake and Wellesley dominated the scene, a little over half a century of conflict brought the Moghul Empire to its knees.

LADY SALE'S AFGHANISTAN *by Florentia Sale*—An Indomitable Victorian Lady's Account of the Retreat from Kabul During the First Afghan War.

THE CAMPAIGN OF MAGENTA AND SOLFERINO 1859 *by Harold Carmichael Wylly*—The Decisive Conflict for the Unification of Italy.

FRENCH'S CAVALRY CAMPAIGN *by J. G. Maydon*—A Special Correspondent's View of British Army Mounted Troops During the Boer War.

CAVALRY AT WATERLOO *by Sir Evelyn Wood*—British Mounted Troops During the Campaign of 1815.

THE SUBALTERN *by George Robert Gleig*—The Experiences of an Officer of the 85th Light Infantry During the Peninsular War.

NAPOLEON AT BAY, 1814 *by F. Loraine Petre*—The Campaigns to the Fall of the First Empire.

NAPOLEON AND THE CAMPAIGN OF 1806 *by Colonel Vachée*—The Napoleonic Method of Organisation and Command to the Battles of Jena & Auerstädt.

THE COMPLETE ADVENTURES IN THE CONNAUGHT RANGERS *by William Grattan*—The 88th Regiment during the Napoleonic Wars by a Serving Officer.

BUGLER AND OFFICER OF THE RIFLES *by William Green & Harry Smith*—With the 95th (Rifles) during the Peninsular & Waterloo Campaigns of the Napoleonic Wars.

NAPOLEONIC WAR STORIES *by Sir Arthur Quiller-Couch*—Tales of soldiers, spies, battles & sieges from the Peninsular & Waterloo campaingns.

CAPTAIN OF THE 95TH (RIFLES) *by Jonathan Leach*—An officer of Wellington's sharpshooters during the Peninsular, South of France and Waterloo campaigns of the Napoleonic wars.

RIFLEMAN COSTELLO *by Edward Costello*—The adventures of a soldier of the 95th (Rifles) in the Peninsular & Waterloo Campaigns of the Napoleonic wars.